Tales of Militant Chemistry

The publisher and the University of California Press Foundation gratefully acknowledge the generous support of the Kenneth Turan and Patricia Williams Endowment Fund in American Film.

Tales of Militant Chemistry

THE FILM FACTORY IN A CENTURY OF WAR

Alice Lovejoy

UNIVERSITY OF CALIFORNIA PRESS

University of California Press
Oakland, California

© 2025 by Alice Lovejoy

All rights reserved.

Cataloging-in-Publication data is on file at the Library of Congress.

ISBN 978-0-520-40293-5 (cloth : alk. paper)
ISBN 978-0-520-40295-9 (ebook)

Manufactured in the United States of America

GPSR Authorized Representative: Easy Access System Europe, Mustamäe tee 50, 10621 Tallinn, Estonia, gpsr.requests@easproject.com

34 33 32 31 30 29 28 27 26 25
10 9 8 7 6 5 4 3 2 1

For Adrien and Élie

CONTENTS

Introduction 1

PART I: BUILDING

Chapter One · The Film Factory 13
Celluloid and Gas · The Model City · Race and Raw Materials · Making Film Safe · Cinema Artificial Silk · The Kodak World

Chapter Two · Story of a Tree 49
Making Use of the Worthless · Chemistry and Empire · Holston · Strategic Materials · Tales of Militant Chemistry · Threads

PART II: UNRAVELING

Chapter Three · Taking Stock 91
Cameras and Guns · A Medium that Turns Ore to Everyday Use · A City Manager in Munich · Cold War, Hot Metals

Chapter Four · Fallout 122
On the Wind · Black Spots · Insidious · Millions of Gallons · Sensitivity Equals Trouble

Chapter Five · A Fine Line 152
A Chemical Problem · *Water and Bones*

Epilogue: The Twenty-First Century 166

Acknowledgements 173
Archives and Abbreviations 177
Notes 179
Bibliography 205
Filmography 229
Index 231

Introduction

EASTMAN KODAK CAME to the atomic bomb through uranium, most of it from the Belgian Congo. It came through what began as pitchblende, chunks of yellow-black ore from the Shinkolobwe mine in the colony's Katanga province. Katanga is inland, hilly and rich in metals like the copper that had been mined there for a millennium. This ore, however, had been discovered more recently, not long after most of the province came under the control of the Belgian mining company Union Minière du Haut-Katanga, which was itself owned by the financial firm Société Générale.

It took years for the uranium to reach the United States. At Shinkolobwe, Congolese miners gathered it by hand, then packed it into drums sent via river and rail to the Atlantic port of Matadi. From Matadi, the ore made its way to New York.[1] It sat for almost two years in a Staten Island vegetable oil warehouse until, on September 18, 1942, General Leslie R. Groves purchased it, setting the drums in motion again to Port Hope, Ontario. There, the Canadian Radium and Uranium Corporation refined the ore and shipped it to the secret city of Oak Ridge, Tennessee, where a company called Tennessee Eastman was operating the Y-12 uranium separation plant—a plant built to make fuel for a weapon that, some thought, would end the Second World War and might even, they hoped, end all war.[2]

At the time, Tennessee Eastman was known best as a subsidiary of the Eastman Kodak Company. Much of Kodak's film could trace its chemical origins to Tennessee Eastman's plant in Kingsport, a few hours from Oak Ridge. But at Y-12, there wasn't any film. There were centrifuges, immense machines that spun uranium in circles so blindingly fast that its nonfissionable atoms, uranium 238, fell away from fissionable uranium 235. When only 235 was left, the uranium was ready to move again. Leaving Tennessee Eastman's hands, it was escorted to Los Alamos, where it was pressed into a bomb, then flown over a vast expanse of the Pacific to Tinian Island in the Northern Marianas. On August 6, 1945, 1,968 feet over the city of Hiroshima, Japan, a neutron in this uranium collided with an atom. The atom split into two, initiating a chain reaction that, starting that morning in August, killed over 280,000 people and sickened countless more.[3] If we think back before the war, though, the cataclysmic reaction was a point in a longer chain. This chain linked a colony and its laborers to a company on whose film that same day, August 6, you might have watched the new Frank Sinatra–Gene Kelly musical *Anchors Aweigh*, a comedy about the war that was, just then, ending in ruins.

This is a book about film as a weapon—not in its images or sounds, but in its chemistry. It asks how Kodak, a company synonymous with photography, came to the Manhattan Project, and it traces the aftermath of Kodak's work at Oak Ridge. Along the way, it recounts how film factories became poison gas and explosives factories, how they monitored for nuclear fallout and were made into spoils of war. Like the chain that brought uranium from the Belgian Congo to Tennessee, New Mexico, and Japan, this story is global. It branches to companies like Germany's Agfa, whose military entanglements were as consequential as Kodak's. It stitches film to rayon, plastics, and cigarettes. It is a story of high political dealings and everyday work on a factory floor, and its characters are scientists, prisoners, soldiers, and spies. Taken together, this frames an alternative history—a chemical history—of cinema and photography in the twentieth century. It shows how film's chemistry was caught up with that century's military, colonial, and environmental violence, and how, as the century wore on and the hazards of industrial chemistry became clearer and clearer, film served as a warning about the same violence.

If you took pictures before there were digital cameras, film's chemistry will be obvious to you. Maybe you remember photo shops, whose heady part-sulfur, part-vinegar smell was a reminder that photography was more than a matter of lenses and light. There was a shop like this in the Massachusetts town where I grew up. Bright boxes of film were stacked behind the counter (some of them Fuji green and red, but most Kodak yellow), and in the back, machines steadily and mysteriously spun out ribbons: someone's retirement party, someone else's first steps. These machines did the precise work of developing film, a sequence of chemical immersions that after a few months in my high school's darkroom, I knew how to follow myself.

What I didn't know then was how finely calibrated film's own ingredients are, both in the base (the flexible strip of celluloid that one loads into a camera) and in the photosensitive emulsion slicked onto this base, a combination of gelatin and silver. I also didn't know that the gelatin in most of the film the shop sold had been made just a few miles away, at a Kodak factory called Eastman Gelatine. But I knew the factory; we drove by it all the time. I remember the chain-link fence that narrowly divided the plant's office from the road. I remember how, when the wind was right, the stench of rot—gelatin's telltale sign—drifted for miles.

Kodak's atomic labor started with materials like these. The company began making film at its Rochester, New York, factory in 1889, first for still photographs and then, in the 1890s, for motion pictures, and this film was an admixture of animal hides and bones, trees, cotton, coal, camphor, salts, and silver.[4] In technical terms, to make emulsion, light-sensitive silver nitrate (silver dissolved in nitric acid) and dyes were suspended in a solution of gelatin and potassium bromide. Most of this emulsion sat on a base of cellulose nitrate, a highly flammable combination of sulfuric acid, methanol, camphor, and the most important ingredient, nitrated cotton (cellulose made from cotton linters, the fibers that attach to the cottonseed, mixed with nitric acid). Film base could also be made from a substance called cellulose acetate, where cotton linters were mixed with acetic acid and acetic anhydride instead of nitric acid. In the late 1920s, Tennessee Eastman started producing this kind of film, usually called nonflammable or "safety" film because it burns much more slowly than cellulose nitrate. Three decades later, another Eastman subsidiary, Texas Eastman, developed a new type of nonflammable film made from polyethylene terephthalate (PET), the same plastic used in plastic bottles, tennis balls, and takeout containers. Its primary ingredients are oil and gas.

For film manufacturers, these substances were, and are, non-negotiable. Without cotton linters, nitric acid, trees, and oil, there would be no snapshots and no movies. But for Kodak, the materials shone with a special allure after 1915, the year the US Department of Justice found that the company had formed a monopoly in the photographic trade and

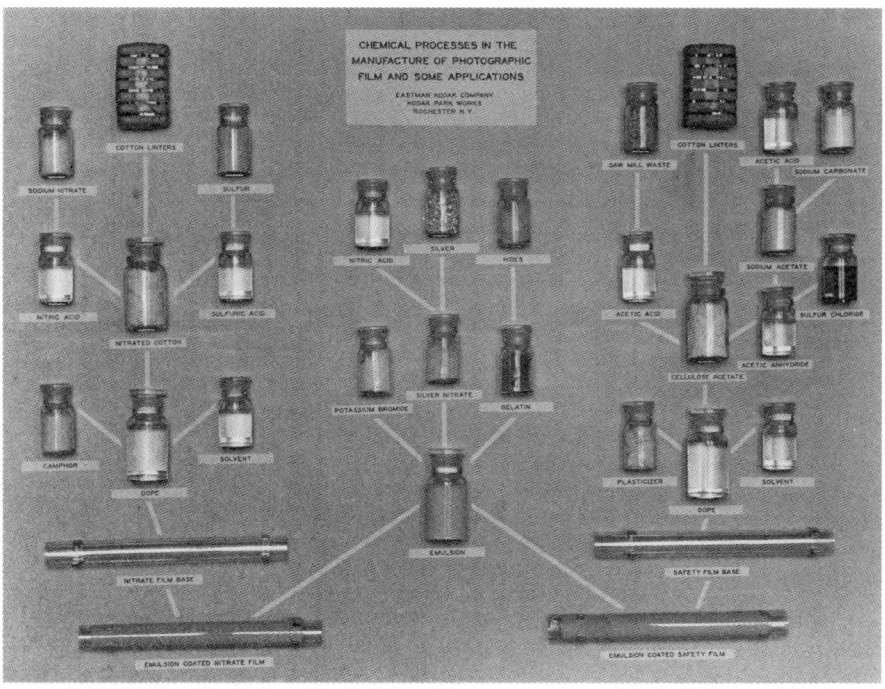

FIGURE 1. The raw materials of flammable (cellulose nitrate) and nonflammable (cellulose acetate) film. Courtesy of the University of Rochester River Campus Libraries Rare Books, Special Collections, and Preservation, and Eastman Kodak Company.

barred it from expanding further. Seeking different ways to grow, Kodak turned to vertical integration. Instead of film and camera companies like the ones it had amassed for more than a decade, it bought factories making chemicals and processing raw materials that were the basics of the business. In 1920, this brought Kodak to Kingsport, where a partially finished methanol plant became Tennessee Eastman. When a gelatin factory came up for sale ten years later, it lured the film company to Peabody, Massachusetts. For Kodak, it appeared to be an unimpeachable strategy, a way to control the business without a glimmer of monopoly.

True to plan, Eastman Gelatine didn't only make photographic gelatin. It made glue, and it made food-grade gelatin, which is different from photographic gelatin: less refined and good for things like yogurt or ice cream. This wasn't unusual at all, because most chemical companies make multiple products. Diversification can be spurred by raw materials' varied uses, like the animal bones that can just as easily become photographs as they can become glue or food. It might be a way to distribute earnings across markets. Or it may be a matter of widely applicable scientific and technical knowledge. In Kingsport, this drove Tennessee Eastman to diversify as well, bringing the company from its beginnings in methanol to cellulose acetate safety film, and from safety film to acetate fibers and plastics. The work was successful and profitable, and in 1942, cellulose acetate chemistry led Tennessee Eastman to the antisubmarine explosive RDX (Research Department Explosive), which it made at a sprawling government-owned factory in Kingsport. Within a year of opening the RDX plant, the company set out for Y-12, shooting up in Oak Ridge's muddy tracts of former farmland.

While Kodak was diversifying, so was its largest competitor, the German company Agfa. Agfa began as a dye maker: Its name stands for Aktien-Gesellschaft für Anilin-Fabrikation (roughly, joint-stock company for aniline manufacturing), and aniline, made from coal tar, is the chemical basis of dyes. In the late nineteenth century, after chemists discovered that dyes could both tint fabric and sensitize photographic surfaces to light, Agfa entered the photographic business. As motion pictures were added to still photographs and the company's film sales grew, it converted land near its dye factory in the eastern German town of Wolfen, outside Bitterfeld, into a film plant.

Kodak and Agfa diversified differently, but they ended up in parallel places. Agfa's Wolfen plant was also built, in part, to make safety film. During World War I, the factory was embroiled with that conflict's defining chemical weapon, poison gas. It began making rayon after World War I, and during the Third Reich, when Agfa was part of the IG Farben chemical cartel, artificial fibers were its most important products. When the Second World War began, many of these fibers, like Agfa's film, were made by forced laborers and concentration camp prisoners from across Nazi-occupied Europe. Esther Leslie puts it plainly: "The chemical industry had it all covered: it produced the bombs and gases and the photographic materials."[5]

These two factories, Tennessee Eastman and Agfa Wolfen, are at the heart of this book. Though they sit on opposite sides of the Atlantic, the plants are hard to disentangle. In times of peace as well as war, they made many of the same products, and they competed to sell these products throughout the world, to make them better and faster. Seen in the factories' light, film looks different than it does in a photo shop or on a cinema screen. It's still something that can entertain or distract us—that hasn't changed. Like books, paintings, or podcasts, photography and cinema help us express and debate things; they chronicle our lives and make sense of the world. Yet the film factory shows us that no matter what is imprinted on its surface, film's meaning also lies in its ingredients, in the hands and machines that touch them, and in how they are transformed. We can compare film to television or radio, but in the factory, it sits just as comfortably alongside synthetic fibers, plastics, pesticides, painkillers, and weapons, to name just some of the products that Tennessee Eastman and Agfa Wolfen made. That is, while film is part of the "culture industry," it is also caught up with "the most powerful sectors of industry—steel, petroleum, electricity, and chemicals," in German critics Theodor

Adorno and Max Horkheimer's words, engines of the mass production that, like cinema and photography, defined the twentieth century.[6]

Horkheimer and Adorno wrote their influential essay on the culture industry in 1944, in exile in Pacific Palisades. Though they were thinking of Germany's flourishing Weimar cinema and of the American studios just down the road, their critique rings true today, as scholars dissect the institutional structures that underpin media. These structures extend beyond familiar places like movie theaters and art galleries to the industries that, since the very beginning, have made it possible for us to watch a film or take a photograph.[7] Consider cinema. We might be fans of a director or connoisseurs of a genre, but what we see and hear in a multiplex, or on the little screens of our tablets, has been shaped just as much by lessons from engineering schools, by labor laws and court proceedings, and by priorities articulated in boardrooms and banks.[8]

The chemical industry is one of the industries that has shaped media, and because chemistry is a science of materials, it shows how deeply film and photography depend on mining, agriculture, and digging for oil, something that Siobhan Angus, Nadia Bozak, and others have explored.[9] The histories of Tennessee Eastman and Agfa Wolfen emphasize how commonplace this extraction was. Throughout the twentieth century, raw materials were the companies' lifeblood, and often a point of pride. Yet these factories also turn the film industry on its head, because the celluloid they made for Hollywood or Berlin was only one of their products. Much more of the plants' film went to less glamorous media: X-rays, microfilm, home movies, and snapshots.[10] Even this paled in comparison to things like rayon, cigarette filters, insulation, and explosives. Alongside petroleum, steel, and electricity, products like these were what kept the film factories—and the film industry—running.

Of course, factories are more than their products. They're intersections of people and materials, science and politics, industry and money.[11] If you've lived near a place like Eastman Gelatine, Tennessee Eastman, or Agfa Wolfen, you know this. You also know that as much as factories matter to a particular place—as much as they mean jobs and community, and as deep as their economic and environmental impact is on a town or a region—they are crossed by larger forces like the ones that brought Congolese uranium to Oak Ridge. Such local and global stories make up this book's chemical history of film, and I draw them from sources in two dozen archives; from memoirs, interviews, films, and newspapers; and from the extraordinary work of historians who have documented the histories of places like Kingsport and Wolfen. Borrowing from Italian author Primo Levi's 1975 book *The Periodic Table,* we could call these stories "tales of militant chemistry."[12]

Levi is a helpful guide. During the years of Tennessee Eastman's and Agfa Wolfen's "militant chemistry," he studied and worked as a chemist, first under the Italian Fascist regime and then as a prisoner and forced laborer in Auschwitz. *The Periodic Table* is a chronicle of this period, each chapter a vignette named for a chemical element: silver, uranium, zinc, tin, and so on. Silver and uranium play roles in this book as well. So do substances like cotton, gelatin, and wood, which, because they aren't elements, Levi doesn't write about, but which the assembly lines at Tennessee Eastman and Agfa Wolfen made into film, and into rayon and plastics and weapons.

Then there are the people. There is Kodak executive Frank Lovejoy, an MIT–trained chemical engineer (and distant relative of mine) who, after jobs making sugar and soap, joined the company's celluloid division at the end of the nineteenth century and, in 1920, traveled from Rochester to Kingsport to visit the location for what would become Tennessee Eastman.[13] There's James C. White, one of Tennessee Eastman's earliest hires, a northern Michigan lumberman who knew wood, and the chemicals that could be made from it, better than anyone else.[14] When he moved to Kingsport, White could never have predicted that twenty-five years later he would be leading a branch of a top-secret military project. Things were different for White's counterpart at Agfa, chemist Fritz Gajewski. Gajewski started at Agfa in 1930, when the film factory was already big, and he was also in charge of IG Farben's Division III, which managed all the film and rayon manufactured in Germany. Gajewski was responsible for the business but not the making. During the war, that was done by people like Oleksandra Lawrik, who was arrested in the city of Dnipropetrovsk (Dnipro) in 1943, one of the countless Ukrainians deported from the Nazi-occupied Soviet Union to labor in Germany. In Dnipro, Lawrik had worked as an accountant at a factory. When she arrived in Germany, she was briefly interned in the Buchenwald concentration camp, then transferred to Ravensbrück, and finally sent to another factory—the film factory in the country's east.

While Oleksandra Lawrik was imprisoned at Agfa Wolfen, a man named Alfred Dean Slack was arriving at Y-12, Tennessee Eastman's complex at Oak Ridge. Slack wasn't hired directly into the Manhattan Project; he was a chemist at Kodak's Rochester headquarters who was transferred south during the war. His time in Tennessee began at the Kingsport cellulose acetate plant. After a few months, he moved to the Holston Ordnance Works, where he supervised RDX production. From Holston, he went to Y-12. In other words, Slack followed the same path that Kodak followed to Oak Ridge—a path charted by nonflammable safety film.

We'll return to Slack later in the book. For now, let's consider where this path began. Safety film wasn't Kodak's invention, but in the late 1920s, when Tennessee Eastman began mass-producing it for the company's new 16 mm cameras and projectors, it was nothing short of revolutionary. As Haidee Wasson has shown, it was suddenly safer and easier than ever to make or project a movie in your home or office.[15] Maybe you caught the end of a picture in a train station, waiting for a delayed connection. X-rays and microfilm used in hospitals and libraries, where fires could be disastrous, were made on the substance. Safety film also transformed Tennessee Eastman and Kodak. It underscored that the film manufacturer was a chemical manufacturer, and it made Tennessee Eastman into a major defense contractor. By 1943, the company that made its name on keeping Kodak film from catching fire had built to enormous size at Y-12, with the bomb, and with uranium that once glinted dully in Katanga's hills.

If we look ahead to 1951, there's another path. That year, Kodak stopped making cellulose nitrate film. After decades of practice at Tennessee Eastman, cellulose acetate was ready to replace cellulose nitrate, even on the 35 mm film used in movie studios and theaters. The company also figured that there were more than enough raw materials for this, since by that point, the nonflammable plastic relied on petrochemicals that Texas Eastman drew from the Gulf Coast oil fields.

Early in the year, however, tiny spots began to appear on this new, oil-based film.[16] The United States was detonating atomic bombs in Nevada, the first explosions on the North American continent since the Trinity test in July 1945. In Kazakhstan, thousands of miles away, the Soviet Union was testing its own atomic weapons. The spots, Kodak determined, were created by fallout from the tests. They were the imprints of radiant particles drifting, in snow and rain, to a company involved in their making: photograms for the atomic age, or as Susan Schuppli has called them, "radical contact prints."[17]

The spots were a warning about the dangers of nuclear proliferation. They unraveled the sense of invincibility that film factories had built between the Great War and the Cold War. And because they began, in part, with Tennessee Eastman's work at Oak Ridge, and because Tennessee Eastman came to Oak Ridge because of its success with cellulose acetate, they were evidence of the deadly consequences of making film "safe." These consequences were layered onto the other violence in film's chemistry: the histories of poison gas, enslaved workers, and fragile and painstaking harvests like camphor, whose trees—grown most abundantly in Taiwan, a Japanese colony from 1895 to 1945—take two hundred years to reach maturity.[18] This reminds us that, as a product of the chemical industry, film is terribly ordinary. It is a cousin to textiles and car tires. It begins with wood, cotton, and oil, substances that can also end in a bomb or in fuel for a warship—like film, essential products of the twentieth century. And as these tales of militant chemistry tell, the places where film was made were both part of a "dream factory" and, simply, factories.

PART I

Building

CHAPTER ONE

The Film Factory

IN 1921, A FILM was made about one of Kodak's factories: its headquarters in Rochester, New York, known as Kodak Park. The war had been over for three years, and cinema had become a powerful form of mass culture—American cinema especially, circumnavigating the globe on Kodak film.[1] This was the year of runaway successes like Chaplin's *The Kid* and Valentino's *The Sheik*. It's understandable that audiences might have been curious about how all that film was made.

A Movie Trip Through Filmland follows the making from start to finish. Workers cart bales of cotton linters into the factory, preparing them to be transformed into film base. In wide, shallow bowls, they dissolve silver bullion in nitric acid. They package finished film in Kodak-yellow boxes. The workers make it look easy, but an intertitle warns the viewer that making film demands "absolute control." Kodak monitors the factory's temperature, humidity, and how much light seeps inside. Its employees are strictly trained and uniformed. Its buildings are fortresses. Dust from a shipment or tracked in on someone's shoes—even the weather—could ruin a batch of film, and so in the 1920s, factories like these were built to filter their air through water, oil, cloth, and finally an electromagnetic field that neutralized the smallest airborne particles. Before emulsion was applied to celluloid, it was washed, rewashed, then washed again.[2]

Kodak's control was absolute because in 1921, film was dangerous. Most of it was made of cellulose nitrate, and cellulose nitrate (guncotton in another guise) is extremely volatile, its history riddled with exploding billiards balls, combustible dress buttons, and cinemas engulfed in flames that were almost impossible to extinguish.³ The hazards began well before cotton and nitric acid became cellulose nitrate. *A Movie Trip Through Filmland* points out Kodak Park's exhaust fans, which "carry off the nitric acid fumes to protect the workmen" from the fumes' suffocating corrosion of the lungs. Connected to smokestacks 366 feet high—taller than the Statue of Liberty—the towers funneled toxic clouds far above the heads of anyone making their way to or from the factory.⁴

Control, then, meant safety. It meant improving processes and machines and managing labor. But because manufacturing mistakes could make film unusable—ruined by premature exposure to light or prone to cracking, shrinking, decay—and waste valuable raw materials, it also meant money.⁵ This was where the film factory floor met the corporate office, since there, too, control was about materials. It was about

FIGURE 2. Exterior, film factory (*A Movie Trip Through Filmland*). Courtesy of the George Eastman Museum.

the bales of cotton and the trainloads of ores and chemicals at the heart of both film and, as Lee Grieveson writes, the liberal political economy of the nineteenth and twentieth centuries.[6]

Few of these materials came from Rochester, where in 1883 George Eastman founded his company to make cameras and dry plates (glass plates coated with photosensitive emulsion). Roll film for still photography followed, then motion picture film. Some of the gelatin Kodak used in its plates and films was from cows raised nearby, and some of the glass and wood in its lenses and cameras was made or harvested locally, but for the rest, the company looked elsewhere. Eastman took a keen interest in this. Perhaps because of his father's premature death, which diminished the family's finances and set eight-year-old George's sights on work instead of school, and perhaps because that work was in a bank, he was powerfully dedicated to thrift. He scouted new sources for materials, kept watch on prices, and as his company grew and the former bank clerk gained political influence, lobbied the US government to adjust tariffs. Take silver as an example. Film emulsion and photographic paper use ore of astonishing purity—99.97 percent, Kodak liked to repeat, purer than the silver held in the United States Treasury—and in the early twentieth century, the company bought more of it than any other US institution except the government.[7] In 1917, about one twenty-fifth of all the metal mined in the country was sent to Rochester, and the same year, Eastman seriously considered buying a silver mine.[8] Over time, the company also imported silver from Mexico, Canada, and Peru, cow and pig bones and hides from South and Southeast Asia, and camphor from Japan.[9] It bought cotton from the markets in the US South.

This was what it took to make film in 1921, and not just at Kodak. Companies like Germany's Agfa, France's Pathé and Lumière, Belgium's Gevaert, Britain's Ilford, and the United States' Ansco also bought camphor from Japan and gelatin from the British and French empires in Asia. They purchased their cotton from the United States and their chemicals from Germany. They compared prices and researched sources and substitutes, testing what made good film and what customers would buy. However, very few of these companies understood raw materials in the way that Kodak did: as keys to controlling the global photographic market, a mission that, as early as 1894, George Eastman saw as his company's "manifest destiny."[10]

A Movie Trip Through Filmland pictures this, too. It's an animated sequence, and on a scale model of Earth, strips of film unfurl from Kodak Park, stretching southeast to New York City, then crossing the Atlantic to France. From there the film turns to Italy, Greece, Turkey, Iran, India, China, and Japan before taking the Pacific route back to the United States. By 1921, each stop on this itinerary was an established market for Kodak: the home of a shop selling cameras, film, and developing services, or an international subsidiary, whose numbers grew as the company expanded. The first of these was Eastman Photographic Materials, established in Britain in 1889. Two years later, the company built a factory in Harrow, England, to make photographic paper and, eventually, coat film base made in Rochester. By 1898, what had come to be known as Kodak, Ltd. directed most of Kodak's activities in Europe, including those of its two largest continental sales outposts: Kodak GmbH (founded in Germany in 1896) and the French Kodak SAF (founded in 1897).[11]

While the animation in *A Movie Trip Through Filmland* is simple, even quaint, Kodak's growth had long depended on a ruthless strategy of purchasing competitors at home and abroad. The British photochemist C. E. Kenneth Mees knew all about this. In 1912, Mees was ensconced at the London photographic firm Wratten and Wainwright when Eastman, inspired by the industrial research taking place in Germany (and, closer to home, at General Electric), invited him to found a laboratory at Kodak Park.[12] Mees wasn't sure. The job was attractive, but he was reluctant to leave his employer. So Eastman purchased Wratten and Wainwright outright, transferring its employees to Kodak, Ltd. Mees himself moved to Rochester, founding the Kodak Research Laboratories and working at the company for the rest of his career.

By the time Mees got to the United States, stories like these had already given Kodak a bad name, a reputation as a trust in the era of companies like Standard Oil and US Steel. The reputation was justly earned. For years, George Eastman had purchased the patents for technologies that would be helpful to his film and camera businesses, and buying patents often meant buying the companies that owned the patents.[13] Kodak was also the only film manufacturer in the Motion Picture Patents Company (MPPC), a conglomeration of US film producers and distributors founded in 1908 to limit competition in the US cinema industry. The MPPC was declared an illegal trust in 1917. By then, the US attorney general's office, which had been investigating Kodak for years, had already found the Rochester company guilty of violating the Sherman Antitrust Act by establishing a monopoly in the photographic industry.

The attorney general's decision arrived in 1915. Kodak appealed it, but with attention turned to the war in Europe, the process spun its wheels until 1921, when it ended with a consent decree that forced the company to sell six of the American photographic firms it had acquired and to stop purchasing US competitors.[14] This hardly touched Kodak's grip on the film industry; nearly all the professional motion picture film made in the United States still came from Rochester.[15] *A Movie Trip Through Filmland* revels in this fact. After its Pacific crossing, the film from Kodak Park ends its circumnavigation in a Hollywood film studio, where we see how this animated sequence was made. A cinematographer perches above a rotating globe as it is garlanded with film, seemingly mocking the attorney general's office with each turn of his camera's crank.

Nevertheless, below this triumphant surface, things were changing for Kodak. Its hands tied by the consent decree, the company was turning its appetite for "absolute control" to an expanding quiver of domestic raw-material suppliers. This led it beyond cinema's cosmopolitan capitals to, among other places, a shuttered war plant in eastern Tennessee. The unfinished factory would soon produce a new kind of film, bringing Kodak to manufacturing on a scale much larger than Kodak Park, to an even greater command of the global film market, and, eventually, beyond photography itself.

FIGURE 3. Kodak film circumnavigates the globe (*A Movie Trip Through Filmland*). Courtesy of the George Eastman Museum.

CELLULOID AND GAS

To understand Kodak in 1921, rotate the globe to Rochester, turn the clock back a decade, and think of George Eastman at the MPPC's height, his confident sway over the US photographic industry undercut, constantly, by anxiety about Germany—in the early twentieth century, home to the world's most sophisticated organic chemical industry. German dyes were Eastman Kodak's largest import, the substances that allowed the company's films and photographic papers to translate light into a gradations of black, gray, and white.[16] The dyes were made of coal: lumps and shards mined in the Ruhr valley's rich seams, then heated until they became the rock-like fuel coke. When a viscous byproduct of coal distillation, coal tar, was distilled in turn, it transformed into mineral acids, alkalis, anilines, and aromatics—the chemical building blocks for dyes as well as products like pharmaceuticals and fertilizers.[17]

In the nineteenth century, German chemical exports had swelled in step with synthetic dyes.[18] Starting with British chemist William Perkin's 1856 discovery of the mauveine tint that became Queen Victoria's favorite, the realization that coal-tar compounds could color materials like fabric and paper better and more reliably than natural extracts transformed the German chemical industry, creating powerful companies like BASF (Badische Anilin- und Soda Fabrik, 1865), Bayer (1863), Agfa (1867), and Hoechst (1863).[19] In 1873, when German chemist H. W. Vogel saw that dyes could also attune photographic emulsion to an array of hues, the synthetic dye industry shaped the new medium of photography, bringing dye makers like Agfa, Bayer, Hauff, and Schering into photochemistry.[20]

Agfa went farther than the others. It began manufacturing developing chemicals for glass photographic plates in 1888. By 1895, the year the Lumière brothers made the first motion picture films, Agfa was making the plates themselves, and soon after that, what was called orthochromatic—and, as it became sensitive to red light as well as blue and green, panchromatic—black-and-white film.[21] The dye maker had become a film maker, and it found a home for its film manufacturing next door to its dye factory in Wolfen, near the city of Bitterfeld, drawn by the chemical industry emerging in the region, as well as cheap land and the proximity of raw materials such as the brown (lignite) coal it needed to power the factory.[22]

Well before Agfa started making film, the dyes that created the German photographic industry had fed Kodak's expanding empire. Throughout the years that George Eastman was building his business, the United States hadn't invested substantially in organic dye making, partly because German products were better and partly because low tariffs made it cheaper to import European dyes than to make them at home. This changed in 1915, around the time the attorney general reached its antitrust decision against Kodak. World War I had already slowed German chemical shipments to a trickle, and that year, the British naval blockade stopped them altogether. Germany was the world's largest manufacturer of dyes, but the United States was their second-largest buyer, and at Kodak Park, the lack of German dyes brought film manufacturing to a near standstill. In response to the crisis, the US government jump-started domestic research and development. When the country finally entered the war in 1917, the Alien Property Custodian requisitioned the American subsidiaries of German chemical companies like Bayer and Agfa, building an industry on their formulas, plants, and techniques.[23]

Eastman—as eager to outrun the German chemical industry as he was to return to the government's good graces—was involved with this work from its earliest days. Mees's Kodak Research Laboratories had opened its Synthetic Organic Chemicals Department in 1914, and the division was in full swing by the time Congress declared war, making more chemicals than Kodak, and the rest of the US photographic industry, could use. It helped develop a marine fuel that, by suspending pulverized coal in mineral oil, burned slowly and economically. For this first air war, Kodak scientists created films fast enough to map enemy territory and positions from the relative safety of an airplane. The company's camera division invented an aerial mapping camera to go with the film, and it opened a school for aviation photography in Rochester.[24] In the spring of 1918, Eastman boasted to an attorney that he was "at the head of one of the most important war industries."[25]

Across the ocean, Kodak's European counterparts had military contracts, too. Just like Kodak Park, Agfa's factory in Wolfen made aviation film, as well as roll film that soldiers used to take snapshots at the front.[26] Also like Kodak, European film manufacturers' largest contributions to the war rested on organic chemistry, the coal-based chemistry of photographs and dyes. This began in the continent's dye factories, which sat idle as the naval blockade wore on, their products and raw materials unused. The materials included chemicals such as chlorine and phosgene, byproducts of dye making that became a new substance: poison gas, the "chemists' war's" terrible legacy, which killed up to one hundred thousand soldiers from Belgium to Poland and wounded more than a million more.[27] In 1917, part of Agfa's dye factory in Wolfen was converted to make poison gas.[28] In France, Pathé's film factory in Vincennes, outside Paris, made gas, too.[29] As *A Movie Trip Through Filmland* showed in 1921, modern film plants' exhaust fans were a worker-safety measure, a way to mitigate the risks of making cellulose nitrate film. Not long before that, the same infrastructure had been used for the deadly work of making chemical weapons.

Let's pause on these substances, cellulose nitrate and poison gas. Each one is a link between film and weapons. Film emulsion is made with dyes, and dyes are a cousin to gas, just as cellulose nitrate film is a cousin to the explosive nitrocellulose. The similarities seem to end there. Explosives like

FIGURE 4. Celluloid and gas (chemical warfare in the First World War, captured on film). © Imperial War Museum (IWM Q 27526)

nitrocellulose are loud and bright, while what made poison gas so frightening and fatal in World War I is that it didn't always announce its presence. Soldiers might not hear or see it in time to don a mask, so their other senses had to be on high alert.[30] Phosgene, soldiers were warned during World War II, smells like freshly cut hay. Yet flames *and* fumes were the reason why the ventilation had to be so good at factories like Kodak Park and Agfa Wolfen. If cellulose nitrate ignited, it burned relentlessly, dissolving into a miasma even more dangerous than the fire itself.

These twin dangers were no secret: Cellulose nitrate had made film fires a common and highly publicized occurrence, in cinemas and outside them. (In November 1914, for example, two people died when cigarette ash ignited reels of nitrate film that someone was carrying, poorly wrapped, in the smoking car of a Chicago commuter train.) As cinema's popularity grew in the late nineteenth and early twentieth centuries, these fires, and the fumes they created, forged an image of film as both a physical and moral danger. There was particular anxiety about cities, home to growing numbers of immigrants and working-class women and children, populations reformers saw as impressionable and vulnerable—to the dangers of industrialized, overcrowded environments and new media like cinema alike.[31]

An alternative existed. In 1865, ten years after cellulose nitrate's invention, French chemist Paul Schützenberger had created a similar substance, cellulose acetate, by combining cellulose with chloroform.[32] Because it contained no nitric acid, it was less combustible—no more dangerous than burning cardboard, it was often said—and within a decade of cinema's emergence, the film industry seized on the idea. In Germany, Agfa, Bayer, and BASF were all working on acetate formulas by 1906. Kodak began making cellulose acetate film in 1909, and starting in 1911, two film projectors ran exclusively on the substance: the Edison company's 22 mm Home Kinetoscope, which used film made by Kodak, and Pathé's 28 mm Kok, sold in North America as the Pathéscope and using Pathé film.[33]

Early cellulose acetate was a substitute for cellulose nitrate, but it wasn't a very good one. It tore and shrank easily, which meant that it had to be coated with emulsion more slowly than cellulose nitrate. This produced fewer feet per hour, making the final product more expensive than the nitrate film that rushed off Kodak's massive film-coating wheels with impressive speed.³⁴ But George Eastman knew that cinema's future could never rest on a material as dangerous as cellulose nitrate, and Kodak marketed its nonflammable film until 1911, when the MPPC put a stop to it.³⁵ Cellulose acetate cost an extra half cent a foot, and since municipal authorities in the United States had failed to require the film's use, there wasn't any incentive for Trust exhibitors to buy it.³⁶ However, Kodak's international competitors were still selling cellulose acetate film in the United States. Pathé's small-gauge (28 mm) film was targeted to amateurs, and Agfa sold its standard-gauge (35 mm) safety film to exhibitors unaffiliated with the MPPC, the so-called independents.³⁷ If Eastman couldn't dominate a market, he preferred to block it, and after the MPPC decision on nonflammable film, he transformed into cellulose nitrate's chief advocate, arguing to the New York fire commissioner in 1915 that "the best interests of the public as well as of the motion picture industry are subserved by properly safe-guarding the use of the nitro-cellulose film rather than by resorting to the use of the so called non-inflammable film."³⁸

Beneath Eastman's bluster, his repeated assurances that Kodak had no desire to make nonflammable film, the Kodak Research Laboratories kept tinkering with acetate, and Kodak Park kept making it. Some of the film went to the French company Gaumont and some to Edison, but sales were lackluster. Eastman began to despair that Kodak's investments in the substance, the factory's stocks of chemicals and raw materials, were a total loss.³⁹

World War I arrived as a deus ex machina. As fighter planes took to the sky for the first time, it became clear that cellulose acetate could replace the cellulose nitrate that was then—perilously, since something as volatile as cellulose nitrate doesn't mix well with shells and bombs—used as a weatherproof coating for aircraft. Acetate was suddenly indispensable. Agfa, Pathé, and Kodak began manufacturing cellulose acetate airplane lacquer (called "dope") and molding gas mask parts from the transparent substance.⁴⁰ When Kodak became the US military's main cellulose acetate supplier, government contracts allowed it to build a new, fully equipped plant in Rochester, an investment that George Eastman estimated at nearly $10 million (some $200 million today). Most of it, Eastman noted, could be written off as a war expense.[41]

THE MODEL CITY

Celluloid and gas. Between 1900 and 1920, the two substances gave rise to a wave of factories.[42] In the United States, there was Kodak Park's acetate plant. There was also Edgewood Arsenal in Maryland, run by the newly founded US Chemical Warfare Service. When the bells of the armistice rang on November 11, 1918, stilling the planes and the gas cylinders, most of these factories stopped, too, and soon, the chemical industry was mired in the brief depression of 1920–21. Workers left for new positions or found themselves out of a job, and laboratories, plants, and raw materials lay idle, tainted by the all-too-recent memory of industrialized death.[43]

The film industry's fortunes were the opposite. After years of wartime austerity, civilian film production was booming, and there was no way to make or show films without film stock. With chemical firms shuttering and others scrambling to find new uses for materials left over from the war, the eagle-eyed Eastman saw an opportunity for vertical integration. Kodak had been doing this for years, working from the principle that amassing control over raw materials would translate into higher quality as well as lower prices. During the war, the company added a new gelatin plant and paper mill, both near Kodak Park. Farther away from Rochester, Eastman toyed with the idea of buying a coal mine, then a silver mine, but neither project materialized.[44] The attorney general's antitrust decision, however, lent new urgency to the idea of buying mining and agricultural concerns instead of film and camera companies, and in the depths of the depression, the stars finally aligned. This time, the material was wood.

Wood is invisible in the depictions of film manufacturing (not a few of them sponsored by Kodak) that appeared as cinemas burst into new life after the war. It's nowhere in *A Movie Trip Through Filmland,* or in *Motion Picture Magazine*'s September 1918 tribute to George Eastman, or in a photo-essay about Kodak published two months earlier in the glossy *Photoplay*.⁴⁵ "Silver—pure silver, and cotton—ordinary plantation-variety cotton," the *Photoplay* essay rhapsodizes, are film's marquee components, its very own stars. But film also couldn't be made without the basic chemicals with impenetrable names that served as reagents or solvents. Many of these ingredients were made from trees. For example, before cellulose nitrate could be pressed into film, the mixture of cotton linters and nitric acid had to be dissolved in methanol, which is created by distilling wood. Methanol is also used in weapons, and in 1920, it drew Kodak to the eastern Tennessee city of Kingsport. There, a half-built factory, a product of the wartime chemical boom, held out the possibility of a cheap in-house supply of the alcohol.⁴⁶

Kingsport in 1920 was a relatively new city. It was incorporated in 1917, though it had existed since 1909. That year, the farmland on which it was built became a waypoint on the Carolina, Clinchfield, and Ohio Railway, which started in Kentucky coal-mining country, stretched across the bituminous fields in southern Virginia, and ended at Spartanburg, South Carolina's cotton mills.⁴⁷ Both this part of the railroad and Kingsport itself were bankrolled by John B. Dennis, a Wall Street financier whose fortune was backed by Progressive visions of rationality and efficiency.⁴⁸ These visions formed a blueprint for Kingsport, as did the idea of a "New South": the post–Civil War project of rebuilding the region around industry instead of agriculture.

The South's natural resources were instrumental to both ideas. Since Reconstruction, Southern elites had pinned their hopes for the region's economic recovery on its raw materials and inexpensive labor force, which they marketed aggressively to Northern industrialists. In Appalachia, where Kingsport was located, these economic campaigns had moral overtones, calling on Northern Progressives to capitalize on Southern resources and in doing so, Ronald D. Eller writes, "'uplift' and 'Americanize' the mountaineers."⁴⁹

For Dennis and his partner, the Tennessean J. Fred Johnson, this played out in a founding myth in which Dennis's money "punched the Clinchfield Railroad through the mountain barrier that had been holding back the Kentucky coal like a dam," bringing industry to, as Johnson put it, "people in the hills wanting an opportunity to use their hands and their native American brains."⁵⁰ Since the point was industry *and* uplift, Kingsport was a planned city: a good, healthy place to live whose single-family homes, churches, and schools revolved around interlocking factories, plants so closely coordinated that one's finished product or waste could "immediately become the raw material of another."⁵¹ The industrial puzzle began with trees: One of the city's earliest factories was the Kingsport Extract Corporation, built in 1912 to make tanning chemicals from oak and chestnut bark.⁵² Next were the Kingsport Tannery and the Kingsport Pulp Corporation, which used the extract

FIGURE 5. Portrait of J. Fred Johnson (1874–1944), 1930s. Photographer unknown. Courtesy of the Archives of the City of Kingsport.

company's products and its wood waste.⁵³ With World War I, the United States' chemical weapons industry reached Kingsport. The Federal Dyestuff and Chemical Corporation opened shop in the city in 1916, making dyes, explosives, and poison gas. Tear gas began to flow from a branch of Edgewood Arsenal in 1918.⁵⁴ When the American Wood Reduction Company of Chicago began building a methanol plant in Kingsport the same year, it was hardly out of place: rooted in timber, reaching into chemicals. Yet before the plant even opened, the 1920–21 depression forced these factories into suspended animation.

By this point, Kingsport's civic institutions were well established. Dennis and Johnson had brought in Columbia University's Teachers College to design the city's school system, and after consulting with the Rockefeller Foundation's Bureau of Municipal Research, they'd chosen the industry-friendly, technocratic city-manager system of government, which Progressives like Dennis favored for its supposed political neutrality. For the most part, though, Kingsport was run by the polite, silver-tongued Johnson and the Kingsport Improvement Corporation over which he presided.⁵⁵ Johnson was ready to spin his tale of the "model city" to anyone who would listen, as a journalist from *The Saturday Evening Post* found out when he arrived in Kingsport in 1938. The journalist was on a southern tour and planning to spend only an hour learning about the city. After parking his car in a garage, he asked the attendant where the chamber of commerce was. No luck. What about the board of trade? Nothing, again. "You'd better," the attendant said, "see Fred Johnson."

This was how Garet Garrett came to spend two days in Kingsport with Johnson—"a native mountain man, doer of old sayings"—and Dennis—"a fine economic realist, Boston by tongue"—learning how, after the war, Johnson set about finding replacements for Kingsport's shuttered factories. Because the goal was to find "something for the town to do that would create northbound freight," Johnson looked to Dennis's circle. Dennis and George Eastman were acquainted from New York City. The financier must have known of Kodak's antitrust troubles and that the company was looking to vertically integrate.[56]

Eastman sent the Kodak executive Perley S. Wilcox south with a delegation. The men were impressed. As soon as they came home, they sent another envoy, telling him that they wanted to know what "that man Johnson" had done to them. "Don't let him do it to you," they added, "but look."[57] Yet not one of the Kodak employees who traveled to Tennessee that year could resist Johnson's "'Kingsportitis' treatment" ("We have seen tight-lipped, hard-boiled New Englanders simmer and melt under a few days' treatment from him," Wilcox recalled later).[58] Johnson spared no expense on these junkets. There were visits to the methanol plant (still government property), and there were banquets, hunting parties at Dennis's estate, and trips to a school whose pupils had been carefully instructed to appeal to the visiting businessmen.[59] The men heard about the city's proximity to coal and trees and its efficient rail links with Southern cotton. They saw its principle of industrial frugality in action, and they studied the spacious "garden city" design being drafted by the Massachusetts city planner John Nolen, admiring its wide streets, hospital, and parks.[60] They learned about its leaders' strict adherence to Prohibition and about the labor force those leaders were devoted to uplifting through work and industry. It was almost too good to be true—nearly a perfect match with George Eastman's vision of what industry, and the city around it, should look like.

Eastman had already experimented with this vision in Rochester, where Kodak was the largest employer and Eastman its primary benefactor. A near lifelong resident of the city, the Kodak founder was deeply involved in Rochester's public life. He gave generously to the university and to civic organizations and applied his Progressive worldview to city governance; in 1925, he, too, successfully advocated for a city-manager government.[61] Eastman's convictions were visible above all in Kodak Park—in Sanford Jacoby's words, a "paragon of welfare capitalism" where there was no room for unions but whose employees were offered generous vacations and insurance plans, company housing, and, on a regular basis, plain cash.⁶² This was what Kodak called the wage dividend, one of the practices that kept workers with the company for their entire careers, often multiple generations of a family.

Through at least the 1930s, even in diverse Rochester, these workers were mostly US born, unorganized, and white (like many reformers, politicians, and businesspeople of his day, George Eastman was a supporter of the eugenics movement).⁶³ The same demographics helped draw Kodak to eastern Tennessee. When Northern industrialists traveled to Kingsport, Margaret Wolfe writes, they heard that the city's residents were "'pure'"—code for white—"Americans who had not yet come under the influence of union organizers." As Perley Wilcox observed later, "It is only natural that George Eastman and Frank Lovejoy should have been concerned about the kind of people to be found in a new location for the company's business—whether they too would have the quality of thinking for themselves and would not be misled by the flood of Bolshevist propaganda that followed the first world war."⁶⁴

Kingsport's founders didn't dispel these impressions, and they knew that if a company like Kodak came to Kingsport, it would secure the city's future. In the final act of courtship, the visitor was George Eastman himself, then sixty-six years old. Eastman was enchanted. On July 29, he wrote to George B. Dryden, husband of his niece Ellen, of the "little town started by the Clinchfield Railroad . . . one of the nicest places I have ever been in." He praised Kingsport's coal mines, its "inexhaustible supply of wood and waste wood for distilling alcohol," its river, its brick and cement factories, and the tannery that, he speculated, could also make photographic gelatin. "It now has about 10,000 inhabitants," he added, "only one of which is a foreigner."⁶⁵

RACE AND RAW MATERIALS

When George Eastman wrote this of Kingsport, his mind may have been on Knoxville, two hours or so southwest. In summer 1920, Knoxville was still reeling from the race riot that had convulsed the city months earlier. Like the other events in what came to be known as 1919's Red Summer, the violence in Knoxville drew on the legacy of the United States Civil War and World War I. It was less than a year after the armistice, and Black soldiers were returning from Europe having experienced racial equality unlike anything in the United States—in Cameron McWhirter's words, with "a broader vision of American citizenship and an appreciation of what liberty and freedom really meant."[66] This sat uncomfortably with some white Americans, including President Woodrow Wilson, who were watching the Russian Civil War nervously and equated Black economic, social, and political agency with "Bolshevism," and "Bolshevism" with "foreigners." The mood was widespread among politicians and industrialists. In June 1919, George Eastman distributed a flyer at Kodak Park warning employees starkly about the Russian Revolution.[67]

At the same time, in the long aftermath of the United States' own civil war and the period of Reconstruction that followed it, Black workers had continued to move north, attracted by better jobs, pay, and treatment. In Southern cities like Knoxville, which had an established Black elite, the Great Migration was coupled with an influx of rural white farmers and mountaineers seeking the industrial jobs that defined the New South. In Knoxville on August 30, 1919, some of these former farmers and mountaineers attempted to lynch Maurice Mays, a Black man who had been accused of rape and murder by a white woman, setting off violence that lasted two days and took many lives, including Mays's.[68]

Kingsport in 1919 was a fraction of Knoxville's size, and at the time of the Red Summer and Red Scare, the war plants had closed and the "model city" was reinventing itself. As it did, it came to look similar to post–World War I Knoxville. Kingsport's Black citizens made up 8 percent of the population, a number that was steadily declining. And although John Nolen's city plan included a Black neighborhood, segregated yet meant to meet the same standards as the rest of the city, Black workers found the barriers to the city's vaunted interlocking industries to be nearly insurmountable. Kingsport, Tom Lee writes, was "built around the availability of white labor."[69]

These racial dynamics were the inverse of the ones that rooted film firmly in the South, where what *Photoplay* tellingly called "ordinary plantation-variety cotton" was inseparable from Black labor: enslaved people's and later sharecroppers' and tenant farmers'.[70] George Eastman was intimately familiar with this. In July 1920, when he wrote to George Dryden about Kingsport, he mused that the city appealed to him because of its factories and raw materials and people, but also because it was on the same latitude as his farm outside Ringwood, North Carolina: a place called Oak Lodge, which Eastman visited three times a year to hunt and ride and host guests. Oak Lodge was a working farm. It was home to about twenty-five Black tenant farming families, and its primary crop was the cotton with which the tenants paid their rent (one bale for a "one-horse" farm, two bales for a "two-horse" farm).[71] Linters from the farm's cotton were not used to make film, at least not directly: Oak Lodge cotton was a cash crop. But Eastman poured as much energy into it as he did into all of Kodak's raw materials. He compared the cost of gins, read up on agricultural techniques, and tracked cotton prices, instructing his proxies in North Carolina to sell when they were high and hold when they were low.[72]

One of these proxies was Henry Myrick, the Black foreman who oversaw Oak Lodge. Myrick, the son of two formerly enslaved people who also lived and worked on Eastman's property, was the rare Black manager in the area. Though this raised eyebrows among the neighbors, Elizabeth Brayer writes, for Eastman, giving Myrick authority was in keeping with the Northerner's abolitionist upbringing. It was also driven by Eastman's belief in Progressive approaches to management, which sought institutional answers to all manner of perceived social problems. The same convictions made Eastman an ardent supporter of the project of Black "uplift" that, following the ideas of Booker T. Washington and others, flourished in the New South.

So, while J. Fred Johnson and the Kingsport Improvement Corporation were making Kingsport into a model city, Eastman was making Oak Lodge into an experimental farm. Myrick was central to the experiment, and Eastman took a paternalistic, almost scholarly interest in him. "It is very interesting to watch the development of this man," he wrote in 1915 to his friend Murray Bartlett. "When I want to do anything new down there I first learn how to do it myself and then teach Henry."[73] Eastman extended similar interest to the children at Oak Lodge, for whom he founded a school—a "model practical negro school," as he described it, which taught things like farming and construction and basic academic skills.[74] When Myrick's son Clyde was a teenager, Eastman paid for him to continue this kind of education at the Hampton Normal and Agricultural Institute in Virginia, where Booker T. Washington himself had studied.[75] Like other historically Black colleges and universities, Hampton (now Hampton University) was founded after the Civil War to educate Black and later Indigenous students, but as Allyson Nadia Field writes, it "was more than a school; it was a concept. Its educational model was intended to correct the former use of Black slaves as human capital." Through agricultural and vocational training, Black students at Hampton would become economically self-sufficient, modest, and "useful," all in slow service of racial capitalism.[76]

George Eastman knew Washington personally, and in 1924, he divided $2 million of his photographic fortune between Hampton and Alabama's Tuskegee Institute, where Washington was head. The donations were the largest the schools had ever received, and like all of Eastman's philanthropy, they reflected his interests, in this case "education of the Hampton Tuskegee type," which Eastman considered "the only hope of the Negro race and the settlement of this problem."[77] The vision of uplift in this type of education was more gradual than that embraced by figures such as W. E. B. Du Bois, and it wasn't as radical as the ideas animating 1919's Red Summer. It also echoed a tenet that drove Kodak's history over the twentieth century and that Eastman may have worked out, in part, at Oak Lodge: the idea that the cornerstones of good society, good business, and good photography were raw materials and the people who worked with them. Absolute control, here, was social engineering.

At schools like Hampton and Tuskegee, Field writes, "raw material" was also an all-purpose metaphor likening students to the materials with which they worked. Most important among these was cotton, the foundation of the United States' plantation economy and, later, film.[78] Three hundred miles to the west, Johnson, Dennis, and the Kodak executives saw a similar potential in trees for Kingsport's white farmers and mountaineers. This was captured in photographs—a pair of snapshots of J. Fred Johnson's neighbor boys, which someone handed to Kingsport's unofficial mayor on August 27, 1921. Johnson sent the photographs to George Eastman that same afternoon. "Perhaps one day," he wrote, "they may help carry on the good things you have started at Kingsport—who knows?" Eastman's reply was brief but warm, thanking Johnson for the pictures of the boys. "If they are fair specimens of the crop you are growing in Kingsport," he wrote, "the future ought to be rosy for that delightful town."[79]

MAKING FILM SAFE

Tennessee Eastman was incorporated on July 20, 1920, and it didn't stray from Kingsport's origins. It was a lumber company first. It cut its own trees and dragged them from hilltops, and it was only scrap (woodchips, branches, roots—60 percent of the tree) that was fed into stills to make methanol for Kodak.[80] In keeping with Kingsport's commitment to reuse, even the waste from distillation was sold: One of Tennessee Eastman's most successful products of the 1920s was the Charket, a briquette made from charcoal dust left over from the wood used to heat the methanol stills. Still, in its first years, the company struggled, and Kodak considered closing it. Plans changed when the focus shifted from methanol to the byproducts of its distillation, three of them in particular: acetone, acetic acid, and acetic anhydride, the chemical foundations of cellulose-acetate safety film.[81]

Although Eastman put his acetate ambitions on hold a decade earlier, safety film had maintained a steady presence in the United States and Canada thanks to the Pathéscope, whose 28 mm had been named the

FIGURE 6. Snapshot of George Eastman with a Ciné-Kodak 16 mm camera, 1926. Attributed to Audley D. Stewart. Courtesy of the George Eastman Museum.

North American safety film standard in 1918.[82] In Rochester, Kodak still made acetate film for Edison, and the Kodak Research Laboratories continued experimenting with the substance. In 1923, the company was satisfied enough to make a larger and more public gamble on acetate by releasing the Ciné-Kodak, the world's first 16 mm camera-projector pair, which exclusively used safety film.[83] The Ciné-Kodak was designed to do what Pathé's small-gauge machines did: take cinema out of theaters and studios, doing away with its professional trappings. Echoing the catchphrase that sold Kodak's Brownie camera—"you press the button; we do the rest"—it was marketed as a motion picture equivalent to that push-button machine, which put photography into amateur hands.

The Ciné-Kodak's film was unique in several ways. It was, of course, nonflammable—a fact that its width guaranteed, since by cutting it to 16 mm instead of 17.5 mm, Kodak ensured that frugal exhibitors or filmmakers couldn't try to split a strip of industry-standard 35 mm nitrate in half. It was also "reversal": You could shoot a strip of film one day, have it processed the next, and on the third day project the same strip, magically transformed in a laboratory from negative to positive. Because it used only one length of film (doing away with the negative that was usually necessary to make both motion pictures and photographs), reversal film was cheaper, theoretically, though the cost of cellulose acetate more than made up for this. In 1923, it cost $3.50—more than $60 in 2024—to shoot a minute and a half of film, putting the Ciné-Kodak out of reach for all but the wealthiest Americans.[84]

Cost was a problem with safety film; Kodak had known this for years.[85] It was many times more expensive to make acetate film than it was to make nitrate film because one of acetate's essential ingredients, acetic anhydride, had to be imported from Germany.[86] This was where Tennessee Eastman came in. The company was already making acetic anhydride from the acetic acid that was a byproduct of methanol distillation, giving it an ample supply of the chemical, practically for free. If you considered the Carolina, Clinchfield, and Ohio Railway, Tennessee Eastman looked like an even better home for safety film, since the coal-to-cotton line put almost all of cellulose acetate's raw materials within reach.[87]

But the rise of Kodak's safety film, and with it 16 mm, wasn't this simple, and it wasn't very fast. Despite George Eastman's long-held (if well-disguised) belief in nonflammable film, and despite the fact that Tennessee Eastman could easily make it, Kodak balked at the idea of mass-producing safety film until the very end of the 1920s. The company's executives considered the demand for acetate to be promising, but unproven. As always, George Eastman would only embrace a new product if he knew he could corner the market, and the only way to keep 16 mm's prices low enough for that was to make cellulose acetate for more than just film.[88]

What else was made of cellulose acetate in the mid-1920s? With the war well over and commercial aviation still a small industry, there wasn't much demand for airplane dope. Yet the Swiss brothers Dreyfus, who had made Pathé's cellulose acetate for years, had begun refashioning dope into acetate rayon, one in a burgeoning line of artificial silks.[89] In 1924, the Dreyfus-owned Celanese company opened an acetate rayon plant in Cumberland, Maryland.[90] Agfa was also making rayon in Germany, and diversifying into fibers would be an obvious choice for Kodak, too, since as film manufacturers already knew from their work during World War I, cellulose acetate was endlessly malleable.[91] Still, it took years before Kodak was convinced. It took until May 1929, when celluloid's kinship to poison gas became unavoidable.

As Kodak Park's architects knew well, when nitrate film burns—when it's merely overheated—it creates a gas. Some describe the fumes as yellow. To others, they're brown. For Dr. William Edgar Lower of the Cleveland Clinic, they looked like phosgene. Lower knew what he was talking about. He had seen gas in Europe during the war, when the clinic's founders volunteered with a team of doctors and nurses from Cleveland and were dispatched to Rouen, France. But he didn't expect to see it in Cleveland, not on May 15, 1929, when a leaky gas pipe in the clinic's basement ignited the X-ray films that were stored there, all of them made from cellulose nitrate. An explosion shook the building, pushing fumes through air shafts and stairwells, shattering windows, warping walls, and forcing patients, nurses, and doctors into hallways, where they asphyxiated on the thick, noxious air.

Lower's colleague, Dr. George W. Crile, was in the operating room at the time of the blast. Afterward, he stood on the hospital's lawn, the muscle memory of the wartime field hospital returning. He spoke crisply but calmly, *The Columbus Dispatch* reported. "'They're all gassed. It's a film gas,' he clipped out and then plunged into a battle hardly less terrible than the horrors he experienced while serving with the Lakeside medical unit of the A.E.F. [American Expeditionary Forces] during the World war. A nurse, almost lifeless, who had served with him in France, was lying on the grass."[92]

Sometimes, film gas kills right away. It's dense in carbon monoxide and nitrous oxide, a treacherous combination. A few victims at the clinic were found sitting in chairs, and they would have seemed to be asleep if not for the jaundiced cast of their skin (this came to be known as the "yellow death").[93] Others, like Crile's colleague, the nurse, were brought out of the building unconscious from the carbon monoxide and died later from the nitrous oxide, which makes the lungs swell, its tissues burst. This was true of gas injuries that Crile and Lower had seen during the war, too. You could walk away from an attack, hardly believing your luck, then drown hours or days later from invisible internal wounds.

The Cleveland Clinic fire killed 123 people. No hospital accident in the United States has ever been as large, with so many fatalities. In the weeks that followed, a team from the Chemical Warfare Service was sent in to investigate. The team, which included a Kodak representative, warned against the "tendency to connect the accident at Cleveland with chemical warfare." They stated, "It is important that our citizens should know that there is no connection with these gases formed by the burning of film and the agents used in chemical warfare." In fact, film gas could be even worse than phosgene or chlorine or mustard gas. "In the Cleveland disaster, there were large volumes of poisonous gas generated in a close space; enormous concentrations were thus possible. Conditions of this sort could not be duplicated in wartime, except by accident." The team observed that even Army-issued gas masks were useless against burning celluloid.[94]

For the public as for people like Crile and Lower, this did little to dissolve the analogy the disaster drew between film and chemical warfare or to quell resurgent fears about cinema fires. The moving-image trade press tried to tamp these down. It reassured readers that film safety was a matter of fireproofing, storage, and ventilation; it was about regulating the places where film was projected, not regulating film.[95] But the outcome was inevitable. From 1930, most of the world's X-ray film was made from cellulose acetate. Kodak had already been producing X-ray film on acetate for a few years, but after the Cleveland disaster, the acetate for these films was made in a brand new plant in Kingsport.[96] A rayon plant followed a year later, making long yarns called Koda for fabrics like satin, as well as the shorter, wool- and cotton-like staple fiber Teca (named for Tennessee Eastman). Both kinds of rayon were sold to the fashion industry.[97] Within a few years, Tennessee Eastman had its own research laboratory, and the factory was making even more things from acetate.

These products ranged from the thin plastic sheets that make safety glass shatterproof to the molding compound Tenite, used to make pens, steering wheels, and the very reels on which film was wound.[98] They were made from trees, coal, and cotton. They were shaped by nativism, by Black labor, by trust-busting and war, and they helped Kodak grow without directly touching the photographic industry, as the consent decree had mandated. But while the products' roots were in film—in the well-founded fear that celluloid could be as toxic as poison gas—the same was true for their branches. Within a decade, rayon would offer Kodak the chance to expand internationally in the very industry from which it was barred at home.

FIGURE 7. Making Eastman acetate rayon. From Schwarz and Mauersberger, *Rayon and Synthetic Yarn Handbook*, 29. Courtesy of the Science History Institute.

CINEMA ARTIFICIAL SILK

Kodak's move into rayon was not a radical development: Film and artificial silk had coexisted for decades. In the first years of the twentieth century, when Pathé began thinking about manufacturing its own film base, it held discussions with the French company that pioneered nitrocellulose silk, Soie de Chardonnet, and with the Italian Viscose Society. Pathé tested viscose base until 1910, when it settled on Dreyfus cellulose acetate. It then built its own plant in Vincennes, where by 1914, three-quarters of the films were made from cellulose acetate.[99] As Pathé consolidated power, eclipsing the legendary Lumière company, the chemist who made Lumière's film base, Victor Planchon, was forced to convert his celluloid plant (Société des Celluloses Planchon) into an artificial silk factory.[100] Around the same time, the Cines film studio in Rome was exploring the idea of manufacturing its own film stock. The company went so far as to purchase a rayon factory, which it later spun off into the fiber manufacturer Cines Seta Artificiale: cinema artificial silk.[101]

All of this was before World War I, and before airplane dope. By the time the war was over, fiber making was standard for film manufacturers, and film making was standard for fiber manufacturers. It made sense. There wasn't much chemical difference between the two products; the difference was in how they were finished, so branching from one to the other allowed companies to use knowledge, factories, and materials efficiently. The same thing was happening outside Europe. While Celanese was adding fibers to its product lines in film and airplane lacquers, the American chemical giant DuPont was expanding from explosives to fibers and film.[102] Japan's Dainippon Celluloid Company, originally a rayon firm, created the Fuji Photo Film Co., Ltd. in 1934, and in 1939, Fuji began making cellulose acetate film.[103]

Yet as Kodak considered diversifying into fibers, it paid closest attention to Agfa. Compared with Pathé, the German company was something of an upstart, but George Eastman saw it as a more formidable competitor. Its film factory in Wolfen had expanded during the war, growing beyond the size of Pathé's in Vincennes, and it had the entire German chemical industry, Eastman's personal bugbear, behind it. More worryingly, the German company clearly held global ambitions that could only be compared to Eastman's own.

Agfa's ambitions rushed into the spotlight in 1920. While Kodak was busy negotiating the Tennessee Eastman purchase and the consent decree, Europe's economies were recovering from the war, and the

FIGURE 8. Agfa Wolfen factory, 1927. © Industrie- und Filmmuseum Wolfen.

continent's film manufacturers had stepped up film sales to the United States, hoping to capitalize on Hollywood's postwar energy. For Agfa, this was the first film the company had been able to sell across the Atlantic since 1914, and between January and August 1921, it shipped enough positive 35 mm to make 150 feature film prints, twenty times more film than Pathé exported in the same period. Practically overnight, Kodak's share of the positive 35 mm used in the United States shrank from 94 percent to 81 percent.[104] The competition that Eastman had squelched came roaring back, and most of it was from Agfa.

After decades of easy dominance, Kodak might have grown complacent, but George Eastman wasn't one to take a fight lying down. In March 1921, he dispatched the film sales agent Jules Brulatour to Congress, where hearings were being held on new tariffs, to argue for a 30 percent duty on unexposed motion picture film. The tax was essential, Brulatour argued, "to the protection of this American industry."[105] Then, at the end of August, Kodak announced that it had purchased three large East Coast film laboratories, Paragon, GM, and Sen Jacq, and would supply them exclusively with its own film. Independent laboratories were offered Kodak film at good prices. If they chose to buy from foreign firms instead, they were threatened with the kind of competition that—as the American film industry knew all too well by now—could only come from Eastman. The scheme worked like a charm, and no European-made 35 mm positive stock was sold in the United States from September 1921 to April 1924, when the Federal Trade Commission grasped the situation and ordered Kodak to immediately sell the laboratories. By then, however, the Fordney-McCumber Tariff Act had been passed, imposing duties short of the 30 percent Brulatour and Eastman wanted but high enough to discourage European film manufacturers from selling to the United States.[106]

Fordney-McCumber, which ushered in the decade of high tariffs culminating in 1930's Smoot-Hawley Act, was sweeping. Starkly protectionist in the face of growing European exports, the act imposed steep duties on all kinds of raw materials and finished goods—including rayon. This, too, affected Agfa, whose involvement with artificial silk stretched back decades. It began experimenting with the fibers at the beginning of the 1900s and expanded its operations during World War I, when there was a severe shortage of wool. After the war, Agfa didn't stop making rayon, alarming the German company Vereinigte Glanzstoff-Fabriken (VGF), Europe's largest producer of artificial fibers. In a compromise, VGF and Agfa formed the Aceta company in 1925, opening an Aceta acetate rayon plant in Berlin in 1926.[107]

VGF returns us to eastern Tennessee, which by the mid-1920s was becoming a center for artificial fibers. This capped decades in which the United States' textile industry had migrated from New England to the South, drawn by the same raw materials and cheap labor that brought Kodak to Kingsport. The tariff had spawned even more growth, as subsidiaries of European companies looked to capitalize on the region's forests while avoiding high import duties.[108] Between 1926 and 1928, VGF opened two rayon factories in Elizabethton, Tennessee, thirty miles from Kingsport: American Bemberg (which made viscose fibers) and American Glanzstoff (cuprammonium fibers). Kodak, which was then considering making rayon at Tennessee Eastman, watched the new competitor warily.

VGF was busy in 1926. In addition to Aceta and American Bemberg, it debuted a third factory that year, a film plant in the southwest Berlin district of Köpenick.[109] The plant, dubbed Glanzfilm, was everything a modern film executive could hope for. Built from the same red brick you could find at Tennessee Eastman and Kodak Park, it boasted one of Europe's largest film-printing plants and a "palatial" board room whose full-moon windows overlooked the Spree—the sparkling river road that led to Glanzfilm's neat cobblestoned streets, bringing raw materials in and sending finished products out.[110] Yet despite the expense of the endeavor, VGF had no real interest in making film; the factory was purely a response to Agfa's foray into viscose rayon, which violated VGF's patent on the fibers. Since Agfa had chosen to compete with VGF on its turf, VGF would compete with Agfa on its own.[111] Unlike with acetate (a smaller market), compromise was out of the question.

Because it knew or cared little about film, VGF called on Pathé to create Glanzfilm, licensing the French company's film patents and paying it to design the plant and train its employees. The arrangement suited Pathé, which was looking for ways to make its film abroad. In 1922, it agreed to help the Italian company FILM (Fabbrica Italiana Lamine Milano) construct a film factory in the Ligurian town of Ferrania, a frustrating partnership that had failed by the time Glanzfilm opened (the FILM Ferrania company would eventually make its home there).[112] In 1924, Pathé struck an agreement with DuPont. The short-lived DuPont-Pathé Film Manufacturing Corporation helped Pathé circumvent US tariffs and produce its films across the Atlantic. In exchange, the Pathé brand gave DuPont a high-profile, consumer-friendly outlet for its nitrocellulose, sales of which had diminished after the war.[113]

In the mid-1920s, these kinds of arrangements were common in the international chemical industry. Mergers, acquisitions, and cartels—most famously Germany's IG Farben chemical conglomerate, of which Agfa was a part—offered ways to use up postwar chemical surpluses, reduce competition, regulate prices, and help companies compete abroad.[114] The VGF–Pathé agreement promised all of this. It allowed Glanzfilm to take over Pathé's markets for unexposed film in Central, Eastern, Southeastern, and Northern Europe, while the Berlin factory was to make 25 percent of the film Pathé needed for the library of titles that could be projected with the small-gauge Kok (or Pathéscope).

This meant that Glanzfilm would also make a new kind of film: 17.5 mm, designed for a projector called the Pathé Rural. The Rural was Pathé founder Charles Pathé's pet project, a dream he had nurtured since 1924, soon after Kodak released 16 mm.[115] Like the Ciné-Kodak, the Rural used cellulose acetate film, and as its name suggested, it was sturdy enough to be lugged to France's villages and farms, community halls and churches. Pathé was optimistic about 17.5 mm since it was cheaper than 16 mm (unlike Kodak's small format, it could be created by cutting nonflammable 35 mm stock in half, so it didn't require special film-casting equipment) and it projected larger images on a screen.[116]

However, Charles Pathé's ambitions for 17.5 mm were doomed by the foreign agreements he struck over the course of the 1920s. The largest of these was with George Eastman in 1927, creating the Kodak-Pathé company and giving Pathé's factory in Vincennes to Kodak. Since the Vincennes factory made cellulose acetate, the Kodak-Pathé agreement specified that it was to begin making 16 mm for the French market (alongside the 17.5 mm film it already made).[117] Later that year, when Glanzfilm's film turned out to be hopelessly mediocre, Pathé sold its shares in the German company. VGF, which had already settled with Agfa over viscose, was only too happy to abandon film manufacturing, leaving the new film factory ready and waiting. It was an opportunity Eastman couldn't pass up: a chance to challenge Agfa at home. Glanzfilm became Eastman's third film plant in Europe, and Kodak transformed into the world's largest producer of nonflammable film, further justifying Tennessee Eastman's move into cellulose acetate. The Berlin factory also gave Kodak's 16 mm another foothold in Europe, slowly tipping the scales away from 17.5 mm and toward the American company's small format.[118]

Now it was Agfa's turn to be alarmed. The company saw Kodak's purchase of Glanzfilm for what it was: a play for influence in the German film industry, which Agfa largely supplied. It responded in kind. Kodak had taken advantage of Agfa's domestic situation, so Agfa took advantage of Kodak's, merging its North American holdings with Ansco, the struggling upstate New York film company with which Kodak had tussled legally for years. The Agfa Ansco Corporation, founded in 1928, allowed Agfa to skirt the tariffs that George Eastman argued for so stridently, bringing its films to American buyers under a familiar brand name.[119] When the company's new film plant opened two years later in Binghamton, equipped with machinery from Wolfen, it immediately became the United States' second-largest manufacturer of film, including 16 mm.[120] Yet Kodak still had the advantage, since it made the chemicals for its film base domestically, at Tennessee Eastman, while Agfa Ansco relied on IG Farben plants in Germany. Kodak couldn't blame it for this, since the material was good. It bought celluloid for its new factory in Berlin from the same plants.[121]

THE KODAK WORLD

As the 1920s turned to the 1930s, George Eastman came to Kingsport less and less frequently. His health was failing, and the once indefatigable man was increasingly confined to his mansion in Rochester. J. Fred Johnson, ever gracious, wrote often, encouraging Eastman to stop by if he ever made his way to Oak Lodge, promising good hunting and better weather: brilliant autumns and early springs. He thanked Eastman for all he had done to shape Kingsport—unquestionably now a Tennessee Eastman town—and the "many people whose lives have been made more useful and happier through the ways you have opened to them here." That thought struck Johnson in particular in January 1932, near the nadir of the Great Depression. "I wish," he wrote to Eastman, "you could stand around and feel the earnest consecration of men to their duties in these difficult times. I have never seen any as good in any plant anywhere."[122]

FIGURE 9. "The Kodak World" at the 1939 New York World's Fair. Manuscripts and Archives Division, The New York Public Library.

Some months earlier in Kingsport, there had been an exhibit of Tennessee Eastman's acetate fibers. Johnson spotted a friend at the opening, a radiologist whom he'd brought his wife to see a few weeks earlier but who had refused payment. Johnson greeted Dr. Hankins warmly and insisted that he take home a bolt of acetate satin—yellow, Hankins's wife's favorite color, and enough to make a dress. Sue Hankins thanked Johnson with a poem about the cloth, and because the poem was for the man who had woven Kingsport's founding myth, it was also about trees and industry. "The magic arts were surely sought," she wrote in the last stanza,

> When this sheer loveliness was wrought
> It seems like some fantastic tale
> To say that once on hill and vale

This satin lived, in sun and breeze;
   reincarnated from those trees
That grew within your country line—
   Trees made sublime by hand divine—
And then the One who made trees grow
   Endowed man with the power to know
How he might make their beauty spread
   Its usefulness in silken thread!

Yet Eastman, to whom Johnson sent the poem, must have seen no magic in it, no divinity.[123] Weeks away from ending his own life, Eastman knew that rayon, like film, was built from the efforts at control that ran through his company's history. This control began in materials like Sue Hankins's trees. It extended to people like Henry Myrick, to Fred Johnson's young neighbors in Kingsport, to the workers at Kodak's factories, and to the factories themselves. By the time of Eastman's death in March 1932, these factories formed a whole "Kodak World," as the company put it at the 1939 World's Fair, made up of Kodak Park, Kodak, Ltd., Tennessee Eastman, and now also the former Pathé and Glanzfilm plants in Vincennes and Berlin, the camera factory Eastman acquired in Stuttgart, Germany, in 1931, and the gelatin plant in Peabody, purchased in 1932.[124] The factories churned out film and cameras but also products that seemed to have nothing to do with photography—products like glue, plastics, and chemicals, which built on the wide-ranging possibilities of film's raw materials. Cellulose acetate rayon was the most important of these products, and the year Eastman died, Tennessee Eastman became the United States' second-largest producer of the fibers. This made it more profitable than its parent company in Rochester. It also transformed Kodak into a chemical giant whose only near rival, at least among those specializing in film and photography, was Agfa.[125]

This would not have happened without World War I and its aftermath. Kodak might never have manufactured 16 mm if airplane dope hadn't made its failed early investments in cellulose acetate profitable, and it would never have founded Tennessee Eastman if Kingsport hadn't become a node in the US chemical weapons industry. There may be irony in the fact that nonflammable film—which made moviemaking, movie-watching, and movie-showing safe and ordinary activities—was forged from these violent conditions, and that in order to make film that could not catch fire or decompose into toxic fumes, Kodak needed a factory built for explosives and gas. The irony recedes when we consider film's raw materials: the camphor, the silver, and especially the cotton, with its roots in plantations and before that, in the Middle Passage. Kingsport, the New South city where Kodak's new subsidiary took root, aimed to overwrite this history in the Progressive vernacular of rationality and science. It also helped prepare the ground for the even greater violence that, during World War II, spiraled from the work of making film.

CHAPTER TWO

Story of a Tree

PICTURE A TREE. As Sue Hankins might have when she wrote her poem in 1932, imagine a maple, an oak, a chestnut, or a loblolly pine, its roots grasping a rocky Tennessee hillside. It's a tall tree, more than thirty feet high, and if you climbed to its highest branches, you'd see mountainsides being cleared, a river soon to be dammed, railways and roads creeping into what, when the tree began growing, was a panorama of farms and forests.

Now picture the tree as it's cut, as it falls, as it's loaded onto railcars and hauled to the outskirts of one of these towns, where it's hewn into lumber. The planks are stacked and carted away, and someone sweeps up the chips and twigs strewn across the sawmill floor. When there are enough of them, they're dropped into a cavernous copper bowl—a still, hot enough that after a while the wood isn't wood anymore, it's carbon and smoke and vapor. Fumes rise out of the still and into a condenser that traps pyroligneous acid. The acid, which takes its name from fire and wood, is mostly water. But if you know how to find them, there are 180 other chemicals in there, too: methanol, acetone, acetic acid, tar.[1]

Things move in fits and starts. Acetic acid is isolated. It's mixed with more chemicals and with purified cotton linters, and this mixture sits, congealing into flakes. When the flakes are dried, then dissolved using acetone also taken from our tree, they become a syrupy solution, cellulose acetate. The solution's placid surface is deceptive, for it contains multitudes. It can be slicked into film, molded into household objects, or extruded through spinnerets until it blooms in a thicket of threads.

Let's say that when this batch of cellulose acetate is mixed, it's summer 1938 in Kingsport. The United States' cellulose acetate industry has continued to grow—more than tripling over a decade—and with it, Tennessee Eastman.[2] Factory buildings have expanded. There's a new power station and a plant to filter water. Hundreds of employees have been inducted into the Kodak system of wage dividends and good benefits. Then, in October, France, Britain, and Italy cede Czechoslovakia's western border regions to Germany. Germany invades Poland the following September. War begins, sending cellulose acetate made at least in some part from our tree across the ocean as film for Europe's militaries, rayon for cargo parachutes, and Tenite for bayonet scabbards and Jeep steering wheels. This is all before Pearl Harbor. By the end of 1942, cellulose acetate has brought Tennessee Eastman and Kodak to high explosives and the Manhattan Project. From trees to safety film to the atomic bomb in the space of twenty-two years.

This is not how the story of film and war usually goes, but its outlines were familiar in the 1940s. Something similar was playing out at Agfa Wolfen, which by 1930 was a central arm of the IG Farben chemical cartel. Like Kodak and Tennessee Eastman, the Wolfen factory still made film and rayon. Now, however, it was also the nerve center for a network of factories, engines for the Third Reich's military expansion. As the chemistry that made film branched into ever more devastating weapons, factories like these dealt in a widening spectrum of materials. There were still trees and cotton and silver, and there were ores like manganese and uranium and plants like flax and straw. These weapons and materials brought new people and places into the factories' orbits: miners in the Belgian Congo, women imprisoned at Ravensbrück, citizens of Hiroshima. This is mostly invisible in the films and photographs for which World War II is so well remembered. But it is the same story.

FIGURE 10. Entrance to Rayon and Synthetic Yarns in Textiles exhibit, Brooklyn Museum. *Rayon and Synthetic Yarns in Textiles,* December 11, 1936–January 25, 1937. Records of the Department of Photography, Brooklyn Museum Libraries and Archives.

We could begin in December 1936, when you might have seen our tree, or what was made from it, on display at the Brooklyn Museum. Three years before the war, photographs of Tennessee Eastman's cellulose acetate fibers and fabrics were mounted on the walls of a sleek Functionalist gallery, enlarged to show the qualities of the yarns, the warp and weft of the cloth. Every year, the museum's Department of Industrial Art put on an exhibit like this, showcasing "the work of men and machines which is the basis of our modern standard of living." In 1935, the subject was glass. In 1936, it was rayon. If it wasn't clear enough that rayon was the avant-garde of textiles, all you had to do was visit the adjacent gallery, where luminaries of modern dance like Mary Wigman, Martha Graham, and Harald Kreutzberg were captured by experimental photographer and filmmaker Thomas Bouchard.[3] Rayon and film, two sides of the same coin.

The 1930s was the heyday of function and design, of Art Deco and Bauhaus style. Artists were engineers, and materials like glass and steel were the stuff of a world that could be organized rationally, a life lived better through industry and technology. There was no better example of this than rayon. In all its forms, the substance was stunningly versatile. It could be cut to any length: lengths of fine, smooth fibers like Tennessee Eastman's Koda or short tufts of Teca. It could take on wool's nub and drag or the gloss of the satin that J. Fred Johnson gave Sue Hankins.

Cellulose acetate—the newest kind of rayon and Tennessee Eastman's specialty—promised even more. The Celanese Corporation boasted that its yarn, Eastman's competitor, "neither shrinks nor stretches in washing and keeps its shape under all circumstances. It does not rot or mold. It launders easily even with cold water because whatever dirt or perspiration there may be on the garment is on the surface and not impregnated in the yarn as in the case of other fibers. It dries amazingly quickly. It never clings and is comfortable under all conditions."[4] Dry cleaners advertised acetate clothing as "hygienic and . . . little affected by bodily excretions and perspiration."[5] It was a miraculous substance, apparently immune from the mess and trouble of the natural world.

We could say, then, that the decade of function and design was also the decade of cellulose acetate; this was how Eastman chemist Donald F. Othmer remembered it.[6] In turn, cellulose acetate embodied the promise of industrial chemistry: the idea that laboratories and factories could make anything found in nature, and maybe make it better. This idea had been a powerful one during World War I, when embargoes and blockades disrupted international shipping and the Kodak Research Laboratories were born. It held sway in the interwar years, when as Tara Zahra has described, the long tail of wartime social and economic upheavals sparked antiglobal sentiments across the world.[7] When Adolf Hitler assumed power in Germany, again throwing trade into question and raising the specter of war, chemistry's possibilities seemed even more urgent.

Everywhere in these years, artificial fibers like cellulose acetate took on outsized importance. Just as the laboratory-made textiles could not shrink or stretch, rot or mold, they were shapeshifters, ready to assume any ideology. They could represent the Protestant thrift woven into Tennessee Eastman's self-image ("Plant Makes Fortune Out of Waste Products," *The*

Knoxville News-Sentinel declared of the Kingsport factories in June 1933), or Fascism's racial hierarchies and nationalism. The VGF-owned company Bemberg advertised its silky underwear in Germany as "sterile," immune to the bacteria that could fester in cotton and silk—as Yvette Lane argues, a ready metaphor for Nazism's fear of racial infestation.[8] At the 1937 National Textile Exhibition in Rome, the Italian-made Lanital, fashioned from casein (milk protein), was heralded as the "new textile of independence." There was a demonstration plant at the exhibition, and on November 24, the state newsreel *Giornale Luce* tracked its workings from beginning to end. Milk was poured into great vats, its casein isolated and dried into something resembling cellulose acetate flakes. Once it was dissolved and extruded, the newsreel showed, Lanital behaved like natural wool. Its fibers could be carded, spun, and woven, slipping off industrial looms in creamy swathes of tartan.[9]

MAKING USE OF THE WORTHLESS

In Italy as in Germany, "independence" meant autarky, the material and economic self-sufficiency that Mussolini and Hitler embraced; wearing "fabrics of the future" like Lanital, Jeffrey Schnapp writes, was one way that citizens could participate.[10] On its most basic level, autarky meant rejecting foreign trade in favor of materials grown or mined within a country's own borders and substances created by its scientists. There was also a mysticism to it, rooted in Fascism's obsession with purity and conformity. Primo Levi describes the Italian chemical laboratory in which he worked in 1938 as "white, anesthetized limbo."[11]

And so we could also begin this story of film and war in Nuremberg, Germany, in September 1936. There, three months before the Brooklyn Museum's rayon exhibition opened, Germany's roadmap for autarky, the Four-Year Plan, was announced at the Nazi Party's annual rally. Because Hitler, then chancellor of the Third Reich, saw Communism and the Soviet Union as existential threats, the plan stated that Germany needed to rearm. Rearmament would only be possible if the country saved its foreign-exchange currency for industrial and military materials. Germany would make everything else from its own land, mines, and laboratories.[12]

In the Third Reich, autarky had the same economic foundations and spiritual overtones it had in Fascist Italy. It was an economic question because Germany imported most of what it needed to make weapons, from iron ore to petroleum, aluminum, and rubber. But to sell the public on the Four-Year Plan, the government needed to inspire everyday Germans to provide for themselves. In the wake of the Nuremberg rally, a raft of books and pamphlets was entrusted with this job. The books were paeans to Germany's natural resources, the materials that were to feed and clothe the country. At the same time, they made the chemical industry out to be what chemistry had been centuries earlier: alchemy, the miraculous transformation of matter. The result was a kind of nationalist science fiction. One of the books was titled *Verwertung des Wertlosen* ("making use of the worthless," translated into English as *Science and Salvage*), and it described a fantastical world in which laboratories could weave new commodities out of factory seconds and byproducts, something Tennessee Eastman had been doing for years ("Plant Makes Fortune Out of Waste Products!"). Cork could be pressed from potato peelings, copper recovered from seawater, and fertilizer conjured from city sewers. Above all of this stood synthetic rubber, fats, fuels, and fibers—the sleek, engineered companions to potato-cork and seawater-copper that would secure "the fundamental conditions for the life of the German people."[13]

Synthetics were the province of IG Farben, the core of Germany's chemical industry and Agfa's parent organization, and Agfa brings us back to our story of war and film. IG Farben was created in 1925, at the moment when cartels and mergers were seen as a way to control the unstable postwar chemical market. As the Great Depression took hold, the cartel was streamlined further, and in 1929 it was split into three divisions, each representing a critical area of chemical production. Division I was responsible for high-pressure chemistry, and Division II for chemicals like dyes and pharmaceuticals. Division III was headquartered in

Wolfen, and for the most part, it made what Agfa had always made: products fashioned from the cellulose in plant walls, like film and artificial fibers, as well as cameras and photographic paper. Now, though, Wolfen also coordinated photochemical and fiber factories across Germany. Given the kinship between cellulose nitrate film and nitrocellulose, Agfa made explosives, too, including at Dynamit Nobel, where Agfa Ansco and Kodak's Berlin factory bought celluloid.[14]

Agfa Wolfen's director, Fritz Gajewski, was Division III's head. Gajewski's youth had been something like George Eastman's. One of many children and too poor to enter university immediately after school, he apprenticed at a pharmacy before attending the University of Leipzig, and he was fascinated by photography and big-game hunting. After he graduated from the university (where he acquired the dueling scar slashed across his chin, a badge of honor for the German elite), he started his career at BASF, where he managed chlorine and phosgene production during World War I.[15] This made Gajewski a good chemist and a better businessman, and when he came to Agfa in 1928—following a gas-to-film ladder not unlike the one that built Tennessee Eastman—he was charged with making the company's factories modern, profitable, in many ways more American. He brought on energetic new employees, helped steer Agfa Ansco through its rocky debut, and built a research laboratory modeled after Kodak's in a gleaming Neue Sachlichkeit headquarters near the Wolfen film factory.[16]

The science of films and fibers was important to Gajewski. As a chemist in the mold of Kodak's own, he knew that Agfa wouldn't survive on the competitive world chemical market if it didn't have the right processes and the right materials. So, although he joined the Nazi Party in 1933, Gajewski had little patience for the Party's more outlandish ideas about autarky—for instance, some Four-Year Plan books' suggestion that cellulose for rayon didn't only need to come from cotton or wood, but that it could also be drawn from German-grown plants like flax or nettles, even from reeds, hops, or milky-white tufts of thistledown.[17] Once, when he questioned Hitler's assertion that rayon could be made from potato leaves, Gajewski was forced to make an elaborate formal apology.[18] This may have been why, in 1936, Agfa commissioned its own Four-Year Plan book about Vistra, its trademark wood-based viscose staple fiber. It allowed the company to follow the Party line while setting the scientific record straight.

The key to threading this needle was the author whom Agfa commissioned to write *Vistra: The White Gold of Germany* (*Vistra, das weiße Gold Deutschlands*), Hans Dominik. Dominik was known best for his science fiction, but he had been trained as an engineer, and his novels—among them *Rubber* (*Kautschuk*, 1930), *The Steel Secret* (*Das stählerne Geheimnis*, 1934), and *Atomic Weight 500* (*Atomgewicht 500*, 1935)—were girded by technical precision. *Vistra* is the same. Like all German books about autarky, it places rayon within a sweeping civilizational drama. Yet it doesn't lose sight of the science.[19] With expensive color

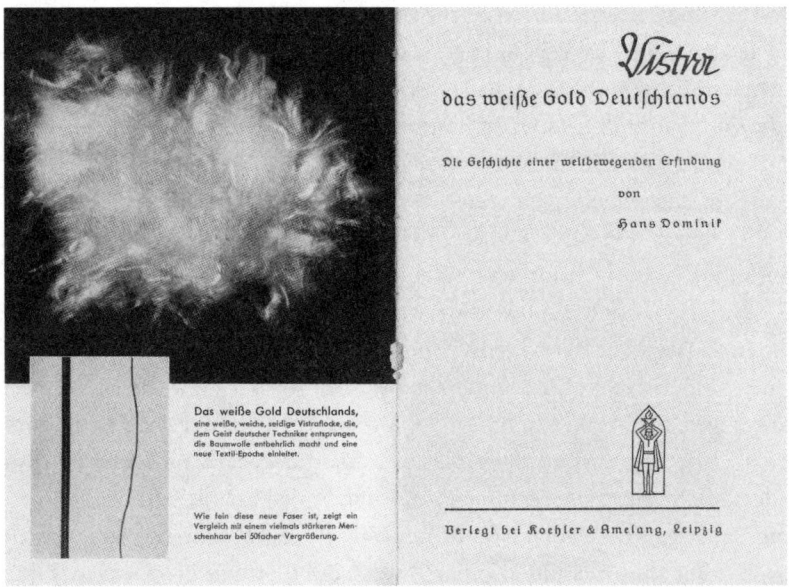

FIGURE 11. Title page to *Vistra, The White Gold of Germany*. The caption reads: "A white, soft, silky tuft of Vistra, which, born from the minds of German engineers, makes cotton superfluous and ushers in a new era of textiles. This new fiber's fineness can be seen by comparing it with a much stronger human hair at 50x magnification." From Dominik, *Vistra, das weiße Gold Deutschlands*.

inserts, photographs, and diagrams, Dominik's book explains what the *Giornale Luce* segment about Lanital would a year later: exactly how a raw material—a German raw material—is transformed into a finished product. It also places Agfa at the center of what Esther Leslie calls the Third Reich's "synthetic world": a world built from rayon and plastics, reflected back to German spectators in the mirror of Nazi film, all of it made by the same company.[20]

CHEMISTRY AND EMPIRE

Dominik's book was designed to sell rayon as much as the Four-Year Plan: There's a sample of Vistra cellophaned inside each copy. Almost ninety years on, the tufts of fine fibers still gleam unnaturally white, and if a reader hadn't caught it from the title, they emphasize that the book is actually about cotton. Cotton was a problem that German autarky couldn't quite solve. The country's cotton industry was Europe's largest, large enough to make cotton textiles Germany's most important export.[21] Cotton itself, however, didn't grow well in Central Europe, so it had to be imported. Staple fibers like Vistra could replace it in some products, like clothing, although low cotton prices in the wake of the Great Depression made it hard to justify the expense of making Vistra.[22] Naturally, Vistra was also no help to film. Like rayon, celluloid needed a natural source of cellulose, and cotton linters were one of the raw materials that Agfa Wolfen had to source entirely from abroad.[23]

Historically, most of Germany's cotton had come from the United States, but the Four-Year Plan's disavowal of trade, especially with America, made these imports politically unpalatable. So, while German books about autarky railed against the idea of "submitting" to foreign empires like the United States' in cotton, they called for an empire of Germany's own. The German Reich, they wrote, should expand into Eastern Europe, commanding Central Asian cotton along with Romanian oil, Ukrainian grain, and Bohemian and Silesian coal.

Autarky would fund military conquest. Military conquest would forge an empire. Empire would make many more raw materials available to Germany, completing the cycle of self-sufficiency.[24] Chemistry would be a partner to it all.

These dreams of empire were built on memory as much as envy. In the early twentieth century, Germany had grown cotton in its sub-Saharan African colonies, on farms built with American assistance—in particular that of Booker T. Washington, with whose support a group of Black faculty and students from the Tuskegee Institute departed in 1900 for the colony of Togoland (Togo) to teach cotton cultivation. While the expedition revolved around cotton, it had to do just as much with the Tuskegee-Hampton idea of industrial education, which George Eastman supported so ardently and experimented with at Oak Lodge. As Angela Zimmerman writes, this folded "techniques and assumptions about agriculture, labor, race, and education from the American South" into the German colonial project, feeding fantasies of the German empire as enlightened, rational, and humanitarian.[25]

Germany's years of colonial cotton farming in Africa showed that these fantasies were far from the truth. They were coercive and violent: German responses to the 1904 Maji Maji rebellion, a revolt against forced cotton cultivation, left 200,000 dead.[26] The years were also relatively short. After World War I, when its colonies were dissolved, Germany again became dependent upon US cotton. When the Four-Year Plan came into effect, its diplomatic and trade offices scrambled to buy from Brazil, Argentina, Mexico, and Egypt, but it wasn't enough.[27] Germany needed an empire of a different sort. Until it achieved that empire, Agfa Wolfen would have to consider using trees in place of cotton linters—local varieties only, of course, like spruce and beech.[28]

Even as it was attempting to disconnect from the United States, Germany continued to see America as a model for its autarkic ambitions—as a model of self-sufficiency, Timothy Snyder writes, and a land empire par excellence.[29] This impression was only partially accurate, since the

United States wasn't self-sufficient. It relied on imports, and imports made American politicians and industrialists nervous. In the late 1930s and early 1940s, American publishers also started to issue books about raw materials. These books, too, listed the country's natural resources and described how they could be used. They emphasized the danger of relying on overseas suppliers and the importance of self-sufficiency, and they praised the chemical industry's power to synthesize. Running through them was the same anxiety about control that had spurred George Eastman to found Tennessee Eastman and scout silver mines, and as in Germany, this anxiety was both inward and outward looking. It worried over domestic materials and industry while yearning for foreign sources close to home. For the United States, "close to home" meant, in particular, a hemispheric economy that would break Latin America's links to Germany while bolstering US supplies.[30]

These were not new ideas. For decades, Megan Black has shown, the US Department of the Interior had used fears about resource exhaustion to justify incursions overseas and on Indigenous land in North America.[31] The same kind of thing happened in the private sector, where it was sometimes hard to distinguish what was vertical integration and what was autarky. Take George Eastman's contemporary Henry Ford, whose dazzling industrial success also lay in mass production. Like Kodak, Ford had been vertically integrating since the company's early years, and in the 1920s, Ford towns were dotted near mines and forests across northern Michigan. Employees made automobile parts while also, on Henry Ford's instructions, growing their own vegetables. Ford's preoccupation with corporate self-sufficiency veered into improbable raw-material experiments not too different from those in the Third Reich—famously, a car made from soy-based plastic—and in 1928, the automobile magnate, too, turned his search for self-sufficiency abroad, building a plantation in Brazil to ensure a captive supply of rubber. The Brazilian community, which Ford modestly dubbed Fordlândia, was a spectacular failure.[32]

Ford's Brazilian project returns us to our story of trees, film, and war. Like cellulose acetate, rubber is made from trees. It is a hardened version of the sap coursing through plants that first grew wild in Brazil's Amazon valley and through vines that snaked high into sub-Saharan African forests. In the late 19th century, rubber had driven the brutal forced-labor system in the Belgian Congo, where the punishment for missed harvesting quotas was dismemberment or death.[33] As Belgium's colonial profits skyrocketed, other European colonial powers went in search of the same thing, building their own rubber plantations in Asia and Africa. By World War I, Britain controlled most of the world's supply.[34] Yet if that war proved anything to industry, it was that raw materials were a precarious possession; laboratories were much more reliable. Germany and the Soviet Union introduced synthetic rubbers in the 1930s, followed by the United States and Britain.[35] The synthetic rubber industry expanded during World War II when Japan occupied the Pacific, cutting off the Allies from Asian rubber plantations.

It was around this time that Tennessee Eastman started working on synthetic rubber. Some years earlier, a scientist at the Kodak Research Laboratories had discovered a way to make the chemical hydroquinone using manganese dioxide. Hydroquinone is a crucial ingredient in photographic developer, the chemical bath that helps images on paper or film appear from the blur of emulsion, and as Tennessee Eastman's capacity grew, Kodak moved the chemical's manufacturing to Kingsport.[36] When hydroquinone turned out to be an ideal arrester for synthetic rubber—something that, added partway through the reaction, kept the substance from becoming too sticky—Tennessee Eastman started supplying the US War Production Board. After World War II, when synthetic rubber became the norm and demand for hydroquinone showed no signs of slowing, the company began buying manganese in Cuba, and in 1946, it founded the Holston Trading Company to oversee its purchases.[37] The United States had occupied Cuba from 1898 to 1902 and again from 1906 to 1909. With rubber as with cotton, the chemistry that promised an escape from empire only tightened empire's stranglehold. And chemistry and empire powered both film and war.

FIGURE 12. Confluence of the Holston River's north and south forks, 1937. Photographer unknown. Courtesy of the Archives of the City of Kingsport.

HOLSTON

The Holston Trading Corporation, Tennessee Eastman's manganese business, was named after the river that forms in Kingsport. If you follow the Holston as it turns out of the city, you'll find yourself heading southwest, almost to Knoxville, where the river—wider and more powerful now—rushes toward the Cherokee Dam. In 1937, a photographer from Kingsport took a snapshot of the place where the dam would be built. The Holston arcs through the photograph, haloed by hills and sky and mist. Below, on a riverbank triangle of land, there are what look like two cars: picnickers or fishermen parked beneath a perfect pair of trees, the only ones thick with foliage.[38] Four years later, both land and trees would be underwater thanks to the dam, which the Tennessee Valley Authority built to generate electricity for the war plants being constructed across eastern Tennessee. The largest of these was also called

Holston: the Holston Ordnance Works, an Ordnance Department facility designed and operated by Tennessee Eastman, the company that helped build the city where the river began.[39]

Tennessee Eastman ran the Holston Ordnance Works from 1942 to 1945, and by the end of the war, the factory was making 570 tons a day of RDX (Research Department Explosive), a powerful mixture of formaldehyde, ammonia, and nitric acid.[40] RDX is highly volatile: The slightest jolt can make it explode, though the risk is lower when it's combined with TNT and beeswax into what is called Composition B. Holston made this, too, nearly 90 percent of all of the Composition B that the United States produced during the war.[41]

When Tennessee Eastman began making RDX, the explosive was indispensable. German U-boats were destroying Allied ships in the North Atlantic, and RDX was the sole weapon that worked reliably against the submarines. Scientists, however, only knew how to make it using a stop-and-start method called batch production. A chemist at the University of Michigan, Werner Bachmann, had developed a new higher-yield method that substituted acetic anhydride for most of the nitric acid, but the process was still slow. It also left large amounts of acetic acid that needed to be converted into acetic anhydride and reused. Acetic acid and acetic anhydride were Tennessee Eastman's bread and butter, since finding a way to recycle and concentrate acetic acid had been essential to mass-producing safety film. In November 1941, the National Defense Research Committee asked Tennessee Eastman to help with the acetic acid and anhydride problem.[42] Within three months, the company had agreed to build pilot plants for RDX and Composition B, and Eastman chemists had the RDX plant up and running weeks later.

Acetic acid was the first reason the National Defense Research Committee turned to Tennessee Eastman for RDX. Thanks to cellulose acetate film and rayon, there were few companies so intimately familiar with the chemical.[43] But for Tennessee Eastman, cellulose acetate was more than the sum of its ingredients. It also represented the company's capacity for mass production, which was essential if the Allies were to make enough RDX and Composition B to win the Battle of the Atlantic. Mass production had been a hallmark of Kodak's manufacturing since 1899, when Frank Lovejoy devised the continuous wheel process that allowed film to unspool nonstop from Kodak Park.[44] The idea was passed along to Tennessee Eastman, first for methanol and then for cellulose acetate, and when Tennessee Eastman opened Holston, the chemicals for RDX were piped continuously from building to building in liquid form, always at the ready. On the other end of the production line, Composition B pellets moved along conveyor belts in orderly rows—a great improvement in time and safety over the manual methods use to shape the explosive elsewhere.

These pipelines and conveyer belts—miles and miles of them, set along military-straight roads—were the arteries in the 6,500-acre, 242-building complex that, by April 1943, Tennessee Eastman was operating in Kingsport. Holston was built a safe distance away from the company's film, rayon, and Tenite plants, since making that much RDX was dangerous, far more so than cellulose nitrate film had ever been. New hires were treated to the cautionary spectacle of TNT and RDX exploded side by side on steel plates—TNT dented the plate, RDX broke through it entirely—and in the hope of extinguishing a fire before it could spread, the factory's floors were constantly kept wet.[45] Despite these dangers, Holston had no trouble finding workers. As it had been in 1920, the Tennessee Valley was one of the country's poorest regions, and the salaries for workers in war plants were many times those of rayon- or brickmakers, schoolteachers, or lumbermen. When you counted thousands of construction workers alongside the 6,146 people Holston employed at the peak of its operations, the plant quickly overwhelmed the city. Households took in lodgers, businesses kept extra hours, and at shift changes, buses from across the region crowded the downtown, closing off entire blocks.[46] For the second time, Kingsport became the center of a chemical weapons industry. Now, however, it was Kodak making the weapons. By January 1944, thanks to trees like the ones overlooking the Holston River, the world's largest film manufacturer was running the world's largest explosives plant.[47]

Holston *was* large. Roughly speaking, 6,500 acres is ten square miles, and the area that made up the factory used to be tobacco farms and cornfields as well as the estate where, twenty years earlier, J. Fred Johnson took George Eastman hunting. The RDX plant also dwarfed both Tennessee Eastman and Kodak Park, which had grown along with their own military contracts. By the time Holston was built, Tennessee Eastman had been churning out fibers and plastics for all branches of the US and Allied militaries for more than four years. It made cellulose acetate for the safety film that ran through military projectors and cameras, the Astrograph machines that allowed fighter planes to navigate by the stars, and the microfilm systems that photographed soldiers' letters onto 16 mm, shrinking military mail to one-fiftieth of its usual bulk. This film was processed in "flying darkrooms" and mobile photographic trailers made, like the cameras and projectors, in Rochester, and it was cut into sheets for map photographs, photolithography, and

FIGURE 13. Aerial view of Holston Ordnance Works, Area 4, undated. Courtesy of the Archives of the City of Kingsport.

medical and industrial X-rays.[48] Tennessee Eastman, that is, was the shining paragon of Kodak's mass production, known for making a lot of products quickly and well. On Christmas Eve, 1942, this brought the company to a project that dwarfed anything it had made in Kingsport.

James C. White, Tennessee Eastman's general manager, was home that day. His wife Vera would have been home, too, or out at Kingsport's shops, busy with holiday crowds. Maybe White's children, young adults, had just burst in the door for a few days at home.[49] Christmas Eve that year was a Thursday, though. Continuous production meant that Tennessee Eastman's plants were always running, and Holston was just getting up to speed, so it wouldn't have been unusual for White to get a phone call. A long-distance call: That was unusual. It was even more unusual for the operator to connect you to Gen. Leslie R. Groves.

White knew Groves, since the general had overseen the construction of Holston, the largest project the Army Corps of Engineers had directed to date. He may not have known that Groves was now heading the Manhattan Engineer District, the top-secret project to build an atomic bomb. The project was ready to move beyond its experimental beginnings. On December 2, a reaction in a squash court underneath the University of Chicago's football field had confirmed that it was possible to harness the energy created by nuclear fission. This energy, scientists knew, could be the basis for a devastating weapon. But a weapon would need much, much more fissionable material.

Groves thought that Tennessee Eastman might be able to help solve that problem by running a factory at Oak Ridge that would separate fissionable uranium atoms from their nonfissionable counterparts. And so he didn't call White on Christmas Eve to wish him the best for the season. He called about an "operating problem" that he wanted to discuss. Groves couldn't say more; could White meet him in Washington next week? The call was a short one, but from that moment, White knew that the holiday was going to look a little different.

On December 30, in Washington, Groves went over the basics: a new factory for a new weapon, based on cutting-edge science that was still mostly theory. White was skeptical. He reminded Groves that this wasn't the kind of work Tennessee Eastman did then, or ever had done. Rochester handled chemical research; Tennessee Eastman was a specialist in chemical engineering. As Pap Ndiaye has described, however, chemical engineering took center stage in the Manhattan Project, and so did companies capable of what Tennessee Eastman already did in Kingsport and at Holston: orchestrating the large-scale conversion of raw materials into usable products.[50] Discussions continued over the next two weeks, eventually making their way to Rochester. Kodak executives agreed that with the project's potential to help end the war, there was no other option but to accept. By early in the new year, both Tennessee Eastman and Eastman Kodak had formally signed on.[51]

STRATEGIC MATERIALS

Uranium was an unfamiliar material for Tennessee Eastman, but not for Kodak, which for years had used uranium nitrate, a salt, as a toner. After it was bathed in the solution, film and paper glowed yellow, lightly radioactive. The metal wasn't seen to hold very much value then, before the war. It was much less important than radium, which sits alongside uranium in ores like pitchblende and carnotite and was widely used in medical settings and to make luminous instrument dials. Yet with the discovery of uranium's use in nuclear fission, what was once a byproduct became these ores' most hotly desired component. In fact, of the 1,200 tons of pitchblende packed into drums at Shinkolobwe, then shipped to Matadi and New York, the Manhattan Project only purchased the uranium. The project held onto the sludge left after refining, promising to return it to Union Minière du Haut-Katanga at the war's end so that it could be used for the company's main business: radium.[52]

The ore-filled drums had been dispatched by Edgar Sengier, Union Minière's director. In 1940, Katanga's uranium deposits were widely believed to be the richest in the world, and Germany, whose scientists were also working on an atomic bomb, wanted to control the ore as desperately as the United States did.[53] When Germany occupied Czechoslovakia's western borderlands in 1938, it acquired the Jáchymov (Joachimsthal) mines, then thought to be Europe's largest uranium deposit. Germany secured more uranium in May 1940 when it occupied Belgium, capturing 3,500 tons of stockpiled Congolese ore.[54] The Congo itself was surely next, so the United States encouraged Sengier to send over what Union Minière had on hand. Sengier arranged for it to be shipped to his company's newly founded office in New York, the African Metals Corporation.[55]

As a gargantuan endeavor in physics and chemistry, Manhattan Project was in the business of resources—an early suggestion for the project's code name had been "Laboratory for the Development of Substitute Materials"—and by purchasing Sengier's uranium, Groves confirmed that the project traversed the same violent histories of empire that defined materials like cotton and rubber.[56] In the Belgian Congo, this violence had begun with the ivory and slave trades, and it continued with rubber under the Congo Free State, the deceptively named colony that Leopold II claimed for himself in 1885. The Leopoldian system's cruelty was widely publicized. In novelist Joseph Conrad's well-known words, it was "the vilest scramble for loot that ever disfigured the history of human conscience and geographical exploration," and the international controversy surrounding the Congo Free State meant that Leopold's endeavor lasted only until 1908.[57] However, Belgium retained the colony, and the exploitation didn't stop. When the Second World War made copper, gold, diamonds, and tin central to the "slaughter of the war," in Raymond Dumett's words, "devoured by the assembly lines that made brass cartridges and cannon shells," Belgian officials extracted these metals and minerals using Leopoldian methods: forced labor, minimal safety measures, and harsh repression of strikes.[58] The mines sent virtually all their copper to the United Kingdom and most of their tin, cassiterite, cobalt, manganese, zinc, cadmium, silver, gold, and uranium to the United States.⁵⁹ The uranium sent to New York had been gathered by hand, exposing the miners, Gabrielle Hecht writes, to "a year's worth of radiation in about two weeks."⁶⁰ To fulfill additional US orders, miners worked night and day. When their shifts were over, they returned to homes built with radioactive materials and to a tainted water supply.⁶¹

This was not the picture the Belgian government wanted to paint of the Congo. The Belgian colony had been synonymous with colonial greed since Leopold's days, and the government remained defensive, paranoid about criticism. Throughout World War II, its propaganda agencies stubbornly repeated the Leopoldian myth: the idea that the king (who never personally visited the colony) was responsible for "pulling the Congo from the shadows of the jungle."⁶² The agencies asserted that the Belgian Congo gave more raw materials to the Allies than anywhere else in Africa, no minor propaganda point in these years when hunger for materials raged. The Belgians hoped it was a point that would guarantee Allied support of their country during the occupation, and that when peace came, they would maintain their colony.⁶³

The point was to be made on film, the lingua franca of wartime propaganda. This was easy enough to arrange, because the Belgian Congo was teeming with filmmakers. Some of them worked for the US Office of Strategic Services, which was in the Congo to make sure that the United States controlled the colony's uranium. There was Armand Denis, under cover as a photographer but in fact a Belgian-born chemist turned filmmaker who had emigrated to the United States and worked in Hollywood on films about "exotic" locations, including the Belgian Congo. Everywhere he went, Susan Williams writes, Office of Strategic Services agent Dock Hogue was said to carry his 8 mm home movie camera, doubtless a Kodak.⁶⁴ The entire operation was overseen by Rudyerd Boulton, an ornithologist who had made ethnographic films during expeditions to the Congo in the 1920s and 30s. The films were

16 mm and, like Hogue's 8 mm, very likely cellulose acetate made in Kingsport.[65]

At the time, Belgium's own best-known colonial filmmakers were Gérard de Boe, Ernest Genval, and André Cauvin. De Boe, a government employee, had lived and worked mostly in the Congo since the late 1920s. Genval was a poet and songwriter who traveled back and forth between colony and metropole and made films in the 1920s and 30s.[66] Cauvin was the man the Belgian government chose to lead the propaganda effort. A lawyer and filmmaker with a taste for drama, Cauvin had the right credentials and the right contacts. Just before the war, he had made two short films about artists that won him acclaim at the 1939 New York World's Fair (*Hans Memling, peintre de la Vierge* [*Hans Memling, Painter of the Virgin*] and *L'agneau mystique* [*The Mystic Lamb*]). He had experience filming in the Congo, where he made the 1939 *Congo, terre d'eaux vives* (*Congo, Land of Living Waters*) and *Nos soldats d'Afrique* (*Our African Soldiers*). He was also a member of the Belgian resistance, and after several members of his network were arrested at a Brussels café in 1942, he fled to London, where he asked his friend Paul-Henri Spaak, Belgium's exiled foreign minister (and former prime minister), for a job. Spaak had just the one. In the shared jargon of war and diplomacy, it became known as the "Cauvin mission."

Because the film was intended to convince the Allies, especially the Americans, to support Belgium's claim to the colony, its crew needed to be British and American as well as Belgian. In London, Cauvin hired British cinematographer Arthur Fisher, Belgian-British secretary Lucienne Harvey Meurisse, and Belgian camera assistant Pierre Navaux. In New York, where he sailed in 1942 to seek money for the project, he made the prize hire: Broadway lyricist John Latouche. Latouche's skills as a writer were ideal, as were his politics, which were farther to the left than Cauvin's own; he was known best for his lyrics to Earl Robinson's 1939 cantata "Ballad for Americans," which was written for the New Deal's Federal Theatre Project and memorably sung by Paul Robeson on CBS radio. In the Belgian Congo, Latouche's job was to follow the crew as they worked, drafting the film's voiceover narration with an American audience in mind.

This was to underline the diplomatic argument: The Congo produced a wealth of raw materials for the war, and the Congo was Belgium's alone.

From the very first week of the Cauvin mission, things didn't go well. The Euro-American crew arrived on October 29, 1942, in Léopoldville (Kinshasa), where they were joined by Congolese assistants. Fisher fell gravely ill soon after their arrival and had to return to London, dying days later. The filmmakers' heavy equipment was difficult to load and unload from the trucks, car, and motorcycle that made up their entourage. The RCA sound discs that they recorded—intending to leave them with the Belgian colonial government as ethnographic documentation—were mistakenly loaded onto an American military plane, "never to be found again."[67]

We know this because Cauvin recounted it in his report on the mission, adventure story style. The finished film also adopts this style. *Congo* begins with the derogatory comparisons that had been used to depict the colony from its inception. The Congo was a "primitive" place until Belgium "civilized" it. Cauvin's camera lingers on hunters in the rainforest, on ceremonial dances and dress, before turning to the Western science and urban planning, the ships and planes and railroads that Leopold and his successors introduced, all of them bent towards transforming the colony's raw materials into the objects of trade.

These materials are *Congo*'s focus—as they were in so many colonial films before it, and in the German and American books about raw materials published around the same time—and the film follows them as they're harvested and transformed for war.[68] In the film's opening scene, a white schoolgirl recites a list of the materials. The colony is endowed with rubber and radium, copper and palm oil. It has elephants, gorillas, rivers powerful enough to produce hydroelectric power, African statues, and precious metals. "The Congo has given all these riches to our Allies during the war," the girl concludes. "It is worthy of Belgium."

The film's concern with Congo's "riches" reaches a climax in the penultimate scene, which turns to the place most important to the Allies:

Katanga, whose mines are the source, the voiceover tells us, of 160,000 tons of copper each year and of masses of tin (the word "uranium" is never uttered). These metals are refined on site, ingots poured and stacked, barrels upon barrels massed neatly at the river port, ready for shipping. The editing speeds up as the sequence draws to a close, paced by a score by the modernist composer and author Paul Bowles, whom Latouche recruited to the project. An orchestra is layered over African drums, and shots of Congolese laborers stacking and rolling goods are intercut with shots of dances. "The song of work," the voiceover intones, "the song of the ancestors." The comparison implies that the movements of these laborers—and they are forced laborers—are exquisitely modern. Because they are modern, they cannot be the product of an inhumane system. Perhaps, *Congo* suggests, the oppositions are not so stark between Congo before colonization and Congo after colonization.

FIGURE 14. Loading barrels of ore at Matadi. Still from André Cauvin, *Congo*, 1942. Royal Belgian Film Archive, Brussels.

Because this was calculated to appeal to Americans, many of whom still remembered Leopold's gruesome rubber campaigns with horror, Belgian diplomats orchestrated *Congo*'s US release as an extravagant media blitz, ensuring reviews in *The New York Times,* the *Chicago Defender,* and other prominent publications.[69] The film was distributed commercially by Warner Brothers and screened to government and artistic organizations. If you were in Washington, you could have seen it at the National Geographic Society, alongside 3,500 others. Or if by some chance you were at the White House, you might have watched it with President Roosevelt, who requested a private screening on March 9, 1944.[70] At the same time, the Belgian Foreign Ministry sent photographs from the film's production across the country, hoping they would both advertise *Congo* and serve as propaganda themselves. Members of the crew, quasi celebrities, sometimes appeared at the exhibitions.[71] Finally, there was a book: an oversized hardback with glossy photographs by Cauvin and text by Latouche, published by Willow, White, & Co. In fact, *Congo* seems to have been the only book that Willow, White, & Co. ever released. The publisher was apparently a fiction, an invention by the Belgian government to give the book an aura of legitimacy. Given the dire wartime shortage in paper, it was also evidence of the astonishing expense to which Belgium was willing to go to lay claim to its sole colony and the materials within it.

Latouche's writing in the book is in the first person, conversational. It follows the parallel arcs of the film and the filmmakers' journey in Congo, concluding in Katanga. There, Latouche meets a mining superintendent for Union Minière, Edgar Sengier's company. The man shows him Union Minière's company housing, its doctors, hospitals, and nurseries—echoes of Fordlândia and of the corporate welfare programs that companies like Kodak offered as a substitute for a closed shop. Standing with Latouche overlooking a mine in Jadotville, not far from Shinkolobwe, the superintendent muses, "There's nothing like it anywhere, I bet. Over 150,000 tons of copper ingots a year. Cobalt—60 per cent of the world production comes from that big place down there. Tungsten, radium, zinc, cadmium . . . oh, I tell you there's nothing like it. And the blacks. They are the best product, perhaps."

In the 1940s, this analogy would have been familiar to Americans, recalling George Eastman's interest in his farm's Black foreman's "development" and in J. Fred Johnson's young Kingsport neighbors—interest that equated people with the material they worked with, cotton for the first, wood for the second. There, on the edge of a mine, the analogy was to metal.

The supervisor turns from the pit and looks straight at Latouche, a question on his lips. "Some of your journalists, *m'sieu l'américain*, are hard to satisfy. Now that they cannot find lurid stories to exploit, they have other complaints." Latouche responds directly to the reader.

> I stated earlier that I have no affection for imperialism, and certainly there is no denying the fact that the advance would be quicker still if the profits not already substantially diminished by governmental taxes were turned back into Congolese improvements, rather than flowing into the oubliettes of abstract absentee fortunes. My personal sympathies are with the former idea. But I am not an economist, and until the colonial administrations change throughout the world (and there seems small hope of that at the moment, alas), the Katanga must be judged from existing standards. And judged from that point of view, it ranks high among the major experiments being made internationally by commercial combines.[72]

With this, Latouche hit on what the entire thing meant for the Allies. Like Holston, Tennessee Eastman, Agfa Wolfen, and Kodak Park, Union Minière was industry on a massive scale, dealing in metals and minerals instead of explosives, chemicals, rayon, or film. And while the United States wanted to distance itself from the Belgian Congo, it wanted the colony's copper, cobalt, and above all its uranium, even more.[73]

TALES OF MILITANT CHEMISTRY

In his report to the Belgian government, Cauvin described the Belgian Congo as "without a doubt the part of the African continent that lends itself best to the cinematic experience." Katanga, he wrote, "stands up proudly, with its opulence, its mining riches, its industrial arrogance, which bring it renown in all corners of the world."⁷⁴ If "mining riches" made the Belgian Congo cinematic, glittering on screen, they did so in a different way at Oak Ridge, where uranium from the Belgian Congo was separated by Eastman scientists and technicians, many of whom had spent their careers thinking about film.

Cauvin's film was probably never shown in the hastily constructed city in Tennessee, where almost no one knew the metal they were working with (those that did used the code name tuballoy). But there were cinemas in Oak Ridge—seven of them, plus a film society, playing first-run releases and repertory fare (at the film society, *A Nous la liberté, The 39 Steps,* even Sergei Eisenstein's *Alexander Nevsky*).⁷⁵ Film was part of Oak Ridge's nonstop complex of leisure-time offerings whose continuous schedules were timed to accommodate the town's three plants' twenty-four-hour operations and patchwork of shifts. The people who came to these cinemas included workers and their families, those who lived in Oak Ridge (population 75,000 at its peak). There were also workers who came from farther afield, taking buses and cars past mountains and farmland not far from where, twenty-two years earlier, Tennessee Eastman was built. Oak Ridge itself had been the communities of Elza, Robertsville, Scarboro, Wheat, and New Hope until October 1942, when, under condemnation proceedings, they were requisitioned by the War Department.⁷⁶

After World War I, raw materials had drawn George Eastman and other northern industrialists to Appalachia, a New South space marketed for its limitless material opportunity. In this new world war, Appalachia became a place where raw materials from elsewhere were transformed for industry. Two thirds of the uranium used by the Manhattan Project—3,700 tons—came from the Belgian Congo, with the rest from Great Bear Lake in Canada's Northwest Territories and from vanadium mined in Colorado.⁷⁷ In Oak Ridge, it was used in three plants, which operated under the umbrella of the Clinton Engineer Works: Tennessee Eastman's Y-12, which used the electromagnetic separation method, the K-12 gaseous diffusion plant, run by Union Carbide and the MW Kellogg company under the name Kellex, and X-10, a graphite reactor that transformed uranium fuel slugs into plutonium and was operated by DuPont—Kodak's old counterpart in film manufacturing, which also made plutonium at the Hanford Engineer Works in Washington State.

Y-12, Tennessee Eastman's operation, was an enlargement of the setup in nuclear physicist Ernest Lawrence's Radiation Lab at the University of California, Berkeley. It didn't deal directly with ore; its work began with the red-orange uranium trioxide sent from the refineries, which it converted into greyish-green uranium tetrachloride. This was what was fed into Y-12's so-called racetracks, which contained "calutrons," machines named for the university where they were developed. Each calutron housed ninety-six four-foot tanks positioned between

FIGURE 15. Alpha track calutron at Y-12, Oak Ridge, ca. 1944. Photographer: Ed Westcott. United States Department of Energy.

electromagnets. When uranium was loaded into a calutron, the magnets made the ore spin. As it circled in the machine, fissionable uranium 235 atoms moved in a tighter circle than the heavier, nonfissionable uranium 238 atoms.[78] After two sets of racetracks, Alpha and Beta, had done their work, the end product was the green uranium tetrafluoride salt that Los Alamos used for bomb charges.[79]

None of this seemed to have to do with film, or with the other products Tennessee Eastman made. The chemical processes were entirely different—acetic acid and acetic anhydride, which linked film to rayon and RDX, played no role in Y-12. Y-12 didn't use continuous production, either; the calutrons, which were prone to electrical, mechanical, and maintenance problems, worked in batches. As Bill Wilcox, a Y-12 chemist who became Oak Ridge's historian, described it, "You run it for three or four days and then you take it apart and you have to clear everything up and start all over again." Yet at Y-12 as at Kodak Park, there was silver: fourteen thousand tons of it borrowed from the government for the calutron magnets, and recovered after the war as painstakingly as the radium-rich sludge left after uranium refining. This was familiar territory to Kodak and Tennessee Eastman, which had long recovered and reused materials like silver and acetic acid.[80] Across Y-12's four main offices, there were also echoes of the division of labor in Kodak's film manufacturing. These offices were scattered throughout the country. One was in Oak Ridge, and the others were in Berkeley, Boston, and Rochester. The Boston office worked with Stone and Webster, Oak Ridge's construction firm, on design and engineering questions. Berkeley, home to Lawrence's lab, advised on technical matters and trained some Y-12 employees. And if Berkeley was home to the physicists, Rochester was home to the chemists. There, upstairs from the Kodak Research Laboratories, the Chemical Group tested methods for the plant's operations, from preparing its uranium to maintaining its miles of equipment. It also operated pilot plants that tried out processes to be used at Oak Ridge.

At this point, this was a settled structure for Kodak, one that it had tested with cellulose acetate in the 1920s. As White reiterated to Groves in late 1942, Rochester was the center of Kodak's experimental chemistry, and Kingsport (though it had its own laboratory) was where chemistry became large-scale industry.[81] For some employees, this translated into distinct professional identities. Kodak Research Laboratories' scientists could be seen as elite creatures, and the same was true for the Rochester-based members of Y-12's Chemical Group. Wilcox was a member of this group, arriving in spring 1943 after graduating from Washington and Lee University. On his first day in Rochester, he was led into a supervisor's office, shown a chunk of uranium, and ordered, under pain of arrest, to forget its name—a fairly standard induction for Manhattan Project scientists, Kate Brown notes.[82] The young chemist passed the summer in a Kodak laboratory teaching himself about uranium chemistry, while downstairs, other scientists were working on Kodachrome. It was top-notch chemistry, Wilcox recalled, and "just as secret."[83]

Robert Ellingson, who graduated from the University of Idaho the same year, had a different experience. After filling out an application to work at Clinton Engineer Works, Tennessee Eastman Corporation, he arrived in Knoxville to be told apologetically that the project had already hired too many chemists. Would he be interested in going into "process" instead? Ellingson said yes and spent the summer in Berkeley, where he learned how to run the calutrons.[84] As he did, he was ushered into Tennessee Eastman's own elite, a cadre of chemical engineers who prided themselves on being "production men." These were people like David C. Hull, the scientist who had helped design the continuous reaction process for RDX and went on to become Y-12's chemical production manager. If you had asked Hull what a production man was, he might have answered that it was someone who got his hands dirty in the factory, someone who didn't sit in his office with a book.[85] In all likelihood, this is what caused White to ask Groves, on Christmas Eve, if Tennessee Eastman was right for the job. It seemed like one for experimental chemists (Groves called them "long beards"), not production men like White himself.

But Y-12 needed both. It needed people to design the processes, people to run the plant, and people to attend to the myriad administrative, practical, and human matters that clustered in a factory that large. These groups began to converge on Oak Ridge at the end of summer 1943, when Rochester's Chemical Group was dispatched to Tennessee.[86] Nearly all the Kodak scientists sent south were research scientists, mostly chemists or engineers. Some were physicists, process-improvement or development experts, and support or clerical staff. In contrast, the Tennessee Eastman and Holston employees transferred to Oak Ridge were primarily foremen and supervisors (overseeing machinists, metal workers, vacuum workers, and welders). Others were office managers and department superintendents, tradesmen, carpenters, and painters, and there were a handful of nurses, doctors, chemists, engineers, and laboratory technicians.[87]

Sometimes, however, these professional divisions weren't so stark. This was the case with a Holston employee who was transferred to Y-12 in 1944. A chemist and a graduate of the University of Rochester, Alfred Dean Slack wasn't really a Holston man or even a Tennessee Eastman man. He was a Kodak man, bonded to the company by virtue of his place of birth and education, and he'd started work at Kodak Park in 1928. In fall 1942, he became a supervisor at Tennessee Eastman's cellulose acetate plants before transferring to Holston to work in the nitric acid division. Slack was named a shift supervisor at Y-12 in fall 1944.[88] It made professional sense, just as it made sense for Tennessee Eastman to move from cellulose acetate to RDX to Y-12. As Slack wrote later, "I was quite familiar with many of the processes and the product being made."[89]

It's true that Slack was a capable chemist. He was also friendly, a good talker, the kind of character treated cautiously in Oak Ridge, where, even if you knew what you were working on, military secrecy ruled. He might drop by your laboratory to gossip, speculating about "what an atomic bomb might really look like." On holidays, he was known for hosting cocktail parties in the nominally dry town.[90]

Slack's liberty to move around Y-12 was a privilege of his position. It was also liberty that relatively few had, since the majority of Y-12's employees weren't scientists but had been hired to operate discrete parts of the factory. Unlike at Holston, it wasn't always easy to staff these positions. By the time the project began, other war industries had stretched the region's workforce, and it would be a challenge to find the twenty-two thousand employees eventually on Y-12's payroll.[91] The Clinton Engineer Works had priority from the War Production Board, however, and the project sent recruiters across the country. It placed newspaper and magazine advertisements and dispatched trucks equipped with loudspeakers that blared music alongside appeals to join the project in Tennessee. Welders, painters, security guards, and cooks came to Oak Ridge from as far away as Massachusetts, California, and Idaho.

The largest single group of employees at Y-12 were women. Some of them were scientists, but many more were just out of high school or college, not yet married or mothers—and so, the government reasoned, capable of working the exhausting shifts that all-out war production required.[92] Most of these women didn't know what Y-12 was making. The veil of silence that shrouded everything at Oak Ridge meant that each process, and each action in each process, stood alone, its place in the whole obscure to all but a handful of people.

Lucille Whitman, who had just graduated from high school in Morrisville, Tennessee, didn't know, and she didn't want to know. She'd been hired as a secretary for Y-12's administrative building, and when top-secret documents passed through her office, she looked the other way. What she did know was that she was working for Tennessee Eastman, and she knew that Eastman made film. A few times, Whitman posed for recruitment photographs—"a result," she concluded, "of working for Tennessee Eastman, being in the film business." When historian Denise Kiernan interviewed Dorothy Jones, another Y-12 employee, about her work at Oak Ridge, Jones remembered being certain that what

FIGURE 16. Calutron operators at Y-12, Oak Ridge, 1944. Photographer: Ed Westcott. United States Department of Energy.

she was doing "had something to do with making those informational war films they played at the movie theater before the main feature. After all, she thought, the plant was being run by Tennessee Eastman."[93] As Bill Wilcox had intuited up at Rochester, the secrecy at Oak Ridge was second nature to Kodak, and it suited the company well for war work.

For one photograph, Lucille Whitman was taken into the plant, the only time she was allowed inside. Instructed to put on a uniform, stand by a calutron, and pretend that she was operating it, Whitman froze in terror. Any wrong move, the photographer had laughingly warned, would cost a lot of money.[94] This kind of thing happened to women at Hanford, too, but for Whitman and Y-12, it had a particular meaning, because the calutrons were where most of the women at Y-12 worked, at stations surrounding the enormous machines.[95] Each woman was responsible for a dial that regulated the temperature in the calutron's racetrack. The temperature was measured by a gauge. If the gauge veered too far in one direction, she was to turn the dial until it returned to normal. Every thirty minutes, she was to record a meter reading on a clipboard. The mysterious work was tedious yet exacting. You couldn't take your eyes off the dial.

The same nimble patience was what you needed to make rayon. Spooling threads or twisting yarn are actions not so different from turning a dial, and it's no coincidence that the young Appalachian women who became the famous "calutron girls" were the same women who had run east Tennessee's rayon factories for decades. Some even came directly from textile plants to Y-12, where everyone was applying for jobs and where it was widely known that the pay was better.[96]

In Germany, Agfa Wolfen's film and fiber plants were also staffed mostly by women. This had been true before the war as well, when close to fifty percent of the factory's workforce was female, and the proportion only grew during World War II.[97] Not all of these women were from the Bitterfeld-Wolfen area. Synthetic fibers and film were government priorities, but when war began, there wasn't enough German labor to make the quantities that Nazi economic plans called for, and so from at least 1939, the factory benefited from government programs to coerce workers from Germany's widening European occupation into domestic industries. At first, Agfa's foreign workers came from the Sudetenland— the western parts of Czechoslovakia that had been annexed to the Reich—and from Slovakia, a Nazi puppet state. There were also Belgian, Dutch, and French prisoners of war, and civilians from those countries who had been pressured by their home countries to labor in Germany.[98]

These workers were not treated well. Rations, housing, and pay: All of it was bad. Conditions were particularly dire for Jews, Roma, and workers from Poland and the Soviet Union, the heart of Germany's prospective new empire, many of whom, as IG Farben's indictment for slave labor at the Nuremberg trials described vividly, had been hunted down.

They were dragged out of beds, movie theaters, or churches, and seized on the street.⁹⁹ By early 1942, Polish women had begun to flee Wolfen. A few left behind apologetic letters, citing homesickness and worry about their families and promising to return. Dorote Rozenau, who left on July 25, 1942, enclosed her butter ration card because she didn't want to "exploit the German Reich." The same month, a woman wrote from Łódź to a friend, Henryka Kaminska, who remained in Wolfen. The letter vibrated with relief. "You don't know how nice it is to be home again," she sighed. "When I was in Wolfen, I always felt so bad."¹⁰⁰

As the factory was drained of workers like these but production targets didn't ease, Wolfen's directors pinned their hopes on programs announced in 1942 that were designed to force more foreign workers to Germany, most of them from the Soviet Union, which Germany now occupied.¹⁰¹ There were special conditions attached to these laborers. Most foreign workers were already housed in barracks, separately from German workers, but since the so-called Eastern workers (*Ostarbeiter*) had "lived for decades under Bolshevik rule and have been trained as enemies of National Socialist and European culture," they had to live separately, in straw-palleted barracks surrounded by barbed wire.¹⁰²

Agfa's treatment of its Eastern workers rested on the imperial designs that underpinned the entire German autarky program. Eastern workers were described as wild and unintelligent, though perhaps moldable, through work, into acceptable colonial subjects. Like the mine supervisor in Katanga and George Eastman at Oak Lodge, Agfa executives documented the workers' behavior with patronizing ethnographic detail. In one report from late 1942, the executives noted that the factory had given the female Eastern workers balalaikas, and that they "like to sing their folk songs, as well as to perform their folk dances, which they do on Sundays after putting on their colorful Sunday clothes." The women had attempted to make the dismal barracks more bearable, decorating them "in a magnificent way, making curtains, wall decorations and the like out of paper and pictures, etc., sometimes with drawings in the Russian style," but to the executives, this behavior was not quaint or charming or a sign of fortitude in the face of adversity. On the contrary, it was evidence of a racially determined weakness and conformity. Once decorations went up in one room in the barracks, they wrote, "the example was immediately contagious, and gradually others followed suit. If, for example, a young Russian woman, not yet sixteen, who has left home to work in Germany starts crying from homesickness, the whole room joins in the crying." "In general," they concluded—parroting popular Nazi theories of crowd psychology—"the so-called mass psychosis is very prevalent."[103]

Agfa's practice was to move Eastern workers through various positions in the film and fiber factories, and sometimes the darkrooms, so that they would learn every step in each industrial process. Some Eastern workers were also sent to work in the plant's photographic division—packaging film, for instance, which factory directors considered "clean and light women's work."[104] But Nazi hierarchies meant that many Soviet and Polish workers were assigned the factory's hardest and most hazardous jobs. Over the course of 1943, these jobs were also filled by concentration camp prisoners sent to work at Wolfen, many of whom also came from Poland and the Soviet Union. In May 1943, the women's camp Ravensbrück established a subcamp (*Kommando*) at Wolfen to make film and fibers, at first with 250 Polish and Russian women and girls. Within a year, the subcamp had 425 inmates, and in September 1944, it came under Buchenwald's management, one of the satellites the sprawling camp built to support German industry.[105]

Among the concentration camp prisoners whom Wolfen's executives described as "Russian," hundreds came from Ukraine, which bore the brunt of Germany's occupation of the Soviet Union. Different paths brought them to the film and fiber factories. There was Walentina Bugajewa, a bookkeeper from Donetsk (then Stalino), who was twenty-three when she was taken to Wolfen. Pelageja Beloschenko, thirty-two, was a weaver from Kharkiv. Tatjana Bondarenko was also from Kharkiv, but the twenty year old was already in Germany when she was seized, working as a driver in Stuttgart.[106]

FIGURE 17. Portrait of Oleksandra Lawrik, April 18, 1940. Photographer unknown. Courtesy of Archiv der Gedenkstätte Buchenwald.

Oleksandra Lawrik's story began in Dnipropetrovsk (Dnipro), the central Ukrainian city where she was working as a factory accountant and raising her eight-year-old son Anatolii when Germany invaded the Soviet Union. Lawrik, who was active in the Communist Party and an elected member of Dnipropetrovsk's Soviet (one of the workers' councils that were key organs in Soviet governance), was detained repeatedly after the occupation began. In 1941, she was forced to register with the Gestapo. In June 1942, she was imprisoned for a month, then let go. When she was arrested again in June 1943, she was held until, in early September, she was deported to Buchenwald along with her father and more than 1,500 other political prisoners.[107] From Buchenwald, Lawrik was sent to Ravensbrück, where she was disinfected for a second time, quarantined, and ordered to work building a road. She had been in the camp for two months or so when, one day in late November, there was a selection. The Ukrainian women were told to line up, and managers from Agfa Wolfen inspected their hands and their arms. By the 23rd, Lawrik was in Wolfen, in barracks and on factory floors locked from the outside and guarded by the SS. The guards knew how to make film and rayon, too, since they had been recruited from the ranks of German women working at Agfa Wolfen.[108]

While Lawrik spent some time in the film factory, she mostly worked with Vistra. Her job was to load wood cellulose into tubs, pour caustic soda over it, and watch for two hours as the solution fermented. Caustic soda (sodium hydroxide) is exactly what it sounds like. It burns the skin and the lungs, and Lawrik had been relieved to find a hot shower in the camp, a relative luxury.[109] The toxic work took its toll anyway. For some of the women she worked with, lung injuries led to tuberculosis. Prisoners were beaten regularly, and they were made to beat other prisoners who had been forced to strip naked and run the gauntlet. Some women died. When illness made others unable to work, they were sent back to Ravensbrück, a death sentence all over again.[110] At a different artificial fiber factory in IG Farben's Division III, the French art historian Agnès Humbert, also a political prisoner turned forced laborer, remembered the work as a blur of "burns and blinding fumes," in which, for her captors, the metal in the factory's spinnerets was more valuable than the lives of the women who worked the machines.[111] This was autarky and the empire it entailed: an expendable source of colonial labor, a scramble for white gold.

THREADS

Film—motion picture film—and textiles are often discussed in the same breath. Film is manufactured in ribbons, and editing means stitching or weaving together frames and scenes. The assumptions about women that brought Ukrainians to Agfa Wolfen and Tennesseans to calutron dials were the same assumptions that, for much of the twentieth century, made film editing practically the only cinematic profession open to women. The idea was that women were naturally patient and dexterous, capable of sitting long hours and performing repetitive, precise actions. While editing, Soviet critic Vladimir Korolevich wrote in his 1928 book *A Woman in Film,* "the fingers of the female cutter and the montagess" moved "invariably and consistently, accurately and faithfully, like the bobbin drivers of gigantic machines."[112]

In the year *A Woman in Film* was published, the rayon industry was expanding everywhere. It's no surprise, then, that for Korolevich, film editing isn't piecework, like stitching or sewing. It is industrial textile-making, performed with "gigantic machines." The work was hard, dangerous, and poorly paid. The year after Korolevich's book was published, this was what made women at American Glanzstoff's rayon factory in Elizabethton, Tennessee, walk out, in the artificial fiber industry's largest strike to date and a pivotal moment for organized labor in Southern textile-making.[113]

Elizabethton returns us for a final time to our tree, to the chemicals that were made from it, and to the deadly histories spun from those chemicals. Just as Nazi Germany's "synthetic world" of films and fibers, a world stitched together by enslaved workers, was built on colonial histories stretching from Africa to Ukraine, this Tennessee tree wove a story of film and war twisted from multiple strands. One of these strands passed through the hands of workers at Tennessee Eastman who made rayon woven into military materiel, and film that, during this war, became ubiquitous in the military. At Holston, another led to RDX, just a few grams of which could destroy a submarine. A thread wound to Y-12, where uranium from Katanga was transformed until it was ready

FIGURE 18. Spooling acetate rayon at Tennessee Eastman, 1933. From Kirkpatrick, "Building an Integrated Industry in Times of Depression," 238. Courtesy of the Science History Institute and McGraw-Hill.

to become the core of the bomb called Little Boy. When this bomb detonated over Hiroshima, creating a fireball that brought temperatures on the ground to more than seven thousand degrees Fahrenheit, the lives of hundreds of thousands of the city's women, children, and men were interwoven with the same thread.[114]

We could add another strand. Sgt. George Caron was a tail gunner, not a photographer, but in the last minute before the warplane *Enola Gay* took off from Tinian Island, someone handed him a K-20 aerial camera. The military was lucky that Caron was there. The sophisticated cameras mounted in one of the planes accompanying the *Enola Gay* didn't manage to capture anything of the explosion, but Caron, positioned just so at the back of the bomber, shot an entire roll of photographs, including the indelible image of the mushroom cloud that was released five days later.¹¹⁵ Like all aviation film, Caron's was cellulose acetate, a material that owed its ubiquity to air war and the need to keep planes from catching fire.

This is one way to tell this story, but there are others. We could tell it through the Gevaert factory in Westerlo, Belgium, converted to make nitrocellulose for the Wehrmacht, or Kodak-Pathé in Vincennes, which supplied film to Agfa.¹¹⁶ In Italy, FILM Ferrania played a central role in Italian autarky. Seen in this light, Tennessee Eastman's and Agfa Wolfen's histories in these years are not exceptional. They are part of what Primo Levi calls the war's "grand chemistry, the triumphant chemistry of colossal plants and dizzying output."¹¹⁷

Levi knew very well what this chemistry was. He knew about its materials, its laboratories, its prisons, and its connections to empire, and he saw it through synthetic rubber, another cornerstone of autarky, which he was forced to make in the massive factory at Auschwitz. Or not make, because, as Levi writes, "the Buna factory on which the Germans were busy for four years and for which countless of us suffered and died, never produced a pound of synthetic rubber."¹¹⁸

For Levi, it was beside the point that nothing was made. What was important was that, as the German authors of *Verwertung des Wertlosen* put it, "Transforming one substance into another and more profitable one" was big business, whatever ideology that business served.¹¹⁹ This was the "big science" of the war that Alvin M. Weinberg described in 1961, when he was director of the Oak Ridge National Laboratory, an institution partly housed in the former Y-12.¹²⁰ Tennessee Eastman and Agfa Wolfen were part of this big science, too, and their factories were core to cinema's gleaming industries, which are often seen as magical, like chemistry. By 1945, however, the silver screen shone not just through its stars, but also through trees, cotton, rubber, and above all uranium, substances that had given Kodak and Agfa more control over film and its chemistry than either company could have imagined before.

PART II

Unraveling

CHAPTER THREE

Taking Stock

A YEAR BEFORE HIROSHIMA, a different story of war and film was unfolding in France. Lacy Kastner, a psychological warfare officer with the Allied expeditionary forces, was looking for unexposed film—nitrate, acetate, anything. He knew there wouldn't be much: After five years of war, most of France's film factories had ground to a halt. But film was a linchpin of Allied military operations, and officers like Kastner needed it to do what they were sent to do: organize screenings in liberated areas, programs of documentaries, newsreels, and feature films plucked from the backlog of Hollywood movies unseen in occupied Europe.[1]

Finding and showing film wasn't Kastner's only task. He was also in charge of retaking American film studios' European subsidiaries, smoothing the way for what the US film industry hoped would be a swift return to the continent.[2] For Kastner, this was the easy part. Like other psychological warfare officers, he was a veteran of Hollywood's European branches, and he already knew the local industry and many of its people. If you didn't count the uniform, his wartime work wasn't very different from his peacetime job.

In American cinema, Kodak had always been as powerful as the biggest studios. So while psychological warfare officers like Kastner were helping bring companies like United Artists and MGM back to Europe, they were doing the same for Kodak: retaking its holdings and devising ways to restore the company's continental markets. This started with Kodak-Pathé, once the largest American film subsidiary in Europe,

FIGURE 19. The liberation of the Kodak-Pathé film factory, Vincennes, France, 1944. Courtesy of the University of Rochester River Campus Libraries Rare Books, Special Collections, and Preservation, and Eastman Kodak Company.

which Kodak had written off at the end of 1941.[3] The Vincennes factory was still functional—it had worked with Agfa during the German occupation—and Kodak was eager to repossess it.[4] Just days after the liberation of Paris, disguised in borrowed military uniforms, Donald McMaster and W. G. Bent of Kodak, Ltd. arrived at the factory gates. They danced with the women, shook hands with the men, showed themselves lords again in their own house.[5]

It was relatively simple for Kodak to retake its film factory with the backing of an army, and it was heroic, good publicity. Restarting production was not so simple. Chemicals and raw materials were hard to come by, and they were hard to transport on France's ruined roads and railways. Electricity was an even bigger challenge. Film factories ran on coal, which, after years of war, was in dire shortage throughout Europe. In the absence of coal, no film at all could be made. Moreover, as Kodak-Pathé's French managers explained testily in November 1944 to the country's Ministry of Information (and not for the first time), you couldn't restart the part of the factory that made film without restarting the more profitable parts, those that made things like plastics, insulation, and explosives: "This would mean starting an enormous set of machinery for a single, minor production stream, when this machinery incurs general costs for steam, water, and electricity, none of which can be amortized through minimal production."[6] Thus, thanks to the privilege of the victor, what little film was made or found at Kodak-Pathé in the months after liberation went to Kastner and his colleagues. A few French film professionals raised weak protests at the requisitions, but most shrugged. This was the price of war.[7]

The price was higher at Agfa Wolfen, which was also on the list of film factories that Kastner and his colleagues were to visit. They had to wait: After the Normandy invasion, it took eleven months, until April 1945, for the Americans and British to reach Saxony-Anhalt. Once they got there, however, their patience was repaid, because while France was an ally, and taking its film required careful negotiation, Agfa was the vanquished enemy. Its products had been pivotal to the chemistry of war, and Roosevelt, Churchill, and Stalin had agreed at Yalta to eliminate Germany's military capacity. At Wolfen, then, there was no delicacy around seizing film. It was retribution and demilitarization.[8] And if for Kodak, repossessing the Vincennes factory offered a chance to restart, Wolfen offered the opportunity to best its longstanding competitor, extending control over the global film market at the end of one war and the beginning of another.

CAMERAS AND GUNS

Throughout the winter and early spring of 1945, Allied bombing runs targeted German industry. By March, American novelist John Dos Passos, seconded to the US Army as a war correspondent, saw the country's modern factories and laboratories—those mainstays of autarky—transformed into a landscape of "tilting girders and steel rods, of smashed concrete twisted like stems of weeds in a pond."[9] Agfa Wolfen, however, was in relatively good condition. The Bitterfeld-Halle area had been spared the destruction Germany had seen elsewhere, and by the time American troops reached Wolfen's outskirts on April 14, the area had been bombed only once, in January 1945.[10] That bombing hadn't hit the film factory itself, and Agfa considered the damage insignificant, never mind the fact that many foreign workers, asleep in the barracks, were killed.[11]

Oleksandra Lawrik survived the January bombing. It was sheer luck, since even if air raids happened during the day, concentration camp inmates were instructed not to seek shelter; they were to work nonstop.[12] A month later, as the factory's raw materials dwindled and production faltered, Lawrik also avoided the transport that brought two hundred of the prisoners in Wolfen's Buchenwald *Kommando* to Bergen-Belsen. She worked until April 17, when the prisoners who remained at the factory were crowded into freight wagons heading in the direction of Dresden. With the countryside in disorder, the trains moved haltingly, with long delays, and at one waypoint, Lawrik and her friend Tina escaped. They crawled under train cars, stripped off the grey striped jackets that would immediately identify them as escapees, and made their way east, in the general direction of home.[13]

Lawrik didn't have much to bring with her when she escaped. That April, though, as the US Army occupied Wolfen and the last German soldiers surrendered, many other fleeing foreign laborers took what they could from the factory.[14] The American forces did little to stop the looting. Perhaps this was out of sympathy for the laborers' plight: A week before it arrived in Wolfen, the US Army had liberated the Nordhausen concentration camp, and the soldiers had seen something of what people like Lawrik had experienced. But the Army also tolerated looting because it didn't interfere with its own interests in the plant. Freed prisoners weakened by hunger and disease could hardly compete with soldiers fed on K-rations, and from the day they officially took Agfa Wolfen, April 20, until the victory parade on May 8, US troops pocketed film, cameras, lenses, magnifying devices, and projectors. While most of the damage to the factory could be attributed to the last, frantic days of Wehrmacht defense against low-flying American aircraft, the smashed glass photographic plates and destroyed workshops could not.[15] In late May, when a British official arrived to assess the factory's state, he didn't even attempt to distinguish what had been looted or destroyed by whom. "Following the cessation of fighting," Sgt. Leader Brock recorded laconically, "extensive looting and wanton damage occurred, for which troops, liberated foreign workers, and criminal German elements are all blamed."[16]

FIGURE 20. Agfa Wolfen after Wehrmacht defense, spring 1945. © Industrie- und Filmmuseum Wolfen.

For forced laborers, looting had a moral logic. American writer Meyer Levin—like Dos Passos, serving as a journalist with the US Army—witnessed this elsewhere in Germany that spring, as he and his French driver Erik were caught up in "a ragged and yet cheerful human flood." "They were on every road," Levin wrote in his memoir about the war, "the liberated slaves undertaking the long journey home to France, the liberated prisoners of war . . . walking, pushing their few belongings in gocarts, lugging their wrecks of suitcases, their packs swollen with a little retribution collected from German households." The stopwatches and light meters stuffed in these packs and carts and sometimes cars—in the hands of ex-prisoners, it was war booty, a more than fair exchange for "entire households of possessions, lifelong savings taken from them by the enemy. It was little enough to take back."

Looting meant something different for Americans. It could be retribution, too, if you were Jewish, like Levin, or a European émigré, or if you had witnessed firsthand the cold alliance of industry and war that played out at factories like Agfa Wolfen. For others, what happened during those three weeks in Wolfen was driven by baser impulses. Levin experienced this himself. Once, in the town of Gotha, he and Erik found themselves breaking down the door of a local photo shop, looking for film for their cameras. The owner had emptied the shop and there was nothing to take, but still, the men were stopped by another Allied correspondent and accused of "plain thievery." The charge caught Levin off guard. After all, "there was an order that Germans had to surrender all firearms and optical items—spyglasses, cameras—the instant a town was taken." "When the going was easy," he recalled, "this regulation became almost a game; in one village I saw the lead tank stationed in the town square while a line of civilians formed, surrendering their cameras, guns, and opera glasses as though this were the primary object of the war."

American troops wanted German cameras as "souvenirs" because everybody knew they were the best machines you could get. In the United States, they were more expensive and harder to find than the ubiquitous Kodaks, and they were small enough to pack home in an Army-issued rucksack. Levin quickly deduced the military hierarchy governing this. "You couldn't give anything less than a No. 3 Contax to the top, and then the souvenirs graded down through No. 2 Contax, Leica, Rolleiflex, Rolleicord, and the minor brands." Guns were equally attractive. He and Erik "passed out our Lugers and Mausers, and ended the war with one of each weapon . . . and with a camera apiece."[17]

Looting quickly gave way to more formal seizures of war reparations. Sgt. Leader Brock had been sent to Wolfen in this new phase. He was a member of the T-Forces of the Supreme Headquarters Allied Expeditionary Force (SHAEF), military intelligence units that followed on the heels of liberating troops, searching German industry for information, technology, and people Allied governments and industries might consider useful. By the time he arrived, little was left. Lacy Kastner and his colleague Lt. Col. Cuthbertson had already been there, as had Donald McMaster from Kodak, Ltd., and with the US Army's help, Wolfen was being emptied of cameras, light meters, film, and nearly all the raw materials needed to make it. Celluloid, gelatin, silver bullion, silver nitrate, potassium bromide, hydroquinone, acetone, camphor: Boxes upon boxes were sent to Kodak-Pathé in France and to Gevaert's factory in Antwerp, kickstarting film manufacturing for American forces and solidifying Kodak's base in Western Europe.[18] With these products and materials gone, along with half of its workforce, Agfa Wolfen was at a standstill. Brock found "only a skeleton staff," none of them working. No one had even attempted to clean up the debris.[19]

The *T* in *T-Force* stood for "target," and German industrial targets were chosen by the American-British Combined Intelligence Objectives Subcommittee under SHAEF command. In June 1945, as SHAEF's liberation operations wound down, the T-Forces were transferred to the new agency FIAT (Field Information Agency, Technical).[20] T-Forces were composed of military and government staff—people like Brock—as well as "technical" personnel, civilians from industry and the academy who took government-funded leaves from their positions. Flown to Europe, given courtesy military ranks, uniforms, drivers, and guards, they searched offices, plants, and warehouses; seized documents, technology, and raw materials; and interrogated scientists and industrialists, writing up detailed reports. FIAT's technical personnel didn't always see themselves as government functionaries first. Some of them phoned or mailed German trade secrets directly to their employers, and like McMaster and Bent at Kodak-Pathé back in August 1944, they often did so with military support.

The T-Forces covered nearly every field imaginable. Some fields had unquestionable links to war production (synthetic rubber, chemicals, aeronautics, machinery). But investigators also visited pencil makers, watchmakers, even Steiff's teddy bear operations—anything that held out the possibility of learning and profiting from German industry.[21] Some of the very first T-Forces to arrive in Germany included representatives of American and British photographic companies. Employees of Celanese, Ilford, DuPont, Kodak, Ansco, Warner Brothers, and the Hollywood Colorfilm Corporation traveled to factories throughout IG Farben's former Division III, lavishing particular attention on Agfa Wolfen. Tennessee Eastman sent someone, too: R. Leonard Hasche, the company's director of research and development, who visited the Wolfen plant on May 25 and 26 with Ray H. Boundy of Dow Chemical.[22] Because the film industry was also the fiber and plastics industry, the report that Hasche and Boundy issued was titled "Fabrication of Plastics at I.G. Farbenindustrie, Wolfen."

At Wolfen, however, the focus was film, which investigators carted away to test in the United States or Britain.[23] Most of the T-Forces agreed that the factory's products didn't measure up to what the Allies made during the war.[24] The exception was Agfa's groundbreaking still and motion picture color film, Agfacolor. For almost all of the Allied visitors to Wolfen, this was the heart of the matter—and possibly the reason, Manfred Gill speculates, why American bombers avoided hitting the film factory itself.[25]

Agfacolor had been made since 1936, although Agfa improved it during the war, and as German color films were captured or fell by other means into American, British, and Soviet hands, the Allies were enthralled by what they saw. Color film was still in its infancy, its technologies young and quickly changing. The colors in one formulation might be too muted or bright; in another, they might be quick to fade. But photographs and films made with Agfacolor's new formula, like Veit Harlan's *The Golden City* (*Die goldene Stadt*, 1942) and Georg Jacoby's *The Woman of My Dreams* (*Die Frau meiner Träume*, 1944), had hues that were vibrant and true, improving greatly on what that had been available before.[26] As foreign soldiers and film executives paraded through the Wolfen factory from April through June, they posed for Agfacolor snapshots with German film factory workers (was one of the soldiers the Central Europe–born Kastner, whose name Agfa officials spelled correctly, with the umlaut over the a?). During his first trip to Wolfen, Lt. Col. Cuthbertson took a copy of Jacoby's 1942 short film *Colorful Dance* (*Bunter Reigen*). During the second, Cuthbertson left with a 35 mm print of *The Woman of My Dreams*.[27] He sent both films to Ansco, which Agfa had attempted to cut off from Wolfen's color film research for years, paranoid about its most valuable intellectual property falling into other hands if the subsidiary was sold.[28] After T-Forces seized the Agfacolor formulas, translated them, and made them available to film manufacturers throughout the world, you could purchase any number of clones: Ansco Color (Ansco, 1950), naturally, but also Gevacolor (Gevaert, 1947), Ferraniacolor (Ferrania, 1949), and the Soviet version of Agfacolor, called Sovcolor (made from 1945 in Agfa Wolfen and from 1948 at the Svema film factory in Ukraine).[29]

FIGURE 21. Agfacolor snapshot of unidentified US soldier and woman at Agfa Wolfen, spring 1945. © Industrie- und Filmmuseum Wolfen.

Although the T-Forces' work was organized by the British and US governments, the investigations were often no less chaotic than the initial weeks of looting.³⁰ When Brock arrived in Germany on May 28, he discovered that two of Agfa's head scientists, Dr. Meyer and Dr. Meskat, were in jail far away in Wiesbaden, outside Frankfurt. Feeling that he should "interrogate these men at once," Brock drove to the jail, where he found the men sitting alongside another Agfa employee, Dr. Schilling. "Neither the men nor the prison authorities could give any reason for their detention," Brock sighed, and he ordered the men released. It seemed someone had mistakenly thought that Dr. Schilling was an expert on the V-2 rocket.

Brock soon learned that Wolfen was a bastion of such rumors, circulated by factory workers, Allied soldiers, former forced laborers, shopkeepers, and farmers alike. The same was true throughout Germany, as the French sociologist Edgar Morin observed while serving as a propaganda officer with the French forces in Berlin. Public opinion in the country, Morin wrote, was formed "not by the ten million newspapers circulated each day, nor by radio broadcasts, nor by large political movements," but by "sounds spread from mouth to mouth."³¹ It was Brock's job to follow these rumors, wherever they led. In Wolfen, he "met an American infantry lieutenant who reported having seen a dump of German aircraft cameras and ancillary equipment in a beer-hall." Asked where the beer hall might be, the man could only say that it was "in a circle of 4 km radius centered on Delitsch [Delitzsch]." Brock located the spot, but the trip was in vain. Just like at the factory, the US Army had already taken everything. And even though he estimated that Wolfen could probably restart production in a matter of weeks, he noted that this was "of only academic interest," since there were no raw materials left, and "Wolfen is in the Russian zone of occupation."³²

Among Wolfen's residents, this generated the most anxious rumors of all. Throughout the winter and spring of 1945, Morin wrote, Germany had awaited the Allied invasion "as a form of deliverance. . . . Deliverance from Nazism and dictatorship? Not even. Deliverance from the plagues of war. At last, to eat, to see family and friends, to no longer fear the bombs: peace." Morin saw a perverse logic through which Germans welcomed American occupation, one rooted in German admiration of the United States' empire. In his words, Germany "did not yet have the superiority complex about the Americans that it did about the Russians and French.... It was very acceptable to be beaten by the USA, by an entire continent, by the world's largest industrial power."[33]

Acceptance of American occupation was matched by fear of Soviet occupation. At Yalta, Saxony-Anhalt had been placed within the Soviet occupation zone, and as the Red Army approached from the east, it was preceded by reports of destruction, pillaging, and rape, many of them carried by survivors of the Soviet campaign in the former German territory of East Prussia. Wolfen's residents, especially the town's women, feared for their lives.[34] The Americans and British, meanwhile, feared losing industrial and military intelligence. And so as the June 30 deadline for Western forces to withdraw came closer, they transported more and more of Agfa Wolfen's equipment, documents, raw materials, and cash westward.[35] They brought scientists and technicians with them, too, anxious to retain the individuals who knew best how to use what they had taken.[36] By the end of the month, forty-three highly placed members of the factory had been transported to Munich, in the US zone, for further interrogation. These included Agfa Wolfen's head scientist, John Eggert, as well as Fritz Gajewski—who would soon be tried on charges of slave labor at Nuremberg, and acquitted.[37]

While some of Wolfen's scientists were eager to go west and avoid what was whispered about Soviet occupation, Eggert was much more hesitant. Agfa Wolfen and its research laboratory were in many ways his creation, and the scientist cooperated willingly with Brock, offering formulas for projects the laboratory had been working on. This wasn't out of character for Eggert, who was no friend of the recently deposed government. A well-known anti-Nazi, he had refused to divorce his Jewish wife, Margarete—a violation of the Reich Citizenship Law that was punishable with a jail term or hard labor. Thanks to Gajewski's protection, however, Eggert not only escaped imprisonment but kept his prominent position at Agfa, and Margarete became one of the few members of Leipzig's once-vibrant Jewish community to survive the war.[38] As Eggert wrote to a colleague some months later, the Allies' arrival released the family from "the heavy spell that has kept us in suspense for more than a decade." Margarete had emerged from the Eggerts' apartment, which they had begun to restore, and some version of life was returning to the city. But "after we managed to get through all this terror, through the looting and confiscation, through the occupation and other consequences of the war," Eggert added, came "the American order to march to Bavaria."

The US Army moved Eggert with the awkward combination of high-minded rhetoric and hunger for profit that characterized its occupation of the film factory. As an Army truck pulled up in front of the Eggerts' apartment and began loading what the family wanted to take, a colleague watched helplessly, recalling that "his huge library did not fit! An American officer had come earlier and told him that he would be taken away, saying, among other things: 'We want to save you and your brain for you, for us, and for all of humanity.'"[39] When he arrived in Munich, Eggert learned that several of his boxes had gone missing. By his account, they included books, scientific instruments, texts on plastics development, chemical materials, and professional correspondence, as well as, more poignantly, the quickly assembled yet carefully listed minimum contents of a life:

2 Pairs of drawers
2 Pairs of shirts
Parts of a desk set
1 Pair of shoes (in good condition)
1 Blanket
2 Neckties
2 Collars
2 Pairs of stockings
1 Cooking-plate
Dinner-service.[40]

These items were inconsequential to the US forces. Eggert himself was the booty, the prize—the key, the Americans hoped, to wringing the last profits from the film factory in Wolfen as the United States' center of reparations moved west.

A MEDIUM THAT TURNS ORE TO EVERYDAY USE

Soviet forces took control of Wolfen on July 1, 1945, and SHAEF was dissolved on July 15. Two days later, the Potsdam Conference began, affirming Germany's division into four zones, occupied by the Americans, British, French, and Soviets. This inaugurated a new phase in the long process of war reparations. The Potsdam Agreement held that each occupying power was to be repaid for the cost of war chiefly in the form of industrial output and property from its zone. In reality, however, reparations had already been haphazardly extracted from Germany for almost three months, which made the accounting difficult. Just as the Western Allies had taken what was available to them immediately after liberation, the Soviet Union had formed its own "trophy brigades" after Yalta. The brigades continued their work in the Soviet zone well beyond early August, when they were meant to stop.[41]

Informal removals also continued. Like US forces, Soviet soldiers were captivated by portable German technologies, which were attractive as souvenirs or just as items that could be exchanged for cash. Watches, as rare and expensive in the Soviet Union as Leicas and Contaxes were in the United States, became an especially coveted prize, and a few soldiers sported several on each wrist. Some of the watches worked and told the right time, others didn't, and it didn't matter. Like carrying a camera around one's neck when there was no film to be found, watches were a status symbol and a marker of power, if a mystifying one to many Germans.[42]

Size, however, wasn't really a problem for the Soviet Union's reparations program. Since the Red Army had railways and roads that led home, the country deemed every German technology portable, and as soon as Agfa Wolfen's new managers, all veterans of the Soviet film industry, arrived at the plant, Lt. Col. Mumzhiev, Col. Kalischkin, and Lt. Col. Iordanskij began shipping what films and fibers were still made to the Soviet Union. Even the plant's most valuable buildings, the ones that made Agfacolor, wouldn't remain in Wolfen for long.[43] They were dismantled, packed into boxcars, and shipped east across Poland and Belarus to the city of Shostka in Ukraine, where the Svema film factory was located. Rebuilt with machines and workers from Wolfen, the factory would eventually produce the color film that the Soviet Union had long been forced to import, not yet having succeeded in making its own.[44]

Throughout the Soviet zone, reparations ranged across a spectrum like this: from seizing weapons, books, money, and art (relatively easy things to move) to transplanting entire factories. By 1948, the Red Army had removed a third of the industry in eastern Germany.[45] This was some measure of compensation for the staggering devastation Nazi Germany had visited upon the Soviet Union, the country that was to form the core of the Third Reich's empire, the source of its raw materials and labor. What unfolded in Wolfen over the course of 1946, then, may have resembled a scene the diarist Marta Hillers described in Berlin, with German civilians "unscrewing things, turning switches off, oiling machines, hauling parts away," hungry and enticed by the offer of extra rations, the men sometimes pistol-whipped by Soviet soldiers, the women catcalled or worse. Freight cars "piled high with machine parts," their metal "gleaming silver," lined the length of rail yards—in theory, at least, the technological and industrial foundations for the Soviet Union's recovery.[46]

The film professionals in the US and British T-Forces also would have liked to take some of the larger machines they found. A "combination slitting and chopping machine" that DuPont executive C. E. Rose saw in Germany would, the businessman wrote home, be of interest to "every company making sheet film or paper." But there was no way to transport machines like this. Shipping space was scarce, and more often than not, film manufacturing equipment was large, a structural part of the factory.⁴⁷ So, in place of machines for making film, the Americans and British contented themselves with film itself as a means of reparations. There was Agfacolor, and there were the three thousand German feature films that the US Army stored in the Bavarian Film Company studios, threatening to strip their emulsion and reuse the base.⁴⁸ Above all, there was microfilm: rolls imprinted with industrial records, chemical formulas, and plant blueprints, the diminutive fulcrum of American and British reparations.

FIGURE 22. Trains at Wolfen filled with factory parts, ready to travel to the Soviet Union in winter 1946. © Industrie- und Filmmuseum Wolfen.

Though it was a century old by the 1940s, microfilm was one of the decade's most hotly discussed media, trumpeted as a revolutionary way to read, record, and store information. The seed for this excitement was a machine called the Recordak, invented by George McCarthy as the Checkograph in 1925. The Recordak was capable of photographing multiple still images onto a single frame of film, and true to its name, it was used widely in banks to keep records of canceled checks. Like hospitals—where, as the Cleveland Clinic fire showed, safety was paramount—banks are busy, public places, and microfilm was one of the film formats behind cellulose acetate's growth in the 1920s and 30s. In 1928, Recordak became a Kodak subsidiary.[49]

Microphotography was not McCarthy's invention, and World War II wasn't the first war in which it was used. In 1870–71, as the Prussian Army lay siege to Paris, French photographer René Dagron (the inventor of the Stanhope, Victorian fashion jewelry containing a minuscule photograph and built-in viewer) tied microphotographed messages to the tail feathers of carrier pigeons and sent them across enemy lines. A single "pigeon post" required painstaking work, multiple steps over several days, but the Recordak was built for speed and volume, and it profited handsomely from this efficiency, becoming the United States' most used microfilm system by the 1940s.[50] This success was partly due to Recordak's business model. It wasn't possible to buy a machine outright; you had to rent one from the company, and the only exception to this rule, the US government, maintained exclusive purchasing contracts with Recordak throughout the 1930s and 1940s. Partly, it was due to Kodak's microfilms, which were part and parcel of the system.[51] Like the rest of the company's safety films, all of their cellulose acetate was made at Tennessee Eastman.

Microfilm's use in Allied reparations built as much on the experiences of banks as it did on those of libraries, which had come to rely on the technology to automate and improve their operations. In 1933, the New York Public Library and Recordak worked together to create a machine that could photograph newspapers in miniature, and a year later, the library's microfilm reading room opened.[52] When the American Library Association's *Journal of Documentary Reproduction* began publishing in 1938, it predicted that future libraries would be spaces of film as much as paper.[53]

Libraries seized on microfilm because of its impressive storage capacity (the reason for microfilming canceled checks). They also saw it as a new way for material to circulate: It was far less risky to hand a reader a roll of microfilm than it was to trust them with a rare book or fragile newspaper.

These qualities made microfilm a darling of the interwar "documentation" movement, which envisioned the technology as the grounds for international understanding. As the University of Chicago librarian M. Llewellyn Raney wrote in 1938, "In the freer flow of record from nation to nation understanding will deepen, hates tend to abate, co-operate become the master word that will once more lift our faces to the sky."[54]

Like the nonflammable film that ran through the Recordak, the documentation movement emerged from World War I, the chemists' war. By inventing poison gas, chemistry had contributed more than any other scientific discipline to the Great War's staggering number of deaths, and for Jean Gérard, head of Paris' Maison de la Chimie (House of Chemistry), the only way for chemistry to begin to atone for this was for the discipline's central institution to become the headquarters of a "universal information network."[55] Gérard argued that sharing scientific information was a path to peace: If weapons such as poison gas could be publicized from the moment of their discovery, it would serve as a deterrent (it was not a coincidence that Gérard involved Fritz Haber, the inventor of poison gas, in his projects).[56] In 1935, the Maison de la Chimie hosted an exhibition of information technologies used by the documentation movement, including microfilm. Two years later, Gérard helped plan the World Congress of Universal Documentation in Paris, at which the author H. G. Wells famously proclaimed these technologies the infrastructure of a "world brain."[57]

As with so many interwar internationalist projects, however, Germany's invasion of Poland upended these plans. Military-scientific research accelerated. Laboratories and factories, beholden to national governments, became secretive, while the war slowed international shipping. The utopian project of sharing information dissolved into espionage. In 1941, Britain's Association of Special Libraries and Information Bureaus (known as Aslib) launched the Enemy Periodicals Project to track German scientific publications circulating in the United Kingdom, and by 1942, the Aslib Microfilm Service (AMS) was cooperating with the United States Office of Strategic Services, the Rockefeller Foundation, and Eugene Power—the founder of Ann Arbor's University Microfilm, Inc., which pioneered the selling of doctoral dissertations.[58]

AMS was headquartered in London's Victoria and Albert Museum, and fittingly for its institutional home, it was led by photographer Lucia Moholy, a veteran of the Bauhaus, that beacon of design born in Dessau, not far from Wolfen. Like the library reading rooms of the 1930s and 40s, the AMS office was crowded with Recordaks: Micro-File Model Ds, which were smaller than the machines in banks and designed to photograph flat documents and bound volumes.[59] Each morning, US Marines ferried foreign publications to the AMS office. They returned later in the day to retrieve finished negatives for the US and British governments and for University Microfilm, Inc., which sold the films commercially. By the time the war was over, AMS had microfilmed more than 5.5 million journal pages, in which you could read about nearly any scientific field in nearly any European language: celluloid in German, enzymology in Norwegian, botany in Italian, obstetrics in Finnish.[60]

AMS's millions of pages were both a triumph and a problem. As Moholy noted in retrospect, despite the project's efforts, microfilm readers were in short supply throughout the war.[61] Even if you could find a machine and read the language (nothing was translated), microfilm was unappealing. It didn't resemble a journal—it had no cover, no table of contents, and no index; it looked and acted like a roll of film. Put differently, microfilm didn't only need a machine to work. It needed radical new approaches to publishing and reading. This was not what had been expected of the technology in 1938, when M. Llewellyn Raney hailed its power to revivify, its ability to transform "a stock of manuscripts" from "a pile of deadwood" ("the confession of an idle plant") into something useful. In the same article, written five years before uranium arrived at Oak Ridge, Raney used another metaphor. Microfilm, he wrote—a technology that depended on the nonflammable film that led Tennessee Eastman to the Manhattan Project—was "a medium that can turn ore to everyday use."[62]

For the engineer Vannevar Bush, one of the period's best-known microfilm enthusiasts, the solution to this technological problem was more technology.⁶³ Before the war, Bush was a professor at MIT, where he had worked on a Kodak-sponsored project to create the "microfilm rapid selector," a machine designed to make it easier to find a microfilmed document buried in a roll of film. He continued to research electronic data retrieval after the conflict began, now for military intelligence.⁶⁴ On July 1, 1945, as T-Forces were retreating from the Soviet occupation zone, he published his famous *Atlantic* essay "As We May Think," describing a machine called the Memex that relies on microfilm to compress, store, and recall "all [one's] books, records, and communications, and which is mechanized so that it may be consulted with exceeding speed and flexibility."

While the Memex is often seen as a proto computer, it was based on the Recordak, then the standard for microfilm. Bush's imaginary machine, however, had many more functions. It created, kept, enlarged, and indexed photographs on what Bush called a piece of "furniture," like the bank- and library-standard Recordaks. "On the top are slanting translucent screens, on which material can be projected for convenient reading. There is a keyboard, and sets of buttons and levers. Otherwise it looks like an ordinary desk." Microfilm, reduced by impressively large powers and containing anything you might want to store, "books of all sorts, pictures, current periodicals, newspapers," was inserted into the Memex. You could also add your own material, placing "longhand notes, photographs, memoranda, all sorts of things" on the machine's platen glass and photographing them with the simple "depression of a lever." Everything was indexed. "If the user wishes to consult a certain book, he taps its code on the keyboard, and the title page of the book promptly appears before him, projected onto one of his viewing positions." Engineered at the nexus of photography, electronics, and library science, the Memex would solve the problem that Moholy and others had identified: "a growing mountain of research" in which "the investigator is staggered by the findings and conclusions of thousands of other workers—conclusions which he cannot find time to grasp, much less to remember, as they appear."⁶⁵ It would connect researchers to material that was sitting at the ready, microfilmed in libraries and archives.

The Memex was never built; it was never really meant to be built. And although Bush understood microfilm's flaws as well as Moholy did, he brought much more of it to the United States. As the head of the Office of Scientific Research and Development, the National Defense Research Committee's successor, he worked with American industries to develop the American-British Combined Intelligence Objectives Subcommittee's target list, sending T-Forces to Germany equipped with microfilm machines—lightweight Micro-File Model Es.[66] Portability, Haidee Wasson argues, is essential to media used in war, and this made Model Es a favorite of US forces, who used them for everything from personnel photographs to map and document photography. They were ideal machines for the field, unpacked and ready to go in a matter of minutes.[67]

Minutes mattered to the T-Forces, who had long lists of targets to visit and millions of pages of paper at each. "Document reconnaissance teams" went first, assessing what was there. They were followed by "document screeners," American civilians from industry or universities. Screeners flagged records to be photographed by the final team, "microfilm units" consisting mostly of German civilians, who, when their work was done, sent finished rolls of film to the FIAT headquarters in Germany to be developed, indexed, and abstracted. Eventually, the documents were published by the US Department of Commerce's Publication Board, part of the Office of Technical Services.[68]

It was plain from the beginning that FIAT's microfilm efforts risked creating the same unscalable "mountain of research" that the Memex was designed to conquer. The agency's operating procedures are filled with warnings to document screeners, the most difficult people to hire since they needed to both read German and understand the technical and scientific context. Screeners were cautioned that "the majority of significant intelligence targets have been visited by qualified field teams," and "many of the documents of real value have been removed." The procedures underscored this last point, noting that "the mere fact that documents are found to be of a scientific or technical nature does not in itself assure that such documents contain intelligence of real value to U.S. science and industry."[69]

This much was immediately obvious to Gunther Stent, an American document screener sent by FIAT to an IG Farben factory in Leverkusen. "I asked my colleagues," Stent recalled, "'How are we going to tell which documents describe hot technical information?... We'd have to be some kind of universal geniuses to do a real screening job on all the paperwork piled up here!' Another member of the team agreed: "'How are we going to keep our Kraut camera crews busy? It takes a lot longer to read a document than to microfilm it!' Thus, before even getting started on any screening, we cottoned on to the futility of our mission, and, indeed, to the hare-brained nature of the whole FIAT document-screening program."[70] Immediately after the war, Germany might have been the site of what American journalists called the "world's greatest treasure hunt," a place where every file or document was a potential prize.[71] Months later, on a medium that could "turn ore to everyday use," the same documents and files threatened to be only fool's gold.

Yet if this was actually the case, it would have been difficult to know. Altogether, from autumn 1945 to summer 1947, nearly thirteen million frames of microfilm were sent to Washington, which Douglas O'Reagan likens to "a stack of paper almost a mile high."[72] Some of this material was listed in the weekly *Bibliography of Scientific and Industrial Reports* and its British equivalent, from which anyone could order copies (the US-based Soviet trade agency Amtorg, or Amerikanskaya Torgovlya, was a regular customer), but most of it remained unprocessed.[73] Even when it was cataloged, it could take months, even years, to receive a report that you'd ordered. A machine like the Memex would have been helpful, but it didn't exist. And so the majority of the information, pursued at great technological, governmental, financial, and human cost, went unused.[74]

At first glance, this seems nothing like the Soviet reparations program, with its trains filled with metal and machine parts. But the differences between the two programs might be smaller than they seem. After all, a chain of overflowing boxcars is not too different from a reel of microfilm, each frame filled with a matrix of smaller images. In both cases, a "mountain" of reparations material had to be unmassed, studied, understood, reassembled, and put to use—whether that meant installing

FIGURE 23. British report on the photographic industry in wartime Germany. From the British Library Collection: Kodak Archive, A 3024.

Agfa Wolfen equipment in Shostka or indexing the documents that held the secrets to Agfacolor. Color film was one of the few real successes of postwar reparations precisely because there was a network of specialists ready to absorb it: the scientists at Kodak, Gevaert, and Ferrania, or the Agfa employees who were transferred to Ukraine. This network had been born amidst the chemical industry's interwar mergers; as Lt. Col. Cuthbertson made clear, Ansco was a special beneficiary of Agfa's color film knowledge because it was a former subsidiary of the German company. Yet Ansco was also equipped to make color film because its US competitor, Kodak, had entered the German market in 1927, purchasing Glanzfilm and worrying Agfa, which created Agfa Ansco in response. After the war, when reels of nonflammable film traveled from the United States to Germany and back again, carrying Agfa's trade secrets, it was Kodak—the US government's microfilm contractor—that stood, above all, to profit.

A CITY MANAGER IN MUNICH

The borders between Germany's Soviet and Western occupation zones hardened after July 1, 1945, but they weren't impassable. From winter 1945 to spring 1946, British and American teams continued to travel to the Bitterfeld-Wolfen area, seeking answers to lingering technical questions, though in contrast to the wild early weeks of spring 1945, they were closely watched, now by Soviet officials. Everyone understood that the visits weren't purely technical in nature and that they weren't only about reparations. They were also stages for diplomacy between the Soviet Union and the West, and the Soviets took their roles as hosts seriously. Just after Christmas 1945, an American FIAT team wrote drunkenly to headquarters in Berlin, recounting the "REGAL SPLENDOR" in which they were housed in Wolfen, where they were received with a lunch "complete with red wine, white wine, and copious quantities of vodka. After eating," they reported, "we met with the directors of the control offices of several of the plants, and were entertained by being shown a German color film. After another enormous repast, which just about finished us, we are only fit for bed, but are writing you anyway . . . ."[75] A week later, another team observed that "our chief difficulty has been the well-known Russian hospitality. Life seems to be just one banquet after another, and one bottle of vodka after another." Nevertheless, "you have in this party excellent diplomatic talent, and the honor, if not the dignity, of FIAT, and in fact the whole USA, is being upheld."[76] Hospitality is a form of power, and when Ilford employees visited Wolfen in spring 1946, their work was overseen by the plants' Soviet military supervisors. In nearby Eilenburg, where they visited the Deutsche Celluloid Fabrik, the investigators were only allowed to meet with the plant's commander.[77]

When this last team visited Wolfen, the factory's dismantling was underway.[78] Some Wolfen employees were happy to accompany it to Ukraine, convinced by the extra rations, decent housing, and fair treatment they were promised. Others were coerced, at times forced to choose between signing two statements—one of which, unthinkable, read, "The undersigned herewith declares his unwillingness to assist in the reconstruction of the Soviet Union."[79] And then, very early in the morning of October 22, 1946, forty-five Agfa Wolfen employees along with their families and possessions were forced into trucks and trains and moved to Shostka as part of a sweeping operation called Osoaviakhim (the name referred to the Soviet Society for the Assistance of Defense, Aircraft and Chemical Construction, *Obshchestvo sodeystviya oboronye, aviatsionnomu i khimicheskomu stroitelstvu*).[80] Panic bubbled among the factory employees who remained. Several visited the Berlin offices of FIAT's Enemy Personnel Exploitation Section, carrying stories that they hoped could be traded for safe passage to the West.

At times, these stories were tinged with the moment's paranoia. In early December, Dr. Erwin Fuchs came to Berlin "to make preparations for an escape in case the Soviets put pressure on him to go to Russia." Fuchs recounted that two weeks earlier, he had applied for an apartment in Wolfen that would soon be available. As he did so, "he had the feeling that he was being stared at as if to indicate astonishment that a man 'already halfway to Russia' should be needing another apartment in Germany."[81] Other stories were closer to the rumors Morin described as endemic to postwar Germany. Several of Agfa Wolfen's color film specialists had fled to Switzerland. But maybe the Swiss agents who spirited them away were actually French—or maybe they were Russian, as had been suspected when V-2 rocket scientists were approached with job offers in Switzerland.[82] Other employees simply disappeared, presumably also to the West. By January 1947 FIAT had found an agent to communicate between Berlin and Wolfen. That month, the agency evacuated some color film staff, and it planned to bring out other employees within weeks.[83]

Brain drain was one of the many problems Agfa Wolfen faced as relations between the Soviet Union and the West soured. By 1946, most Agfacolor specialists had left, and the disorder of the early postwar months, during which the factory's raw materials and machines were confiscated, looted, or lost, had given way to more permanent dislocations that stranded Agfa's camera, paper, and film factories in different zones. The company's headquarters remained in Berlin. The Munich Camera Works was in the US zone, the Leverkusen paper plant in the British zone, and Wolfen in the Soviet zone. The plants were allowed to keep functioning in no small part as sources of reparations, and they were managed by the Allied Control Council's IG Farben Control Commission, whose job was to dismantle the cartel. However, the Americans, British, French, and Soviets had different ideas about how this should be done, which made reparations, operations, and supply problems worse.[84] Often, matters could not be separated: Because the factories didn't work well, neither did the reparations.

Supply problems were some of the most intractable, as Wolfen shows. Although the Soviet zone was rich in chemical companies and photochemical firms, the factory had always depended on materials made throughout Germany. It bought cellulose nitrate from nearby Eilenburg, cellulose acetate from Dormagen (now in the British zone), plasticizers from Ludwigshafen (French zone), gelatin from the Schweinfurt Gelatin Works (US zone), and so on.[85] Now, due to zonal borders and postwar shortages, only some of these materials were available.

Bruno Uhl saw this dysfunction clearly. The son-in-law of longtime Agfa executive Wilhelm Otto, Uhl had been a sales manager for the company for years. He started his career at the Munich camera factory in 1923. In 1931, he was made Agfa's director of sales, one of the executives Fritz Gajewski brought on to modernize the company as IG Farben's Division III took shape. Uhl was energetic and experienced, and as he built up Agfa's marketing programs, he looked to the big US firms.[86] His esteem for the United States lost no luster at the end of the war when, having fled Berlin, holed up with his family in a monastery, he heard that there was an American soldier at the gate, asking for him by name. The soldier turned out to be the son of a Jewish journalist whom Uhl had helped secure emigration papers before the war. On his father's stern instructions, the soldier offered Uhl cocoa, tea, coffee, shoelaces, and toilet paper. He also gave him the use of his Jeep. Wearing beige worker's coveralls taken from Wolfen, Uhl drove with the soldier back to the film factory to find what might still be left. Eventually, he made his way to British-occupied Leverkusen, which was to become Agfa's West German film factory. In fall 1945, he was named Leverkusen's new sales manager.[87]

Uhl, then, might have thought himself on friendly ground when, on February 23, 1946, he, his wife Greti, and Fritz Felber, the American-appointed custodian of the Munich Camera Works, found themselves in the US zone meeting with Major Elmer W. Prince, the once and future city manager of Morgantown, West Virginia, and the current US sub-control officer for IG Farben in Munich.[88] There was a problem: Agfa Wolfen had begun requesting payment on past accounts from its customers in the British and US zones. The accounting was impossible for the Americans and British to verify. Even more confounding, to evade restrictions on exchange between zones, Wolfen had ordered the money to be sent to a location in the British zone close to the border with the Soviet zone. There, it was said, an agent would be waiting to collect the funds.

The transcript of this meeting captures Prince's confusion at the arrangement. "How," he asked, "can the British zone representatives collect accounts in the American zone?"

Uhl, speaking English honed during his years at Agfa, corrected him: "Not from British, from Russian zone!"

"But what about the American zone?" Prince insisted, continuing: "I still cannot understand how any firm in the British zone can collect money for the Wolfen plant which is payable in the American zone."

"You are right," Uhl explained, "that is impossible. That is on the black way, but I have stopped it." He paused, then spoke again, trying to appease Prince: "I think it is not right when this money from American and British zone goes into the Russian zone."

Prince's frustration only mounted. "It is not right under the principles which have been set up by the Allied Control Council. It is just complicating things more to have the money go from the American to the British zone."

"And then to the Russian zone," interjected Greti Uhl, whose English was pure Oxford, even better than her husband's.[89]

"Even if it stops in the British zone it is not right," Prince repeated. "No money can go out of the American to the British zone."

There was a related issue: Felber was on his way from Munich (US zone) to Leverkusen (British zone) with silver. "You take that silver," Prince warned Felber, "that is going to be a hard thing." American officials needed written confirmation from the British that the silver would be exchanged for photo paper for the US Army.

Amidst the "world's greatest treasure hunt," in which, Norman Naimark writes, "the vaults of some banks and loan houses [were] simply emptied into large sacks and shipped off to Moscow," Prince might have seen Felber's silver as currency, like the money Wolfen was requesting.[90] It wasn't. As Felber put it, it was "to be considered as raw material for the fabrication of photographic sensitive material," and more silver was at the Reichsbank in Frankfurt awaiting transformation into silver nitrate.

In fact, the problem wasn't even that silver was a precious metal. Prince was equally concerned about a batch of gelatin that Felber was due to deliver to Leverkusen, which also could not leave the US zone without a release stating that it would be returned in kind by the British. Similarly, he told Uhl, there was no way the Munich factory could sell cameras to British zone civilians—no doubt eager to replace the devices that had been taken in such great numbers by the Allies—without an exchange for another commodity. It seemed to come as a surprise to Prince when Uhl hesitatingly suggested the most valuable thing of all: food.[91]

Perhaps the encounter with Prince was a surprise to Uhl, too, revealing the limits of the country the Agfa sales director had so admired. What's certain is that it confirmed Morin's diagnosis of occupied Germany as a fractured system in which everything was potential currency. In this system, the only way that anything—whether it was silver or photo paper, factory parts or potatoes—could leave an occupation zone was with a promise that it would benefit the occupier. Prince, an American city manager, was one of the many functionaries sent to coordinate this system, and he brought with him Progressivism's moral and economic assumptions, its commitment to rationality and "scientific" management. This was no match for postwar Germany, whose concurrent occupations were bent on breaking the Third Reich's own history of empire. And so even though Uhl, Felber, and others like them were charged with establishing independent industries in the reconfigured country, their work was stymied by, in Morin's words, the "real contradictions between the victors' democratic aspirations and the economic imperialism of the power of money."[92]

COLD WAR, HOT METALS

The money that Agfa Wolfen would have earned by reconciling accounts in the British and US zones would probably have been insignificant for the Soviet Union. Silver was a different matter, and not because it was a raw material for film or a form of currency. In the Soviet zone in spring 1946, silver was meaningful above all as a harbinger of uranium—an infinitely more valuable metal, and an element in the emerging Cold War.

Silver had been mined for centuries in the Ore Mountains, the mineral-rich natural boundary between Saxony and Bohemia, east of Wolfen. This was the area that Oleksandra Lawrik walked through after she fled the transport out of Wolfen. After separating from Tina at the Czechoslovak border, Lawrik continued alone as the hills rolled more steeply and farmland gave way to forested cliffs, the entrances to centuries-old mines cut into their sides. The mountains have a climate of their own, and though it was the end of April, it was sleeting. Lawrik—lost, hungry, her lungs permanently damaged by caustic soda—collapsed under a pine tree. When two Czech women stumbled upon her, offered her sandwiches, and revealed a hidden path to a village, it might have felt like a second chance at life, or given all that she'd survived, more than that. After two weeks of convalescence in the Sudetenland, Lawrik was on a train to Warsaw, then Kyiv, and finally Dnipro, where she arrived on May 28 to find Anatolii waiting for her.[93]

During her journey home, Lawrik had unwittingly passed through one of the world's most geopolitically sensitive regions at this moment when the Second World War was turning cold and the Soviet Union's atomic bomb project was accelerating. The Bohemian town of Jáchymov wasn't far away. Jáchymov was where Ore Mountains silver had led to the discovery of uranium, and later, its ore fed Polish-French scientist Marie Curie's groundbreaking research on radioactivity. In August 1945, Soviet officials began meeting with the Czechoslovak government, fresh from its wartime exile in Moscow, to assure that Jáchymov's mines came under Red Army control. The Soviets were also interested in the German side of the Ore Mountains, but they didn't start prospecting there until late September. When it became apparent that those uranium deposits were even richer and more extensive than the ones in Czechoslovakia, the radium spas in which Russian soldiers had relaxed in spring 1946 were closed, and the area transformed into a heavily fortified military zone. Known as Wismut (for the metal bismuth), it became one of the world's largest uranium mines, and for the Soviet Union, a source of reparations far more meaningful than Agfa's film and fibers, silver and gelatin.[94]

By 1946, then, in eastern Tennessee and this part of what would soon be East Germany, film manufacturing and nuclear bomb making sat shoulder to shoulder. This was a chemical matter and an industrial matter, and it was a matter of film's ingredients and their multiple uses. Like the trees that could be made into safety film and RDX, silver was at once a metal that turned fleeting encounters with light into permanent recordings and a sign that uranium was near. Such layers of meaning drove film's use as reparations throughout Germany. Film and its raw materials could be used by occupying forces. They could be taken as trophies, substituting for violent urges. They could be counted in ledger books or packed into trains, compensation for impossible losses. But despite successes at Kodak-Pathé and with Agfacolor, it was difficult to make film truly work as repayment for what the war had taken because its components, formulas, and technologies only became valuable when all the ingredients were there; when there were cameras or projectors through which it could run; and when scientists and technicians knew how to assemble a piece of machinery or read a chemical formula. Reparations on microfilm also only meant something when the film had been indexed, when microfilm readers were plentiful, and when people had learned to use them—in Lucia Moholy's and Vannevar Bush's view, an unlikely series of events.

Were reparations simpler in other forms? Maybe. When Marta Hillers's radio went out in spring 1945, after the Red Army had washed into Berlin on a tide of fear, electricity cuts, and tinned food unseen in the city for weeks, she thought about this. "Once again," Hillers wrote, "we see what a dubious blessing technology really is. Machines with no intrinsic value, worthless if you can't plug them in somewhere. Bread, however, is absolute. Coal is absolute. And gold is gold whether you're in Rome, Peru, or Breslau."[95] Hillers's diagnosis of technology was correct, and she was correct that coal, as a source of heat, was absolute. But as a raw material—as the basis for dyes, for film, for the entire field of organic chemistry—it was not, and neither was gold just gold. Like silver and uranium, these elements often took on radically different meanings when they were "plugged in" to new scientific, cultural, and economic systems.[96] When Soviet forces sent trains filled with film, factory parts, and later uranium on the same path Oleksandra Lawrik followed out of Germany, they set another process of transformation in motion, as reparations for the war that had just ended became the materials for the one about to begin. Soon, the uranium would be airborne, drifting from the Soviet nuclear testing site to Kodak's film factories in the United States.

CHAPTER FOUR

Fallout

THE SNOW THAT FELL on Rochester on November 1, 1951, was a record. Even there, on Lake Ontario's southeastern shore—where there is often snow, and a lot of it—it almost never started so early in the season. Halloween had been crisp and seasonable, a good night for trick-or-treating. By the next afternoon, pumpkins grimaced under a slushy mantle, and even those most hardened to upstate weather were eyeing their shovels, already weary of the winter ahead.[1]

Kodak knew that the storm was coming. The company had been watching the weather since January, when the United States sped up its nuclear testing program in response to the Soviet Union's first successful bomb test. Although Rochester was two thousand miles away from the Nevada testing grounds, it was proving to be something of a trap for fallout from the explosions: a "radiation sewer," as an Atomic Energy Commission (AEC) scientist put it a few years later. This was an accident of air and water. After each test, westerly winds swept radioactive particles northeast across the country toward the Great Lakes. When the winds met Lake Ontario's warmer climate, the same lake effect that created so much snow in Rochester caught the particles, driving them earthward.

November's "hot" snow was front-page news in Rochester, and it alarmed Kodak because the company knew that even the smallest radioactive particles could damage photosensitive film and paper. In the industry, these effects were known as fogging or black spots. Snow had been the culprit the first time Kodak Park found fallout in its air filters, after the January 1951 tests. The company had alerted the AEC's New

York Health and Safety Laboratory. That laboratory's director, Merril Eisenbud, called the medical director of the Nevada test site, who scoffed that Kodak's report was nonsense: there was no radiation there, in Nevada; why should there be any in Rochester? Eisenbud didn't give up. He phoned the AEC's Washington headquarters, which admitted that beyond the test site, the agency was doing little monitoring of the bomb's effects. So Eisenbud and his colleagues called all the university and industry contacts they had in the Northeast, and sent them out in the cold to collect ice-cream containers of snow, which were rushed to New York for analysis. There was confirmation from the Rochester *Democrat and Chronicle* a few days later: "The cloud of 'hot' products formed by the atomic bomb blasts presumably was swept in this direction by high-altitude winds, and then was caught in the snow that fell widely over the Northeast."[2] Soon, Eisenbud's team had created a network across the region to monitor for fallout—Rochester was one of its stations—and the AEC had agreed to give the US photographic industry advance warning of weapons tests.[3] Rochesterians, meanwhile, were told not to worry.[4]

Rochester may have been a radiation sewer, but it didn't drain the westerlies of their radiant content. The winds swirled through New York State, east, northeast, across New England and the Maritimes and then the Atlantic. Tendrils twisted around Kodak Ltd. in England and Kodak-Pathé in Paris, across the border between the two Germanies and into Wolfen, particles drifting to the ground when it rained or snowed. Within a week or so, they passed overhead the Kazakh steppes.[5] When bombs exploded at the Soviet testing site there, they also sent radiation into the atmosphere. Those clouds moved westward over China and the Pacific, past Hollywood and Los Alamos. They skirted Oak Ridge and Kingsport, and, joining the clouds made by American bombs, drifted toward Lake Ontario—on whose Canadian side, just northwest of Rochester, there is another lake, called Crawford.

Geologists see Crawford Lake as a sentinel: evidence of the earth's transition from the Holocene to the Anthropocene, the period in the planet's history shaped irrevocably by human activity. The transition is visible in the lake's sediment, which is layered. A probe pressed deep into the muck and raised to the surface carries a remarkably detailed cross section of at least a thousand years of history, each layer revealing something about what was happening on Earth at a given time. In the layer that corresponds to 1950, the lake's sediment begins to change. Ash from burning fossil fuels appears, and so does the same radioactive dust that fell over Rochester in winter 1951. All of this, some geologists argue, means that 1950 was the year Earth shifted decisively from one geological epoch to another and that Crawford Lake merits the designation of a "golden spike," a metal stake in the earth marking this change.[6]

If you were to take a microscope to a cross section of film, you would see that, like Crawford Lake's sediment, it is layered. And like Crawford Lake, film around 1950 was a sentinel. This started with its top layers, the emulsion. As fallout turned Kodak's factories into a de facto nuclear monitoring network, spots and fogging on this emulsion became markers of the atomic age. Below the emulsion is the base. Starting in 1951, nearly all of Kodak's film base was made from cellulose acetate, and cellulose acetate was increasingly made from petrochemicals processed at Texas Eastman, a new Tennessee Eastman subsidiary in Longview, Texas. Tennessee Eastman's employee newspaper, *TEC News*, chronicled the factory's emergence alongside listings of births, marriages, and the factory's daily film screenings. The movies were anodyne: cartoons, slapstick comedies, World War II dramas. Quietly, chemically, however, the film on which they were printed was chronicling the world that companies like Kodak helped create, a world marked by the joint upheavals of the Cold War and the Anthropocene.

ON THE WIND

The storm in Rochester that November lasted for days. While it was sending cars into tailspins and luring children to late-season raspberries frozen on the branch, a crisis was brewing at Rochester's photographic plants (beyond Kodak, there were a few: Bell and Howell, DuPont,

Dynacolor, Haloid). The systems and protocols that had promised "absolute control" over the factory environment were beginning to fail, and radioactive dust was making its way inside. At first, the companies insisted that it wasn't a problem, just a matter of workers wiping their shoes more carefully at the door. By the 6th, Kodak admitted to the *Democrat and Chronicle* that the radiation had forced changes at its photographic paper mill. The news would have gotten out anyway: So many of the city's residents worked at Kodak that its factory walls were more permeable to gossip than to dust.[7]

The fact that radiation could damage photographic paper or film didn't catch Kodak off guard. Radiation is a form of energy, part of the same electromagnetic spectrum as visible light, and it exposes film and paper the way light does. This had caused problems for Kodak years before 1951's hot snows. Early in World War II, the company found fogging on film that had been sitting, packaged, for weeks. Salvage campaigns meant that the cardboard used to pack film could contain waste paper from war plants, and sometimes the plants used radium paint to create instrument dials. It became evident that even a minuscule amount of radium in the waste paper used to make cardboard was enough to damage film, and so Kodak changed tack. It found new packaging in strawboard—a material pulped and pressed at Midwestern factories that Kodak hoped it could control as absolutely as its own.

The plan worked for a while. It worked until August 6, 1945, the day of the Hiroshima bombing. That day, at a mill in Vincennes, Indiana, something got into a run of strawboard. It did so invisibly and without fanfare, and no one knew it until the board was finished and layered between sheets of X-ray film. A few weeks later, the same film developed fogged areas—tiny ones, no more than a millimeter in diameter, but deep, penetrating several layers of emulsion. Within a month or so, similar damage appeared on film packaged with strawboard made two states away, in Tama, Iowa.

For Julian H. Webb, a Kodak physicist who worked at Y-12 during the war and later returned to Rochester, this became an experiment.[8] Since whatever was causing the spots emitted only beta and gamma rays, and no alpha rays—the signature of natural radioactive elements like radium or uranium—Webb deduced that it was human-made, like plutonium. It probably didn't come from the straw; batches of film packed with strawboard made weeks earlier showed none of the same contamination. When it started to appear after every heavy rainfall, he concluded that it came from the water the factories used: the Wabash River in Vincennes and the Iowa River in Tama. If it was in the rain, it was also in the sky. And what was in the sky in Vincennes, Indiana, on August 6, 1945, could not have been radiation from Hiroshima, not yet. It must have been from the Trinity test three weeks earlier. "It is readily conceivable," Webb wrote in a 1949 article on the damaged film, "that radioactive atoms projected into the stratosphere, and carried by winds, could collect on dust particles and be brought down by precipitation and be washed into streams." Volcanic ash was known to travel in exactly this way.[9]

This was a possibility that the Manhattan Project's leaders had known about since shortly after the Trinity test.[10] The detonation created a cloud of atomic dust, and clouds like that could travel. But Webb went out of his way to emphasize that they were nothing to worry about: "The magnitudes of the radioactive effects observed were exceedingly minute and were detected at all only because of unusual circumstances that resulted in very great sensitivity." In fact, he added, "the main reason for presenting the data at this time arises from the thought that the results obtained, and the experimental procedure used, might be of interest to other physicists who are concerned with detection of minute quantities of radioactive materials."[11] From reading Webb's article, it would have been easy to conclude that fallout was merely a curiosity: a matter of "film health," as a journalist put it later, not public health.[12]

It was a curiosity that film manufacturers took deadly seriously. When the first series of Nevada tests was announced in late January, 1951, William C. Babbitt, managing director of the National Association of Photographic Manufacturers, contacted the AEC. The industry was worried that the tests might have the same effect on film and paper that Trinity did, and it wanted the government's help. Fallout showed up, as expected, and Kodak called Eisenbud. Eisenbud's team confirmed

Kodak's findings. On February 13, Julian Webb was invited to Washington. He secured a promise from the AEC that the agency would give the photographic industry "an approximate idea of the date of future tests." When he returned to Washington on March 8 for more meetings, Webb was handed a copy of a map that Eisenbud's office had made of fallout from the January tests, and promised more maps in the future—predictions of how wind might move after a test and where radiation might fall. The maps, the AEC emphasized, were for industry eyes only.[13]

Like Kodak's switch from cardboard to strawboard packaging, this system worked, sometimes. Sometimes it didn't. It was around this time that Hercules, Inc. got a call from Kodak. Hercules was a descendant of DuPont, spun off when the US government feared that the explosives manufacturer, like Kodak, was getting too large, and its cellulose plant in Hopewell, Virginia, purified more cotton linters than anywhere else in the world.[14] A recent shipment of Hopewell cotton had left Kodak with a batch of motion picture film speckled with radiation, and the Hercules chemists were baffled. They ran test after test but found no problems. So, like Webb at Kodak, they began an observational experiment, waiting, watching, and concluding that the contamination came from something that appeared in the atmosphere about every eight days: "atomic clouds that floated around," in the words of Hercules CEO C. A. Higgins. "And if it rained, you got an extra dose."

Hercules was told not to say anything, and it didn't, but it kept an eye on the sky and listened to the warnings the AEC sent photographic manufacturers. "Eastman only got the stuff from the days when the air was clear," Higgins recalled. Cotton linters for other products weren't a problem. Your pocket comb could be lightly radioactive. So could your plastic cups or the lacquer that protected your car from rust. But not the film you used to photograph your children or the slides you taught with in a classroom because there, in the products of a prominent and popular American industry, radiation's hazards could appear with startling clarity. As Hercules showed, these hazards were not just revealed by film's top layers, its emulsion, but also by the base that supported them—like straw, made from the fibers of a thirsty plant.[15]

FIGURE 24. Kodak Park air filters, 1950s. Courtesy of the University of Rochester Rare Books, Special Collections and Preservation, and Eastman Kodak Company.

BLACK SPOTS

Film manufacturers like Kodak were too large for the AEC to ignore, but they were also too important to the agency's work. To see this, peel back another layer, one laid three weeks before fallout landed near Vincennes and Tama. Early in the morning of July 16, 1945, the day of the Trinity test, dozens of cameras were arrayed across the desert in Alamogordo, New Mexico. The machines were poised to photograph the explosion that would send beta and gamma rays high into the atmosphere on desert dust, then to rivers, straw, and cotton, unwittingly damaging film.

Although in 1951, fallout would shake the photographic industry's sense of control over its factory environments, photographing the first atomic explosion had been a sweeping demonstration of photography's capabilities.[16] The Los Alamos Laboratories Weapons Physics Division had planned the test for over a year, and it was intended partly to document the event and partly so that the new weapon's effects could be measured and studied. This wasn't easy to do. Capturing an explosion unfolding in fractions of fractions of a second required cameras and films that could operate at extremely fast speeds. The machines also needed to be sturdy enough to withstand the bomb's heat, which scientists knew would be unbearable, and the sand and debris that, even when there wasn't an explosion, the desert site constantly kicked into the air. The sand could jam the cameras' shutters; it could get stuck in the gates.

In all, there were fifty-five cameras at Alamogordo, mostly motion picture cameras, stationed at set distances from the bomb: a half mile, six miles, twenty miles. Since the most important action would unfold so quickly, the cameras were automated, their shutters tripped by the same mechanism that loosed the weapon. Some of them used 35 mm and some used color film, but for the most part, Trinity was photographed on black-and-white 16 mm. In milliseconds, this film captured a fireball that appeared to bubble from the ground, its outline growing hazy as dust clustered around its base. Later, aerial cameras flatly revealed the blast's crater on an expanse of desert.[17]

As revelatory and terrifying as they were, these motion pictures and photographs only showed part of the picture. The film on which they were made contained a fuller image of the new world the bomb test brought into being—since, as Jennifer Fay writes, the Trinity explosion suggests another point of origin for the Anthropocene.[18] The past and the future were both visible here. The past: Because it burned slowly and calmly, 16 mm cellulose acetate was the film that helped Tennessee Eastman expand into rayon, leading the company to Holston and the

Manhattan Project, which brought those fifty-five cameras to Alamogordo. The future: When it was developed, photographers discovered that the explosion's heat had singed some of the emulsion, leaving telltale traces on the prints—black spots, as Julian Mack and Berlyn Brixner put it shortly after the test, not so different from the ones fallout from the same explosion would soon create.[19]

In other words, the future was in atomic testing, with which the US photographic industry remained involved for years after Trinity. In early 1946, while he was unraveling the story of the black spots, Julian Webb sat alongside representatives from Bausch & Lomb, Fairchild Camera, and other companies in meetings convened by the Navy's Bureau of Aeronautics, planning how to photograph the first set of postwar tests, Operation Crossroads, scheduled for that summer at Bikini Atoll in the Marshall Islands.[20] The plan's scale was massive. Multiple photographers were employed, as was a complete array of still and motion picture cameras. The cameras were positioned at every possible angle on the ground, in the air, and on the water. They shot photographs and films, and they made scientific measurements. Following guidelines devised by Kodak Research Laboratories, among others, they tried to avoid the problems that had surfaced at Trinity: singed film, black spots.[21]

The first bomb test in Operation Crossroads, called Able, was exploded in the air. The second, Baker, was designed to measure the effects of an explosion on a naval fleet, and it was detonated underwater, near specially equipped ships. As far back as January, the team on which Webb served had been warned that the water explosion, the world's first, would be dangerous and unpredictable. It was expected to create a "tidal wave possibly 100 feet high," a radioactive surge that would inundate the islands nearby, perhaps even those miles away. The only way to protect film from the radiant wave—to make sure that images of the explosion could be viewed and studied later—was to entomb cameras in a solid foot of lead. "The worst conditions," Webb recorded in his notes from the meetings, "must be expected in this case."[22]

Baker was even worse than predicted. It sent a wide column of water six thousand feet in the air. There was radioactive spray, and the predicted tsunami. As a landmark *Life* magazine article put it a year later, the test also "demonstrated a terrifying new possibility of atomic warfare," underscoring that atomic bombs' danger didn't end with the explosions themselves; the aftermath was just as perilous. The color photographs for which *Life* was so well known (there's an advertisement for the new Ansco color film in the same issue) showed the dissected corpses of some of the thousands of animals held captive on the ships as stand-ins for humans: the enlarged blood vessels and organs, the hemorrhaging muscles in rats, goats, pigs, mice, and guinea pigs. These effects were just the obvious ones, those that appeared relatively quickly. In the days and weeks after the explosion, radiation became "pervasive." It entered the marine food chain, and on X-rays, tropical fish glowed unearthly bright.[23] The area of contamination grew to the point at which soldiers' bunks had to be moved, inch by inch, away from the ship's walls, and the radiological safety team was monitoring "almost every bite of food, every drink of water, every piece of laundry, the handrails of ships, the beaches where the men went swimming."

"Some of us have reflected," that team's head, Dr. Stafford L. Warren, wrote in an accompanying article, "what might have happened if Bikini had been a populous harbor with a wind blowing in from the sea. Fission products equivalent to tons of radium would have been spread over the city. Most of its people would have inevitably died. A smooth-working evacuation system might have saved a few of them, but no defense would have been effective. The only defense against atomic bombs still lies outside the scope of science. It is the prevention of atomic war."[24]

Coming from Warren, the Manhattan Project's former chief medical officer, this was significant. A professor at the University of Rochester's medical school who studied radiation's effects on the human body, Warren had joined the project in 1943, after the Kodak executive Albert K. Chapman introduced him to Leslie R. Groves. Warren was initially tasked with leading a university research group to study how to protect Manhattan Project employees from the radioactive materials they handled, and to determine how much radiation workers' bodies could safely bear. That was hard enough to do in factories and laboratories at Oak Ridge, Hanford, and Los Alamos, but it was impossible in the Pacific.[25] Warren's description of Bikini Atoll as a "harbor with a wind blowing in from the sea" also wasn't hypothetical. Although the island's inhabitants had been evacuated, the tests irreparably contaminated or destroyed their homes, livelihoods, and sources of food, seeding health problems passed down through generations. Yet even if Warren had mentioned this, such warnings didn't carry very much weight, and neither did the photographs that accompanied them.[26] For the US government, preventing atomic war meant deterrence: building bombs powerful enough that no other country would dare strike first.[27] As the years went on and nuclear explosions grew larger and more sophisticated, the photographic industry kept pace with the AEC, creating faster cameras, and films sensitive enough to match the breakneck speed of proliferation.

For the photographic industry, atomic testing was a double-edged sword. As with airplane dope in World War I, the opportunity to experiment in the name of defense was useful for photography, even civilian photography.[28] But at the same time that the industry was sending cameras and film to test sites in the Pacific and Nevada, it was struggling to protect itself from fallout from the same tests. The redundant plant design and vertical integration that, until World War II, had protected film factories' products, materials, and factories—none of it was enough in the era of constant nuclear explosions, which, as the *Life* article warned, had made human-made radioactivity ubiquitous.

In March 1951, Kodak president Thomas J. Hargrave wrote to the AEC about this, warning that if bomb tests caused enough damage to the company's products, "we will very likely have to file claims for redress against the Government." He pointed out that the risks spilled beyond Kodak Park, since photographic factories depended on "such basic material as wood pulp, cotton linters, gelatin, and many others, as well as air and water," and these substances came from across the United States and beyond. Contamination in any one of them or the places they were found could damage film.²⁹ Hargrave publicly reiterated the threat of litigation the next year, telling *The Evening Star* that fallout was "so insidious we can never tell whether to expect it in the water, in the emulsion, the film base or at a thousand and one other places." He added that it was costing Kodak a great deal of money. "So far we have filed no formal claim against the Government for repayment, but we are trying to adjust the matter with the AEC."³⁰

The AEC was a difficult agency to argue with. The successor to the Manhattan Project, it had inherited that project's secrecy and power, and through the early 1950s, it publicly denied that atomic testing was a health hazard. Even though the Manhattan Project had studied radiation's effects on animals, documenting the damage that small exposures could cause, the agency held that there was a level under which it was essentially harmless.³¹ This notion of a "tolerance dose" had driven Warren's team's research in Rochester, and it was behind the "film badges" that workers and soldiers wore at Manhattan Project sites and during tests in the Pacific. A combination of personal identification and radiation monitor, the playing card–sized badges (there were also ring- and pencil-shaped versions) contained packets of highly sensitive film, much of it Kodak dental X-ray film.³² The films were designed to be popped out of the badges at regular intervals and developed. The darker the image that appeared, the higher the wearer's exposure, the more quickly, in theory, something could be done about it.³³

Perhaps it was because of this that discussions of atomic dust at Kodak Park played out so publicly. Kodak's clout, and its involvement with the United States' nuclear program, meant that the AEC couldn't avoid the subject, but agency officials were quick to qualify complaints about film damage with reassurance that fallout posed no threat to humans. After all, film was the substance that could detect radiation before it caused harm. Yet the black spots that conveniently confined fallout to an industrial problem also eventually helped reveal the extent of fallout's danger to public health. As Eisenbud recalled years later, his office, the one that built the radiation monitoring network, "might not have been involved in further fallout studies were it not for the fact that Eastman Kodak needed information to protect its processes."[34]

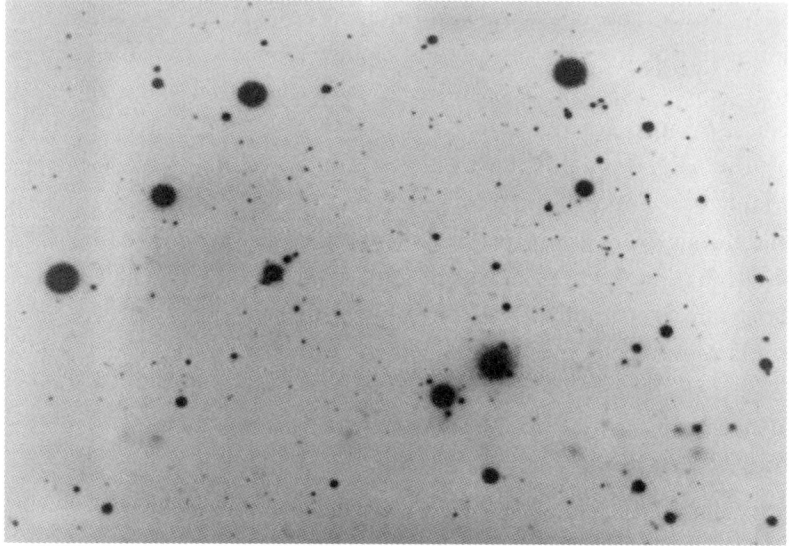

FIGURE 25. Black spots. Courtesy of the University of Rochester River Campus Libraries Rare Books, Special Collections, and Preservation, and Eastman Kodak Company.

INSIDIOUS

When Thomas J. Hargrave called radiation "insidious," he may have been playing to the political moment, in which the word was a key metaphor—not for fallout but for Communism, about which anxiety was escalating again. The Soviet Union finally had the bomb, and by the time hot snow first fell on Rochester, J. Edgar Hoover's Federal Bureau of Investigation and the House Un-American Activities Committee were investigating whether the Soviets had procured uranium from the United States, posturing at controlling a material whose remnants were already in the air and the water, steadily creating a new layer of earth. In December 1949, the FBI's Buffalo office phoned Kodak. Had the company ever sold the metal to the Russian government or any of its agencies, such as Amtorg (the Soviet company that bought so many microfilmed reports on German industry, and a long-standing target for right-wing accusations of spying)? No, Kodak replied: The only kind of uranium the company had ever bought or sold was uranium nitrate, the toner.[35] Strictly speaking, this was true, even if Kodak and the government knew that the company's knowledge of uranium went much deeper.

As it turned out, there had been a Soviet spy at Kodak. This was Alfred Dean Slack, the chemist who was transferred from Kodak Park to Tennessee Eastman in 1942 and from there to the Holston Ordnance Works and Y-12. Slack began photographing company files and formulas for a Kodak colleague, Richard Briggs, in 1936. At first, he didn't know that Briggs was sending the photographs to a Soviet spy named Gaik Ovakimian, though if he had, it might not have dissuaded him: Slack got into espionage for the money, not politics. When Briggs died, Slack began handing information directly to Ovakimian, and a few years later, he got a new handler, a man named Harry Gold. Gold's network included informers working in the US atomic program. He himself reported to Semyon Markovich Semyonov, a Soviet spy—and an employee of Amtorg.[36]

Harry Gold's clandestine career was cut short in 1950 when the Los Alamos spy Klaus Fuchs was arrested in Britain and named Gold as his courier. After Gold was caught, he named names, too. Slack was just a bit player in Gold's stable of informers. Much more important was David Greenglass, a machinist who was stationed at Los Alamos for more than a year. Gold's testimony led to Greenglass's arrest, Greenglass pointed the government to his sister Ethel Rosenberg and her husband Julius, and both Greenglass and Gold were witnesses for the prosecution in the Rosenbergs' espionage trial. The couple's execution on June 19, 1953, made terribly clear the paranoia into which the United States had descended because of the bomb, and the Cold War of which it had become the most potent symbol.

Slack was also arrested in 1950, and while he was never part of the atomic core of Gold's network, his career traced the same industrial steps that led Kodak from film to the bomb. Early in the war, when he was still at Kodak Park, Slack passed Gold things the Soviet Union wanted: documents related to Kodachrome and aerial photography.[37] After he was transferred to Kingsport, Gold stayed in touch. Every few months, the agent would take the train from Philadelphia to Kingsport, stepping off at the old CC&O station, where cotton and coal and wood once crossed. He usually appeared unannounced at Slack's home and stayed for a couple of hours. Sometimes the two men played chess. Sometimes they argued, with Gold giving Slack what he called "pep talks" about his responsibility to the Soviet Union, a country that Slack wanted little to do with. In his penultimate visit, Gold threatened to reveal Slack's spying at Kodak unless he gave Gold something useful.

So, on a spring evening in 1944, Slack stayed late at the office. Close to midnight, he snuck into a part of the factory he didn't usually visit and pocketed a handful of RDX.[38] Sweating, nerves taut, Gold carried the powder to Philadelphia, then New York, where he passed it to Semyonov.[39] He only saw Slack once more. In 1944, he arrived in Kingsport to find that the chemist had been transferred, apparently to work on a poison gas project somewhere near Knoxville. Semyonov told Gold to "forget Slack," but in reality, Slack's move—to Y-12— would have brought Semyonov closer to what the Soviets were really interested in.[40]

Slack returned to upstate New York at the end of the war and began an unremarkable life as a chemist in Syracuse. In June 1950, he stood in federal court in Greeneville, Tennessee. The former Eastman employee pleaded guilty to violating the Espionage Act and was sentenced to fifteen years in prison. This was five years longer than the Department of Justice had recommended, citing Gold's blackmail, Slack's reluctance to spy, and how mild his betrayal was in comparison to Greenglass's. As Slack pointed out in the many attempts he made to appeal his sentence, sharing the RDX formula during the war, when the United States and the Soviet Union were allies, didn't mean what it would have at the present moment, in 1950. What's more, RDX had been described by German chemists as far back as the nineteenth century, and it was first used during World War I.⁴¹

Slack laid this out in letters to the presiding judge, Robert L. Taylor. Written in neat, dense script on prison-issue stationery, the letters showed the knowledgeable scientist behind the slightly-too-easygoing colleague. On Taylor's desk, they crossed other letters that praised the judge's gumption in flouting the government's sentencing recommendation. Letters came from across the country, but many were from Johnson City, fifty miles to the east and a stone's throw from Tennessee Eastman. Some were xenophobic and antisemitic (even though Slack, a US citizen, wasn't Jewish), and they showed how little some things had changed since the end of the last world war, when Kodak chose Kingsport for its methanol factory in part because of the town's "pure American" population."⁴² As Perley S. Wilcox reflected three years before Slack's sentencing, at a celebration of Tennessee Eastman's first quarter decade, "Then, it was Bolshevism. Today, it is Communism. There is not much difference between them; both are un-American and repulsive to us. And let me say that the threat of Communism now is much greater than the threat of Bolshevism was then."⁴³

Even if Slack had been an atomic spy, the Soviets had little interest in uranium in Rochester or Tennessee. By that point, it was clear that the ore was far more abundant than anyone had thought during the war, and the Soviet Union had set up mining operations across its territory—in Central Asia, Ukraine, Siberia, and elsewhere.⁴⁴ In 1949, when the FBI approached Kodak about uranium, Soviet sights were set with particular intensity on deposits in Eastern Europe, above all the Ore Mountains.

On the German side, the Ore Mountains' foothills begin about ninety miles southwest of Wolfen, starting in the coalfields that originally drew Agfa to the region, becoming rich in silver, radium, and uranium as they approach the Czech frontier. Just as much as geology, economic and industrial connections knit together this southeast stretch to the border, as Rainer Karlsch has shown, and these connections intensified as the Soviet occupation zone came into its own. The factory at Wolfen was proof of this. While it had been Soviet property since July 1945, in February 1947 it was transferred to a new Soviet joint-stock company, SAG (Sowjetisch Aktiengesellschaft) Photoplenka, whose holdings included the former Agfa Wolfen, celluloid factories in Eilenburg and Leipzig, and a rayon finishing plant in the village of Sehma in the Ore Mountains. Photoplenka was a small-scale version of Division III, an umbrella organization for the inseparable industries of film and rayon.[45]

The Sehma rayon works—formerly Richard Schubert, AG—was the joint between these industries and uranium. Founded in 1911, the factory had grown along with artificial silk. In 1926, it was folded into IG Farben, and eventually into Division III, where it was administered from Wolfen. By 1947, it was a textile outpost in a landscape of shafts, pits, and barracks—the haphazard tableau into which the Ore Mountains were dissolving as Wismut's uranium operations grew with immense speed.[46] There had been mining in the area forever. But there had never been anything like this: the "total mining" that, in the Ore Mountains as in the Belgian Congo, took over streets, homes, and villages, reorienting communities and families in the pursuit of a single raw material. "Uranium, every hour uranium," as a seasoned miner puts it in Konrad Wolf's *Sun Seekers* (*Sonnensucher,* GDR 1958), a film set in Wismut in 1950.[47] Even after the German Democratic Republic (GDR) was established in October 1949, Wismut was Soviet military domain, its laser focus on uranium at times sustained by forced and prisoner labor.[48]

The GDR was founded two months after the first Soviet bomb test. Like Trinity, that test took place in a desert, and it was filmed. The clips you can find on the internet begin with a flash of light that resolves into a fiery cloud shooting straight upward. On the horizontal, a blast wave incinerates everything in its path. What the film doesn't show—what no test footage could show—is the origin of the ore used to make the bomb, which in August 1949 was mainly Wismut and Jáchymov.[49] Between the end of the war and 1953, as the arms race accelerated, about 60 percent of the Soviet Union's uranium came from the Ore Mountains: 15 percent from Czechoslovakia and 45 percent from East Germany.[50] Wismut alone sent 9,500 tons of uranium to the Soviet Union, more than any uranium mine in Soviet territory. Like Photoplenka's film and rayon, each of those tons was considered war reparations.[51]

And so, while the FBI and HUAC were kicking up controversy about Russians taking American uranium, and Kodak was battling the AEC about the Nevada tests, film—still a sentinel—told a more complex story about the Cold War. Because weather patterns kept radioactive dust aloft until, over months and years, everything drifted to the ground, fallout was global, and dust in one country might very well be from a bomb exploded in another. Merril Eisenbud's fallout studies had shown this, and in 1954, Eisenbud urged the AEC to start sending what information it had about foreign tests to the US photographic industry.[52] This meant that some of the black spots on Kodak film were surely made by Ore Mountains uranium. At the same time, they were imprints of uranium from the Belgian Congo—from Katanga, where the United States had guarded the Shinkolobwe mine as jealously as the Red Army did Wismut—and from Central Asia, where the Soviet Union eventually mined most of its uranium.[53] As much as the spots were traces of the atomic world, they were evidence of the "radioactive colonialism," in Ward Churchill's and Winona LaDuke's words, that brought the United States, and before it Belgium, to the Congo; the Soviet nuclear arms industry to Central Asia and the Arctic; American testing to Nevada and the Pacific; and uranium mining to the Ore Mountains.[54] This offers a different chronology for the Anthropocene, one that begins well before 1950, as Sylvia Wynter and Kathryn Yusoff remind us. Among other moments, it begins in the 1400s, when Africans were first enslaved by Europeans in service of materials such as silver and cotton—the materials woven, centuries later, into film.[55]

FIGURE 26. Tennessee Eastman in 1947. Courtesy of the University of Rochester River Campus Libraries Rare Books, Special Collections, and Preservation, and Eastman Kodak Company.

MILLIONS OF GALLONS

Yet film was changing in the early 1950s. Kodak stopped making nitrate film base in 1951, completing the turn to cellulose acetate that had been underway since the Ciné-Kodak's 1923 release. Cellulose acetate was also changing, as oil replaced coal as industrial chemistry's central raw material. So, while the emulsion on Kodak film was registering the radioactive sediment of the Anthropocene, the same film's base, made at Tennessee Eastman, was marking the second decisive transformation in the Earth's stratum, as fly ash from burning fossil fuels came to lay alongside atomic dust.

Someone who had seen Tennessee Eastman only in the 1920s might not have recognized it in 1951. The sawmill and distillery were gone, and the rayon and acetate buildings had grown into Tennessee's largest industrial plant, employing 9,500 people across seven departments. Each department marked a chapter in the company's history, an industrial layer forged by the film industry, by the textile industry, by two wars. One department made acetic and other acids. Another made cellulose acetate. The others were responsible for Tenite, Koda yarn, Teca fiber, hydroquinone, and plasticizers.[56]

Since its early years, Tennessee Eastman had made the basic chemicals for most of these products from wood and coal. In chemistry, however, you can sometimes use a different feedstock—a raw material—to make the same product. This was true for oil. To make acetic acid, the crucial ingredient in cellulose acetate, you needed an alcohol. Ethanol (which is distilled from oil instead of wood) served the purpose just as well as methanol, and before World War II, Tennessee Eastman started buying ethanol from Standard Oil.[57]

The American oil industry was already large by this point. Petroleum products had been part of the US chemical industry since the late nineteenth century, and as cars proliferated on US roads, companies like Standard Oil and its successors began making gasoline. The byproducts of oil and gas refining include olefins, a multifaceted group of chemicals that includes ethylene and polypropylene. As the automobile industry grew, more and more olefins were available to be made into other products. During World War II, the most important of these was synthetic rubber, and just as the First World War had left chemical weapons plants idle and ripe for reinvention, after 1945, a forest of derricks, pipelines, and refineries reached from the Gulf Coast into Texas and Oklahoma.[58] Moving from military to civilian hands, this war infrastructure fed fantasies of postwar abundance: as Stephanie LeMenager writes, the sense of freedom and possibility one might have felt in a car speeding down a newly built highway to a suburban house and postage-stamp yard, "all made possible by oil."[59] Abundance brought lower prices, and by the end of the war, it no longer made sense for Tennessee Eastman to cut, hew, and distill any wood, originally its raison d'être. Instead, the company bought millions of gallons of ethanol every year from the United States' petrochemical giants.[60]

With this, Tennessee Eastman's nonflammable film base, its acetate rayon, and its plastics became some of the many postwar consumer, chemical, and industrial products made from cheap oil and gas. There was much more nonflammable film by then, too. Kodak had continued to work on its cellulose acetate film formulas since the 1920s, trying to remedy the brittleness, weakness, and shrinking that kept the film industry faithful to cellulose nitrate. In 1948, Tennessee Eastman devised a cellulose triacetate formula that was reliable enough for professional 35 mm motion picture film. At the 1950 Oscars, cellulose acetate won Kodak an Academy Award.[61] After forty-plus years of 8 and 16 mm, of still photographs, X-rays, and microfilm, nonflammable film had conquered Hollywood. To keep up with its growing footprint, Tennessee Eastman needed millions more gallons of ethanol.[62]

Since its earliest days, Kodak had distrusted this kind of dependency. Relying on another company for raw materials was risky. That company could raise prices, go out of business, or send defective products. In addition to the antitrust ruling, this was the reason for vertical integration, and it was why Tennessee Eastman had been founded in the first place. In 1950, the same fear of dependency led the company to the Gulf Coast, where in Longview, Texas, Texas Eastman cleaved from Tennessee Eastman in the same way that Kingsport cleaved from Rochester thirty years earlier: in search of a supply of alcohol it could call its own.

If you squinted, Longview was a little like Kingsport. It also began as a railroad town and became a cotton and lumber town, until, in late 1930, it turned to oil.[63] In 1919, it was the site of one of the race riots of Red Summer. But it had none of Kingsport's parsimony, the dedication to thrift and uplift that grew an industrial city from trees and enthralled George Eastman. Oil came to Longview all at once, when the city's first well flooded its rooming houses and hotels with fortune seekers prospecting, and buying and leasing land.[64] World War II disciplined that early torrent, and in 1942, Longview became the origin for the Big Inch, a government pipeline that snaked three hundred million barrels of oil every day from East Texas to the East Coast's refineries. By the time Tennessee Eastman arrived, Longview hardly resembled the boom town it was in the early 1930s. It was a city of almost thirty thousand residents, and its pipelines, the products of war, had become permanent fixtures, templates for the long-haul transport of oil and gas and the backbone of the United States' petroleum era.[65]

As was the case when Tennessee Eastman, Holston, and Y-12 were built and when parts of Agfa Wolfen were shipped to Shostka, the new factory needed experienced workers. Many of these workers came from Kingsport, a few from Rochester, and some from Holston or Oak Ridge, whose wartime work had solidified Tennessee Eastman's expertise in large-scale chemical production.[66] *TEC News* tried to reassure the employees who were being transferred. When construction on the plant began in 1950, an article likened Longview to Kingsport as "a city of churches and homeowners," the dream of a planned middle-class good life on which the Tennessee city had been built, and which oil now promised.[67] For some Tennessee Eastman employees, though, Longview felt like the Wild West, lawless and bigger than life. They joked about this in the newspaper in an occasional column called "Tall Tales from Texas," where oil was rumored to be unavoidable, wells sprung just by digging factory foundations.[68]

The column had a point: Longview wasn't really the same. Just west of the Louisiana border, it was disconnected from the railways that linked Kingsport to cities like New York and Rochester. You could drive between Tennessee Eastman and Texas Eastman, but it was faster to fly, in planes that ran on the same gas flowing through the pipelines below. The new factory was also almost outlandishly modern. In place of Eastman's traditional red bricks, there was a gleaming tangle of pipes, valves, stacks, and silos, hardly a building anywhere. On a clear day, if you gazed at it across one of the artificial lakes that surrounded the factory, Texas Eastman shone in double, an industrial castle reflected in its moat. This so-called open system was cutting-edge plant design. Intended to make chemical manufacturing safer than ever, it was the opposite of the enclosed factory floors that had at first guaranteed Kodak control but whose air vents and doorways, in 1951, threatened calamity.[69]

When Texas Eastman stripped away familiar plant architecture, it also did away with consumer products. Chemicals like alcohols and aldehydes were what ran through its pipes and valves, and those pipes and valves were actually a series of smaller factories. There were cracking plants, a synthesis gas plant, polyolefin and chemical plants. Their products could be made into any number of things: toys, twine, insecticides, adhesives, paints, perfume, plasticizers, insecticides, herbicides, drugs, disinfectants, antifreeze, detergents, brake fluid, pipe fittings—and, still, Kodak's and Tennessee Eastman's films and fibers.[70]

As the 1950s progressed, however, a smaller percentage of Eastman's fibers and films were made from cellulose acetate. The universe of human-made fibers had changed since the 1930s. In 1938, DuPont began selling nylon, a fiber that is fully synthetic: neither natural like wool or cotton, nor made from cellulose, like rayon, but fashioned entirely from chemicals in a laboratory, like synthetic rubber. At Wolfen, Agfa also made nylon under the brand name Perlon. The work sped up when the plant became part of Photoplenka, and most of its products were sent to the Soviet Union.[71] As nylon's star rose, cellulose acetate's fell. Once the most modern of fibers, it was now dismissed as too absorbent and difficult to dye (it was better suited, Tennessee Eastman saw, to things like cigarette filters, one of the company's most profitable postwar products).[72] In contrast, nylon was strong and elastic, perfect for products such as hosiery because it could be made at once strikingly sheer and difficult to ladder. It was also economical, requiring neither a cotton plant nor a tree: just coal or, later, oil.[73] In 1950, DuPont introduced polyester, another synthetic fiber made from oil, and in 1955, it made polyester film. By the end of the decade, polyester fibers had joined Tennessee Eastman's stable of chemical products, and Kodak was also making polyester film—a nonflammable film stronger than cellulose acetate and especially well suited to the wear and tear on projection copies (the film prints shown in cinemas). In turn, Longview's pipes and retorts became the pure raw material supplier that George Eastman might once have imagined, realized in the seemingly inexhaustible resources of oil and gas.[74]

In 1958, the year before Kodak introduced polyester film, the French director Alain Resnais made a short film called *The Song of Styrene*. As its title announces, the film is about plastic. In French, however, where it is *Le Chant du Styrène,* it plays on the idea of the siren's song (*le chant des sirènes*). Plastic, it hums, that irresistible substance. *The Song of Styrene* was commissioned by the French company Pechiney, which like Tennessee Eastman and other firms in the 1950s, was moving into petrochemicals—in Pechiney's case, from its traditional base in aluminum. Pechiney wanted to interest the film's French viewers in plastic and its uses. It wanted viewers to buy plastic, a threshold to the world of easy come, easy go objects that had taken root in the United States soon after the war but came to Western Europe somewhat later.[75]

Resnais wasn't known as a director of advertising or industrial films. At the time Pechiney proposed the project, he had built his career on short documentaries, including two films that came out in 1957, *Night and Fog* (*Nuit et brouillard*) and *All the Memory in the World* (*Toute la mémoire du monde*). *Night and Fog* is a meditation on Auschwitz and the Holocaust; *All the Memory in the World* traces the inner workings of the French National Library. Both films have been widely interpreted as critiques of the French state during World War II and decolonization.[76] What Pechiney must have seen in them, then, was their visual style, built on tracking shots in which the camera rolls fluidly from one point to another. In *Night and Fog,* these shots were created on the railway lines threading through Auschwitz, the horrible architecture of the camp's transports. In *All the Memory of the World,* the camera follows books as they are carted through the library's warren of shelves, call slips shooting through pneumatic tubes. It was an aesthetic well suited to the Pechiney factory's sinuous silver system of pipes, stacks, and retorts, the petrochemical industry's emerging international style.

In *The Song of Styrene*'s lens, Pechiney's plastic *is* seductive. Sensuously, magically, the company's polystyrene sheets morph into bowls and cups, toys and boxes, glowing against a velvety black background. Working backwards, Resnais shows that this is chemical transformation, *petrochemical* transformation: All these objects are melted from polystyrene pellets, which themselves are made through mixing and drying, pulverization and dyeing.

Because film base is plastic, and it is also made through mixing and drying and pulverization, there are echoes here of *A Movie Trip Through Filmland,* the film Kodak made about its Rochester factory in 1921. Edward Dimendberg argues that *The Song of Styrene* is about celluloid. Yet Resnais asks about the oil and coal in Pechiney's polystyrene what *A Movie Trip Through Filmland* does not about Kodak's cotton and silver: where on Earth it comes from. It comes from underground, *The Song of Styrene*'s narrator muses (reciting a text by poet and novelist Raymond Queneau)—from the remnants of prehistoric fish, or maybe plankton. More to the point, it comes from Pechiney's global network of suppliers. By the 1950s, Dimendberg writes, these may also have included French petrochemical companies in Congo, sections of which were part of French Equatorial Africa until 1958, the year *The Song of Styrene* was released.[77]

There they were again: the colonial histories that made materials like film, disguised now by wells and pipelines, multinational organizations, and factories so modern and seemingly transparent that they needed no walls. The very fact that petrochemistry was largely an underground business, hidden from view, was a talking point for Texas Eastman, which mused that sometime in the future, archaeologists working in the land around the Longview factory, or what was left of it, "may be fascinated to discover that a few feet below the surface is a complex grid of pipe lines—pipes of various diameters and directions. They will reason that something useful and important to earlier man must have been made to flow through those pipes."[78]

Yet those archaeologists might also be geologists, and they might be interested less in the pipes than in the soil around them. They might look at those feet of land and say *here, here it is.* The beginning of a new geological era, an era in which substances taken from the earth were incinerated or exploded until they reached the sky, and fell back down again. Ashes to ashes, dust to dust, they might say.

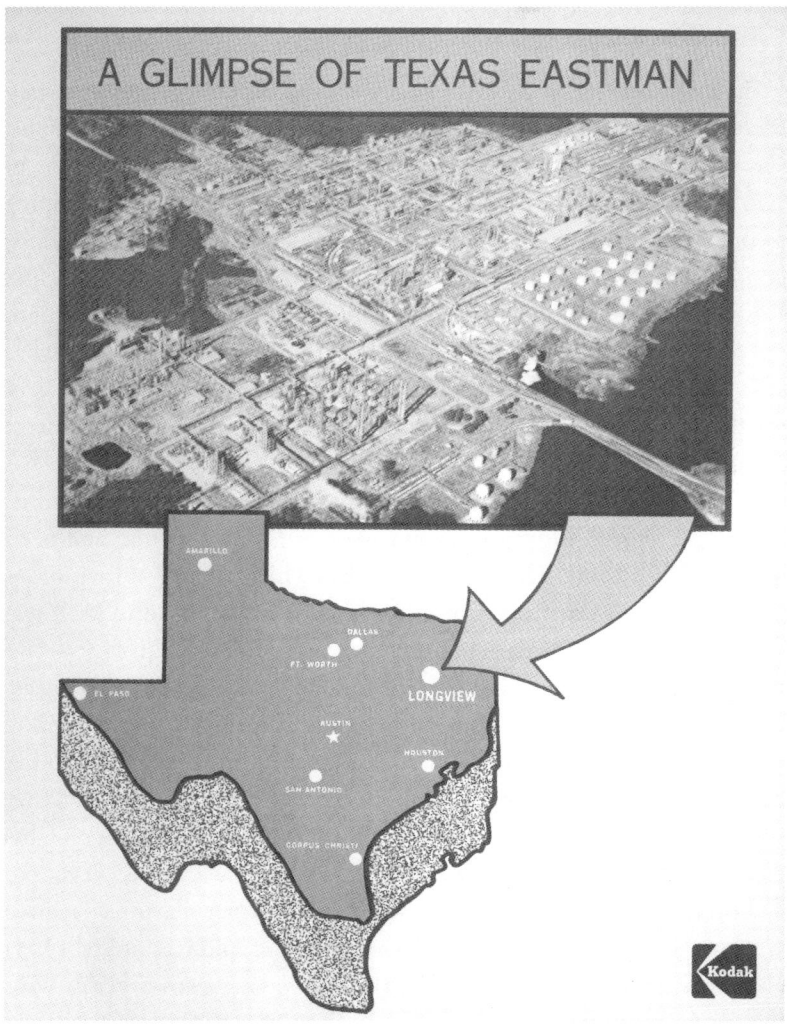

FIGURE 27. This is Texas Eastman. Courtesy of the Science History Institute and Eastman Kodak Company.

SENSITIVITY EQUALS TROUBLE

"You saw nothing in Hiroshima. Nothing," begins *Hiroshima mon amour,* the film that Alain Resnais made after *The Song of Styrene*. On screen, shimmering dust (fallout, maybe) settles on the limbs of two entwined bodies. "You saw nothing," insists the voice belonging to one of these bodies, a Japanese architect; his lover, a French actress, counters that she saw everything. The camera comes to her defense. Resnais's tracking shots glide through Hiroshima: the hospital, Peace Memorial Park, the museum, where the actress insists that she has seen "the photographs, the photographs, the reconstructions, for lack of anything else." "You saw nothing in Hiroshima," the architect maintains.

The architect is correct. Photographs showed little in Hiroshima, where the "visual order," in Akira Mizuta Lippit's words, had been destroyed by "atomic light and force."[79] But while fallout was invisible—nothing like the crust that glitters on the lovers' arms—film itself pictured the bomb's aftermath plainly. X-ray film did, the film so sensitive it could reveal a blood clot or fracture hidden beneath the skin, or measure how much radiation someone's hands absorbed while they were scraping uranium from the sides of a calutron. X-ray film, which didn't even need light to say something about the world.[80]

Primo Levi tells us something about this in the chapter of his chemical chronicle titled "Silver." Many years after the war, Levi goes to a dinner, a college reunion organized by a former classmate named Cerrato. The two men spend the evening talking, and Cerrato tells Levi about the time after World War II when he was a guest worker in West Germany, making X-ray paper at a photo plant. One day, a letter appeared. A clinic in Vienna had discovered bean-shaped spots on their X-rays. More letters arrived with the same complaint, and Cerrato's employer tasked him with determining the origin of the so-called bean effect, which had put the whole business in jeopardy.

In the same way that Julian Webb did, and Merril Eisenbud, and the chemists at Hercules, Cerrato became a detective. He sifted through batches of paper and determined that all the damaged material was manufactured on a Wednesday. Then, chatting with a guard at the photo factory who fished in a nearby river, he heard that a tannery had opened upstream. Cerrato visited the tannery and learned that it released its wastewater into the river every Monday night. The next morning, Tuesday, the photo plant washed its workers' overalls in water from the same river. Cerrato realized that it must be dust from the supposedly clean overalls that, every Wednesday, floated to the paper's still-wet emulsion, carrying molecules of tanning chemicals—polyphenols that damaged the silver bromide.

For Levi, this is a story about matter and its "cunning intent": how the polyphenols lurk in the river before hitching a ride on a cotton or rayon fiber and wreaking gleeful havoc on the stuff of humans. It is also a story about X-rays. On this, Cerrato is modest: Making X-ray paper is nothing like making X-ray film. Film is infinitely more sensitive, and, as he puts it, "sensitivity and trouble are proportional."[81] This does not mean that X-ray paper isn't sensitive. Like film, it is coated with an emulsion of gelatin and silver, and as Kodak showed in 1946 and again in 1951, the combination of silver and gelatin carries imprints of the environment even when it isn't developed. These imprints—spots, sometimes—tell their own story of rivers, straw, cotton, wind, and ore. They tell a story of bombs and the governments and industries and people that made them; a story of how minuscule marks on film and paper stood in for a vast history of human and environmental harm. They also tell of how, without that same film and paper, some of the harm might not have been uncovered, or perhaps not as quickly.

The material from which X-ray base is made tells a story, too. After the Cleveland Clinic fire, Kodak's X-ray films—always the first in Kodak's product line to be made safe—were made from cellulose acetate. By the late 1930s, there was oil in the company's acetate. Within a few years of hot snow's 1951 debut, the acetate in X-ray film no longer contained trees, and at the end of that decade, X-ray film was fashioned from PET.[82] These changes unfolded in step with wars and weapons. During World War I, airplane dope and poison gas made cellulose acetate essential.

With World War II and synthetic rubber, oil became inevitable to cellulose acetate's future. Tennessee Eastman broke ground in Longview within months of the first Soviet nuclear explosion, and Kodak's polyester films had their roots in these first, tense years of the Cold War.

For a different view of how this ties together—safety film and the Cold War—we can turn to the Berlin factory that Kodak bought in 1927: the former Glanzfilm, later known as Kodak AG. After a tumultuous start amidst Agfa's and VGF's rayon patent wars, the plant steadily manufactured motion picture, photographic, and X-ray films and papers for Kodak's European business. Kodak wrote it off as enemy property during the war, but the factory kept working until air raids damaged the premises on the cusp of 1944. Between postwar plunder and Soviet dismantling, it was only in summer 1946, when it was part of Berlin's Soviet zone, that the factory began producing again. Plastic for shoes was the first thing it made (in the first months after the war, shoes were more important than film). Cellulose nitrate film followed later.[83]

In 1953, what was now the East German company Kodak AG Filmfabrik Köpenick turned to nonflammable 35 mm. At first, this was a research question. Like Kodak's factories and Agfa, Kodak AG had a laboratory, and at the end of the year that laboratory published reports on its work. One report was titled "Development Work to Improve the Mechanical Properties of Triacetate Film Bases for Cinema," and it began by discussing Kodak's Oscar-winning 1948 triacetate base before quickly veering to DuPont's polyester film and the factory the company was building for it in Parlin, New Jersey.[84] Synthetics were the future of safety film everywhere, including at this film factory four miles from the Berlin border between East and West Germany: four miles from the Iron Curtain, the mostly imaginary wall that, like the bomb, stood in for the Cold War's divisions.

The idea of the Iron Curtain became part of the worldwide lexicon on March 6, 1946, the day after Winston Churchill's "Sinews of Peace" speech. As Patrick Wright and Cristina Vatulescu tell us, however, it wasn't Churchill's invention, a rhetorical flourish intended to express or inflame the moment's geopolitical drama. It referred to a device used in actual drama: the metal-laced curtains that had been installed in British theaters since the late eighteenth century to stop stage fires (from a tipped-over candle, say, or an incendiary prop) from spreading to the audience.[85]

In other words, the iron curtain was to theater what nonflammable film was to cinema. It was a way to prevent the fires that, in the eighteenth century as in the early twentieth century, reformers held up as examples of the pastimes' danger. Cellulose acetate, which Kodak made widely available and which the former Glanzfilm factory had been designed to manufacture, helped make cinema "safe," safe enough that the heirs to theater's Georgian-era reformers welcomed it into their offices and schools, even their homes. Soon, the chemistry behind cellulose acetate was used to make RDX, which wasn't safe at all, bringing Kodak to the atomic bomb. With the advent of nuclear weapons, cellulose acetate's counterpart, the iron curtain, became shorthand for the Cold War.

Each device—the film, the curtain—carried this double history, a history of diversion and danger, of fire and preventing fire. This was exactly the catch in the black spots that appeared on Kodak's film in 1951: They were both a document and a warning of a world that the company, and the many other private businesses involved in the Manhattan Project, had shaped. But it took too long for that warning to sound outside the factory. The same day as the November snowstorm—which, Kodak informed the AEC with alarm, contained five hundred times the level of radiation found in February's first hot snow—the *Democrat and Chronicle*'s first page pictured a three-year-old boy beaming as he pressed the wet, heavy stuff into a snowball.[86] As bomb tests continued and hot snow kept falling, the AEC assured the public that it was "all right for Rochester kiddies to build radioactive snowmen if they want to."[87] By spring, the snow that hadn't melted into mittens and scarves was splashing through storm drains and seeping through thawing soil, the layer formed just that year.[88]

CHAPTER FIVE

A Fine Line

WATER WAS WHAT BROUGHT Charles Fordyce to the municipal building in Olean, New York, on March 4, 1963. Olean is south of Buffalo, just over the border from Pennsylvania, and the Eastman Kodak chemist had driven the two-plus hours from Rochester to speak at a hearing about nuclear waste. A few years earlier, the New York State Office of Atomic Development had bought 3,500 acres of farmland nearby, in the hamlet of West Valley. Eisenhower's "Atoms for Peace" program was promoting the "peaceful development and use of atomic energy," and the state planned to transform the land into the world's first privately owned nuclear fuel reprocessing plant. It was to be something like a space-age version of 1920s Kingsport: spent material from nuclear reactors remade into plutonium and uranium, part of a clean, efficient economy.[1]

Fordyce might have been nervous that afternoon. He was a member of the National Association of Photographic Manufacturers' Committee on Radioactivity, which formed in the wake of 1951's black spots, and the committee had doubts about the nuclear waste project. A few weeks earlier, Fordyce had written to the Atomic Energy Commission (AEC) on the committee's behalf, asking the agency to reconsider building the plant. His letter noted that western New York had "a greater concentration of photographic manufacturing than anywhere in the world." Beyond the factories in Rochester, there was Ansco in Binghamton and the DiNic Chemical Company in Honeoye.

Fordyce's letter bore the anxious hallmarks of the era of fallout, the years when photochemists became meteorologists.[2] With technical precision, he observed that all the plants were east of the West Valley site and "would thus be exposed to some degree to possible airborne radioactive by-products traveling in the direction of prevailing winds." The association was worried about water as much as wind: liquid seeping from the plant, making its way "from Lake Erie to Lake Ontario or through the New York State Barge Canal to the Genesee River and then to Lake Ontario." "Over a long term, any potential contamination of underground water would also be most serious," Fordyce added.[3]

Fordyce came to the Olean hearing equipped with notes that put this more succinctly. The association, he said politely, would prefer it if the proposed plant were built elsewhere. In fact, it believed that as much space as possible should be created between nuclear plants and film plants: "As nuclear power activities expand, we believe it may be necessary for the photographic industry, with the help of the Atomic Energy Commission, to establish some area as free as possible from potential contamination hazards."[4] But it was too late; the reprocessing plant was a done deal. Its manager was announced two days later: Wesley H. Lewis, a nuclear chemist from Powell, Tennessee, who had worked for Tennessee Eastman at Y-12 and stayed on after the war when the factory was transferred to the AEC.[5] On hearing this, maybe Fordyce shook his head with recognition, because Fordyce knew Tennessee Eastman well. A specialist in cellulose chemistry, he had joined Kodak in 1929, the same year as the Cleveland Clinic fire, and he was responsible for the cellulose triacetate formula that brought nonflammable film to Hollywood.[6] Fordyce helped win Kodak its Oscar, and his research shaped Tennessee Eastman. Tennessee Eastman shaped Lewis, the man who was to run the nuclear waste plant.

When Fordyce spoke in Olean, anxiety about radiation was pervasive. Over the years since the black spots' first appearance, it had become plain that nuclear proliferation threatened much more than film, no matter what the AEC said. Public concern had grown over the first part of the 1950s, coming to a peak in 1954 when fallout from the Castle Bravo test at Bikini Atoll gravely sickened the crew of the Japanese tuna boat *Lucky Dragon* and killed its radio operator. By the end of the decade, fears clustered around strontium 90, a product of nuclear fission that fell to the ground with "hot" precipitation. From the ground, it got into plants. From plants, it made its way into people and animals. Bones—especially children's growing bones—can mistake strontium 90 for calcium, transforming the radioisotope into an invisible internal source of cancers, leukemia, and thyroid disease. Strontium 90 has a half-life of almost thirty years. In this sense, nuclear testing didn't make early-50s Rochester a radiation sewer. It made the city a radiation lake.[7]

Panic calmed somewhat in November 1958 when the United States and Soviet Union announced a mutual agreement to suspend nuclear testing, but the moratorium was short lived. On September 1, 1961, the Soviet Union began testing again, and at the end of that October, Tsar Bomba, a thermonuclear weapon more powerful than any the world has seen since, was detonated high in the Arctic, in Novaya Zemlya. As the superpowers careened toward nuclear war during the Cuban Missile Crisis a year later, it was clear that things couldn't continue this way. In August 1963, the Soviet Union, United Kingdom, and United States signed the Limited or Partial Test Ban Treaty, agreeing to move nuclear testing underground.

Fallout levels dropped after the treaty was signed. They had fallen after the 1958 moratorium as well, but by 1961, the United States' radiation monitoring system was reading hot again. By then, that system had grown, reaching well beyond Rochester, and it was shadowed by a second monitoring network: cows, whose milk was sampled for iodine 131 and strontium 90 at sixty stations across the United States.[8] One of these stations was planned for West Valley, on the grounds of the future nuclear waste plant. It wouldn't be out of place there: West Valley is dairy country, and by the time the plant was approved, there couldn't have been a farmer in the United States who didn't know about the links between strontium 90 and milk. But while the cows were there as reassurance, when Marian Reynolds, a reporter for the *Olean Times Herald*, surveyed reactions to the West Valley plans in June 1963, she didn't find many people reassured. Mark Bobseine, the owner of forty prize-winning

Holsteins, planned to "see it through" and continue to improve his farm, "the same as I have done for 45 years." Another farmer, Elon Zetwick, replied flatly that it would cost him more to move. Marjorie Hollenbeck and Marle Jones, co-owners of a tearoom, were more voluble, though they still spoke in code. Jones worried that "superhighways, shopping plazas and heavy industry will spell the end of the pastoral life."[9]

The unease may have stemmed from the fact that, by spring 1963, Americans were starting to view chemical plants like West Valley with mistrust, even if the plants didn't handle nuclear waste. The spark for this was Rachel Carson's *Silent Spring*, an exposé about chemical pesticides that had been published six months earlier, provoking widespread alarm. For Carson, the clearest analogy to pesticides was fallout: As she famously wrote in *Silent Spring*'s first pages, "Chemicals are the sinister and little-recognized partners of radiation in changing the very nature of the world."[10] The same words opened *The Silent Spring of Rachel Carson*, the CBS Reports documentary that aired less than a month after the Olean hearing, indelibly linking fallout and chemicals even for those who hadn't read Carson's bestseller.

Carson's book pointed to something that was absent from Fordyce's testimony: how contamination like what the photochemists feared about West Valley could be caused by plants like their own. This was something Stafford L. Warren thought about years after the Manhattan Project ended. While the project was "running scared" from radiation, he recalled, it paid less attention to the toxicity of the chemicals used at Oak Ridge and elsewhere.[11] Chemicals' dangers were plain to the people who worked with them, however. On October 4, 1960, sixteen Tennessee Eastman workers died and more than two hundred were injured when an aniline dye installation exploded in Kingsport and the fire spread, igniting nearby chemical tanks. With the mushroom-shaped cloud hanging over the city, schoolchildren feared a nuclear disaster.[12] In Rochester, where Fordyce was worried about radiation from West Valley silently entering the groundwater, chemicals regularly spilled and seeped from Kodak Park. As Alison Feser has chronicled, residents of neighborhoods near the factory started noticing clusters of rare diseases and cancers, and so did Kodak employees. In spring 1988, the *Democrat and Chronicle* began to report on the leaks, and Kodak was forced to admit that it was aware of them.[13]

This exploded into catastrophe at the end of the same year when a pipe burst at the film factory, sending thirty thousand gallons of methylene chloride, a solvent used to make film base, in the direction of an elementary school at the factory's southern edge. The substance, a carcinogen, was found in groundwater and in the soil beneath the school, as were other solvents: methanol and acetone, the kinds of toxic irritants that Kodak Park's exhaust fans and smokestacks had been engineered to remove, at least from the factory's inside. Things escalated to the point that when Kodak met with families at School 41, a journalist for *The New York Times* showed up. The journalist recorded a Kodak spokesman's practiced condescension in the face of parents' fear and outrage. "We've never been thought of as a chemical company," the spokesman remarked coolly, "we just made the yellow boxes, so there's an element of surprise and unfamiliarity."[14]

A CHEMICAL PROBLEM

This was bigger than a Kodak problem. As Carson put it starkly, it was a chemical problem. It was a problem, in the spokesman's words, of the film industry as part of the chemical industry. And the problem was the same at film factories on the other side of the Iron Curtain. By the end of the 1980s, the region stretching from Wolfen to the Ore Mountains, the most industrialized part of East Germany, was also the country's most polluted, its air choked with coal dust and its forests withering from exposure to acid rain. The area around Wolfen had become a focus of East Germany's unofficial environmental movement, and in 1988, as Kodak's methylene chloride crisis was unfolding, a group of East and West German environmentalists were working together, secretly, to make a documentary about the area's devastation.

Bitterness from Bitterfeld: A Stocktaking (*Bitteres aus Bitterfeld: Eine Bestandsaufnahme*) was filmed shot around the factories and mines that powered East Germany's chemical industry, and in the bleak interstices between industry where, the voiceover notes dryly, at least the price of schnapps is discounted in the winter. Early on, the filmmakers visit the former Agfa factory, which in 1964 redubbed itself ORWO (for "Original Wolfen") after Agfa's West German factory in Leverkusen retained the brand name. It would've been impossible to film inside the factory itself, and the filmmakers turn their camera on Silver Lake (Silbersee), the site of the former Grube Johannes open-pit lignite mine in which, starting in 1921, the factory collected wastewater filled with sulfur, metals, and cellulose, diluting it before releasing it into the Mulde River. The camera lingers on the lakefront, which is clogged with foam, its water a sulfurous shade of gold. The lake stinks, the voiceover tells the viewer, from uncontrolled chemical reactions.[15] What the filmmakers may not have known is that, during the war, there'd been a camp for soldiers and foreign workers next to the pit-turned-lake. For the women housed in the workers' barracks, exhausting days making fiber and film were followed by night after night of inhaling the same materials' toxic residues.[16]

Bitterness was shot on VHS video instead of film. By 1988, magnetic tape had replaced 16 and 8 mm safety film as the premier small audiovisual technology, and for clandestine work like this, the technology was essential. It required neither lights nor sound equipment, and it was easy enough to conceal (or at least its book-sized cassettes were). The filmmakers secreted the tapes into West Berlin, edited them, and slipped the finished video back into East Germany, where it was quietly screened and fervently discussed in environmental and church circles, key spaces for dissent. Since like fallout, TV signals care little for national borders, East German viewers also tuned in when *Bitterness* was broadcast on the West Berlin television program *Kontraste* on September 27, 1988. GDR authorities scrambled to contain the damage.[17] Even then, when East Germany's months were numbered, it was risky to make a video as critical as *Bitterness*—a video that accused the East German government of deliberately deceiving its citizens about the Bitterfeld region's environment and what it meant for their health. Environmentalism in East Germany was a carefully managed matter, given lip service in state policy but trumped by the needs of industry.

In East Germany, you couldn't argue with the government. In the United States, you couldn't argue with industry. *Rachel Carson's Silent Spring* had shown this back in 1963, when CBS framed the documentary about Carson's book partly as a debate: Carson versus Dr. Robert White-Stevens, a tall man in a white lab coat who worked for the American Cyanamid Company, which began in pesticides and, like so many other chemical firms, diversified into fibers, plastics, dyes, perfumes, weapons, and more. If readers accepted Carson's conclusions about DDT and other pesticides, White-Stevens foretold a return to biblical conditions: plagues of locusts, fleas, and pestilence of livestock, pictures of which CBS managed, incredibly, to supply from its library of stock footage.

Yet in both the United States and East Germany, government and industry were tied closely together, and a company as big as American Cyanamid could usually count on the government's support. State support even allowed American companies dismantled by trust-busting to grow to immense size, as Kodak showed at Holston and Y-12. This continued beyond World War II—private business' great entry point into military business—through the first years of the Cold War, when Atoms for Peace enshrined the same military-civilian partnerships. Take Holston, which Tennessee Eastman left after the war ended. In 1949, on the AEC's request, it began operating the ammunition plant again, through a new Kodak subsidiary named the Holston Defense Corporation.[18] It made explosives there until 1994, the year Tennessee Eastman separated from Kodak, becoming the Eastman Chemical Company. Eastman Chemical ran Holston, the United States' sole producer of RDX and Composition B, until 1999.[19]

And so maybe a reason why Charles Fordyce's 1963 protests about the nuclear waste plant didn't carry much weight is that Kodak was still caught in the bind of the black spots, uncomfortably navigating the consequences of its work for the Manhattan Project and the AEC. The delicacy of the company's position was on display the next year, 1964, when

Kodak's medical director, James H. Sterner, spoke at the Third International Conference on the Peaceful Uses of Atomic Energy in Geneva, Switzerland. Like Fordyce, Sterner had been with Kodak since the 1930s. After a few years in Rochester, he had gone to Tennessee, becoming medical director at Oak Ridge. He had advised on the radiological safety of the Bikini Atoll tests and was a longtime consultant for the AEC. Sterner was also a member of New York's General Advisory Committee on Atomic Energy, a committee that must have known about the state's plans for West Valley from the beginning.

Sterner titled his paper "Atomic Energy for Society and the Balance Between Hazard and Gain." The essence of his argument was, in his words, "not that we should ignore the evidence of hazard for radiation, but rather should place it in proper perspective in relation to other environmental factors affecting health so we do not unduly penalize a development with such great promise of benefit."[20] Sterner was trying to walk a very fine line. He couldn't criticize the atomic energy industry, with which the photographic industry was deeply involved. He also had to avoid saying that atomic energy was entirely safe. By then, no one could deny that nuclear technology threatened not just cataclysmic war but also millions of cancers and premature deaths. Anyway, Kodak had warned Sterner not to claim that atomic energy was harmless, since more nuclear facilities could spell danger for Kodak's films and factories.[21] So, to cast atomic energy as *relatively* safe, Sterner played with *Silent Spring*'s equation between fallout and pesticides. Those "other environmental factors affecting health," the ones that Sterner insinuated could be more dangerous than atomic energy, were chemicals—a word that he didn't speak once. After all, as the spokesman pointed out twenty-five years later in the meeting at School 41, Kodak was a chemical company.

If this was a debate, we might say that Carson won. She won because she established the terms of the argument so effectively: You could no longer talk about radiation without talking about chemicals, and vice versa. Still, just as it took years for the AEC to acknowledge the dangers of fallout, it was a long time before the warnings in *Silent Spring* forced the US government to do something about the chemical industry's widespread pollution. The Environmental Protection Agency was founded only in 1970, and another decade passed before the Comprehensive Environmental Response, Compensation, and Liability Act created the Superfund. Many of Kodak's factories eventually became Superfund sites—sites so polluted that they merited government intervention. These included Kingsport after the aniline plant explosion and Texas Eastman in Longview, but Kodak Park was the largest. In 2014, Kodak settled with the Environmental Protection Agency and Department of Justice to fund a forty-nine million dollar cleanup of the factory site, as well as of the neighboring Genesee River and other locations in New York and New Jersey, remains of the fading photographic giant.[22]

WATER AND BONES

Some of the Kodak factories that became Superfund sites had their beginnings in the company's great expansion of the 1920s and 1930s, the years after the antitrust ruling when Kodak acquired what would become Tennessee Eastman, then the former Glanzfilm, then Kodak-Pathé: factory after factory after factory.[23] One of these sites is Eastman Gelatine in Peabody, Massachusetts, the factory that I knew growing up, although I didn't know what it made. Kodak bought Eastman Gel, as it's still known, in 1930, and soon the plant was making two-thirds of Kodak's gelatin.[24]

Like Tennessee Eastman, Eastman Gelatine began with local industry and its raw materials—in its case, animal carcasses. From the eighteenth century to the early twentieth century, Boston's North Shore was a world center for shoemaking, and at the start of the 1900s, there were more than one hundred tanneries in Peabody. Industry begat industry, as it did in Kingsport, and the city was also home to smaller companies that used leathermaking's byproducts. At the Densten Felt Hair Company, hair pulled from cowskin became felt, upholstery, and plaster. The Newell and Knowlton Extracting Works used tissues scraped from animal hides to make grease for soapmaking and leather currying.[25] Leather scraps also gave rise to a handful of glue companies, and one was founded on the Eastman Gelatine site as early as 1808, becoming the American Glue Company in 1900. Natural glue and gelatin share most of their ingredients—animal remains, water, some chemicals—so it made sense when, in 1908, American Glue expanded into gelatin, first for food and then for photography. When the factory went up for sale, Kodak, a longtime buyer, purchased it. Eastman Gel was still a major employer in Peabody well past the tanneries' heyday.

After it acquired Eastman Gel, Kodak imported the industrial organization that governed its Rochester and Kingsport factories. Its employees were issued handbooks nearly identical to the ones distributed at Kodak Park, Tennessee Eastman, and later Y-12, describing the benefits the company offered in exchange for hard work and the expectation of a long, loyal tenure.[26] According to a 1950s article in Kodak's employee magazine, *Kodakery*, even the factory itself was modeled after Kodak Park; it, too, had "its own power plant, water system, sewage disposal plant, and its own trucking, maintenance and yard department."[27] The plant was fully self-contained, the article noted, because with a substance as critical and yet finicky as gelatin, Kodak couldn't afford to outsource anything.[28]

Nevertheless, at Eastman Gel and Kodak Park alike, the idea of absolute control was a fantasy. As with the trees in rayon or the cotton in film, in gelatin, as Nicole Shukin has written, you could see the very life of the animal. Kodak was thoroughly aware of this. In 1925, the company traced a series of failed emulsion experiments to a herd of cows that had avoided the mustard plants on which cattle typically graze. Their bones, it turned out, lacked the sulfur that sensitized film to yellow light.[29] Later, Kodak kept detailed records of where Eastman Gelatine's hides and bones came from. During World War II, "the Japanese invasion of Southeast Asia completely disrupted the collection of Water Buffalo hides," and in 1944, "the Peron military dictatorship took over the Argentine government," placing an embargo on the export of bones that lasted until 1945. "Wars or revolutions, political or economic embargoes, natural calamities, radio-active contamination, technological changes, or other unforeseeable events," the company warned, could "suddenly cut off one or more of the major gelatine raw stock supplies, most of which come from abroad."[30]

FIGURE 28. This is Eastman Gel. Courtesy of the University of Rochester River Campus Libraries Rare Books, Special Collections, and Preservation, and Eastman Kodak Company.

These records were for the files—internal use only. There were no wars, revolutions, calamities, or contamination in the public stories Kodak spun around Eastman Gel. "Quite frankly," the author of the *Kodakery* article wrote, "I went to Eastman Gel expecting that I would find offensive odors and perhaps some raw materials and processes that might be a bit unpleasant. Not so. I knew gelatine was made from animal bones and I anticipated the worst. Untrue, again. The bone Eastman Gel uses (from cattle only) comes neatly cut into lengths of 8 inches or so. The bone is snowy white; it has been entirely 'degreased' by a boiling process before it's shipped to Peabody. There's no odor. As a matter of fact, it's said that a dog will evince no interest whatsoever in these bones which are so clean that they apparently have no canine 'sniff appeal.'"[31] White bones, like the "white gold" of Agfa's Vistra rayon: clean and harmless, thanks to chemistry.

This doesn't square with the situation in Peabody recently, or in the 1950s. When Alec Klein, a *Wall Street Journal* reporter, wrote about Eastman Gelatine in 1999, he began with the sentence, "The stench of death rises from 16-foot-high piles of cow bones chopped into popcorn-sized nuggets."[32] A *Salem News* article from 2003 called Eastman Gelatine a "Good Neighbor, Despite the Odor."[33] This odor persisted after 2011, the year that Kodak, winding down its film business, sold the plant to the French gelatin company Rousselot. In January 2020, Peabody residents filed a class-action lawsuit against Rousselot for the reek that permeated nearby neighborhoods. The company brushed off the complaint. According to a spokeswoman, the source of the smell was "an accumulated level of solids in the system" resulting from a problem with a wastewater treatment tank, but anyone who lived within a few miles of the factory knew that the odor was no fleeting occurrence.[34] Neither was it benign. Eastman Gel's lime waste lagoons (widely known locally as the origin of the smell) overflowed in 1954, spilling industrial waste onto Peabody's streets and inciting fears of a dysentery outbreak. In the 1970s, there were concerns that the lagoons had created a pancreatic cancer cluster, but researchers couldn't find any direct connection. Later, the lagoons were designated a Superfund site.[35]

If you're at the Rousselot site today, if you drive east from the factory down Washington Street into Salem and keep going, you'll find yourself on a bridge overlooking the city of Beverly's harbor. Turn onto Goat Hill Lane and veer down to the water, and you'll see the harbormaster's office, a restaurant, and beyond them, some new-build apartments. You can't tell that there was nuclear waste where the apartments stand, but there was. From 1942 to 1948, the site was home to Metal Hydrides, a Manhattan Project contractor whose employees worked with uranium

238, converting oxide into powder, recovering metal from scrap. Metal Hydrides was tightly linked with the Manhattan Project's major plants. Some of its materials came from Oak Ridge and Hanford, leftovers from reactors that Beverly workers recast into new fuel, prefiguring the work that West Valley would later do.

What was once Metal Hydrides isn't a Superfund site. As a former nuclear installation, it's the equivalent for the US Department of Energy (the AEC's successor, formed in 1977). The precariousness of the place where the factory was built is evident just from looking at it: It sits on a spit of land that juts out from under the bridge into where the Danvers River joins the Atlantic. The tides are large here, around nine feet from high to low. When the Department of Energy began its cleanup in 1995, officials walked past the seawall and found that radiation extended well beyond where the buildings had stood, into the harbor and the mudflats at its edge.[36] The factory itself had been too radioactive to be disposed of in any ordinary way. It was disassembled, and its parts were hauled twelve miles from shore to a watery grave in cod-fishing waters and lobstering grounds.

Metal Hydrides' employees already knew how dangerous the factory was. In Beverly, unlike Peabody, it was easy to pinpoint the source of the cancers that they contracted years after they left the company. They had often worked with bare hands and unwittingly inhaled and ingested the uranium powder. But the Manhattan Project didn't require film badges in Beverly. They weren't tracking how much radiation was building up in workers' bodies, and they weren't sampling the air.[37]

The tissues that connect Metal Hydrides to Eastman Gel are invisible but dense. The factory sites are only fifteen minutes apart. During a morning of errands, you could pass one, then the other. Members of the same family, close friends, could easily have worked in the two places. Once again, and no matter what the photographic manufacturers said, it was hard to separate film plants from nuclear plants. You could see this in the people the factories employed and the communities with which they overlapped. You could see it in their processes, built on an abhorrence of waste that saw no material, no scrap of bone or metal, as too small to be salvaged. And you could see it in the industry built on these materials, the chemical industry, which two wars and counting had ballooned to enormous size. But as Rachel Carson had foreseen, the consequences of this industry's growth came into sharpest focus outside the plants' walls, with each flood, each tide, and each deep breath.

Epilogue

THE TWENTY-FIRST CENTURY

I MADE THE DRIVE from Eastman Gelatine to the old Metal Hydrides on a brisk afternoon in March. In the late winter sun, flanked by green sod lawns and a seawall walk, the apartment complex gleamed with clean, nautical luxury. Someone living there could gaze out of its windows onto working piers and boat lifts without feeling a crust of salt on their skin. Parking is easy and amenities are plentiful. Rentals go for thousands of dollars a month.

It's a predictable story: When industry moves on, sometimes factories become housing. The Beverly complex is where it is because the United States' nuclear industry left a wide stretch of waterfront property in a place where that kind of land is at a premium. Elsewhere, it's the film industry that's moved on. In Berlin at what used to be Glanzfilm, there's an air of accessible luxury, too. Brick walls from the 1920s sprout sleek metal patios. Glassy atria have been built, and new elevators. But while the Beverly apartments don't advertise the site's past, the opposite is true in Berlin. Living in a former film factory has cachet, and the architects retained both the plant's buildings and its footprint. Its cobblestoned streets still bear names like "To the Film Factory" and "To the Film Warehouse," and there are two playgrounds called "Kodak."

What there isn't is film, or very much of it; this is true everywhere in the era of digital images. Kodak declared bankruptcy in 2012 and shrank to a fraction of its former size. Agfa has contracted as well, focusing on business-to-business sales and medical products. At the end of 2023, Rousselot closed the Peabody gelatin factory's doors for good. Nevertheless, celluloid enthusiasts are blowing small embers of life into film manufacturing. There's the company FilmoTec on Wolfen's "X-Ray Street," which offers motion picture and photographic films and bills itself as ORWO's successor, not Agfa's. In Italy, lovers of cinema have led a successful crowdfunding campaign to revive Ferrania, the film of classics such as *Bicycle Thieves* and *8 ½*, whose factory, in 1964, was acquired and subsequently absorbed by 3M (the Minnesota Mining and Manufacturing Company, makers of Scotch and cassette tape alike).[1] A handful of powerful directors and actors refuse to work on anything but film, and they're crucial to present-day photographic manufacturers. Bringing things full circle, Christopher Nolan's 2023 film *Oppenheimer*, a story about one of the men behind the Manhattan Project, was shot on Kodak's 70 mm: the film that requires the largest amount of cellulose acetate, the slow-burning substance that led Tennessee Eastman to the atomic bomb.[2]

For some enthusiasts, the actions required to shoot a film or take a photograph—choosing the right film and the right speed, measuring light, adjusting focus—stand firm against the automated images we make now that our cameras are our telephones, and our telephones are mobile. For others, films like Super 8 or Kodachrome might capture a sense of nostalgia for a time before the digital turn and the climate crisis. These feelings are understandable. We know well that our phones and computers and the batteries on which they run depend on metals and minerals that grow scarcer with each new machine and its planned obsolescence. Their extraction depends on dangerous, vastly undercompensated labor, the backbone of a global economy that is still—not unlike when Kodak and Agfa built their photographic empires—shot through with violence and inequity and inseparable from war.[3] Yet lest we think film simpler and less implicated than digital technologies, we can remember the black spots that appeared in 1951, signs that film factories didn't only shape cinema's golden age. They helped create the chemical age, in which toxic waste, forced labor, and proliferating weapons were inseparable from industrial society's dependence on mass-produced materials like film—even as film itself grew increasingly "safe." Safe, we could ask, for whom?

You can see the long tail of the film factory's history in a century of war in some of this book's locations. Katanga, where uranium for the atomic bomb was once mined, now produces more than two thirds of the world's cobalt, which is used to power cellphone cameras and electric cars. Mining in Katanga is still hazardous, precarious work, and it's still commanded by powerful foreign countries.[4] In Wolfen, not far from FilmoTec, a corner of the film and fiber complex has been purchased by the Dutch company AMG and turned into a lithium hydroxide refinery. Like cobalt, it's a newer source of energy but an old idea. As the European Union attempts to dodge China in the global market for rare earths, Wolfen's industrial spaces are once again seen as vital to economic self-sufficiency—now an entire continent's.[5]

While the film plant is turning to lithium, down the road, the Grube Johannes is being filled. In the former mine pit where film and fiber runoff once festered, the province of Saxony-Anhalt is piling slag made from household waste, layering soil and grass on top. The area is regularly tested for emissions, and the air is better; the region is dotted almost ostentatiously with wind farms.[6] Something similar is happening in what used to be Wismut, where portable fencing and placards announce the area's remediation, and nineteenth-century hotels next door to mine shafts are open again, freshly renovated and filled with tourists seeking healthy mountain air.[7] Yet this is all too late for many of those who passed through Wolfen and the Ore Mountains in the twentieth century. Oleksandra Lawrik, again. Like others who returned to the Soviet Union after the war, she was treated with suspicion because she'd been imprisoned in Germany, and she was kicked out of the Party and sent to a work camp in the Donbas region. She returned and had two more children, a profound gesture of hope. In 1986, after a reactor at the Chornobyl Nuclear Power Plant exploded, one of her sons was sent to clean up the aftermath and was poisoned by radiation.[8] The damage is deep and impossibly entangled, beyond the reach of any remediation.

Film can't escape these legacies, but it might still be able to change. That's the idea, at least, behind something happening at Eastman Chemical, the former Tennessee Eastman, which bills itself as a specialist in the "circular economy." In some ways, this is old wine in new bottles. From the beginning, reusing byproducts and waste was central to the company's identity, a brand of prudent austerity that sounded as good in a war economy as it does amidst the climate crisis. Eastman has three new factories now, in Kingsport, Longview, and Normandy, France, built to dissolve petroleum-based plastics into their molecular building blocks. Broken down in this way, they're ready to be retransformed into plastic—the beginning, the company emphasizes, of a potentially endless cycle. The chemical that Eastman uses to do this is methanol, the process was first used at Kodak Park in the 1970s to recycle PET X-ray film, and the significance of these facts isn't lost on Eastman Chemical. In a corporate video about the recycling process, the voiceover notes that the new factories' work builds on the company's history. Just then, the video cuts to a photograph of George Eastman.[9]

While these twenty-first century factories are rooted in film's past, it's not clear what, if anything, they mean for film's future. Eastman executives think molecular recycling will be lucrative (the new plants were generously subsidized by the US Department of Energy), and they downplay environmentalists' warnings about greenwashing, about the plants' toxic emissions and hazardous waste, about the prodigious amounts of energy that they use.[10] This, too, is nothing new. Conservation in the film factory was always as much about the bottom line as it was about environmental or political concerns. At the same time, it had to do with chemistry, since reusing materials—silver, for example, or acetic acid—is fundamental to the science and the industry it created. Primo Levi writes about this as well. One of his arguments in *The Periodic Table* is that while the periodic table codifies the elements, the point of chemistry is the elements' transformation, whether that happens through laboratory reactions or factory processes or in more mundane ways. In Auschwitz's synthetic rubber plant, Levi recalls, the iron-cerium rods with which the prisoners lit their industrial torches could, clandestinely, become flints for cigarette lighters. Their meaning was never fixed.[11]

We can end with another of Levi's stories about transformation. It is the story of a glass of milk and an atom of carbon in that milk. It is Levi's glass of milk, and he swallows a mouthful. The atom of carbon enters his bloodstream, and from there, a nerve cell in his brain. Before this, the same atom, or one like it, has been many places. It has been encased in limestone, "caught by the wind, flung down on the earth, lifted ten kilometers high." It has been part of a grape plant turned into wine, swallowed by a different man, a man who isn't Levi, and breathed out again as carbon dioxide. It has been the body of an insect and loam on the earth. When it reaches Levi's brain, the atom does something new. It becomes part of "a gigantic minuscule game which nobody has yet described," a game that, after the centuries and miles of the atom's journey, from Levi's brain to his hands, creates words on a page.[12]

Like many of the stories in Levi's book, this one is a parable. It's a parable about chemistry and the people and things it touches, about its inherently global scale, and about its materials, which change into myriad things with just as many, sometimes irreconcilable, meanings. In fact, if we alter the details a little, we could turn it into a story of film. Let's make it a version of the one with which this book began: of how uranium mined in the Belgian Congo is sent to New York, then Canada, then Oak Ridge, where it is transformed into a bomb. This bomb explodes in Nevada or the Marshall Islands, and after fallout has circled the earth one, two, three times, it comes to rest in a pasture in West Valley, New York, whose cows and their milk are an early-warning system. Maybe these cows are descendants of the herd Kodak kept in upstate New York long before it founded Eastman Gelatine, and maybe, in their bodies, what is left of the uranium—strontium 90 or iodine 131—gravitates to bones instead of milk. Months or years later, the bones are pulverized to make gelatin in which silver salts are suspended, and the spots burned in this emulsion show the film factory how much its raw materials matter, and just how much they reveal. But nothing at all would be visible without the base: the translucent surface that holds film steady, giving it purchase in the world that made it; the world that it has changed, over and over; the world of which it will be an inescapable part even when film is entirely obsolete, eclipsed by technologies of culture and war that we cannot begin to imagine.

ACKNOWLEDGEMENTS

I had been working on this book for about three years when, on July 28, 2020, the US government announced that it was loaning Eastman Kodak and Fujifilm millions of dollars to manufacture pharmaceutical products, part of an early-pandemic bid to make the country's drug industry independent of China. To some, the loans seemed outlandish. As economist Robert Reich put it, "Kodak isn't even a pharmaceutical company."[1]

By that point in my research, I knew the outrage was misplaced: Kodak has long been involved with pharmaceuticals, as Fujifilm is now. The Kodak subsidiary Distillation Product Industries made vitamins A and E starting in the 1930s. Tennessee Eastman manufactured chemicals for pharmaceuticals, and so did Texas Eastman. While the 2020 loan was a flash in the pan, it underscored how much this book—the story of factories that have always made much more than film—had to do with the present.

The years around 2020 were a challenging time to research and write a book, and both before and after that moment in July, I incurred many debts. The first is to the remarkable archivists and librarians across North America and Europe who, over the past decade, guided me to sources and patiently answered countless questions. My thanks in particular to Ashley Augustyniak, Shane Bell, John Elsbree, Rene Emendörffer, John Falconer, Anita Ganzenmüller, Manfred Gill, Uwe Holz, Kenton Jaehnig, Bruno Mestdagh, Sarah Newhouse, Sven Sachenbacher, Stéphanie Salmon, Michael Stallo, Brianne Wright, Melinda Wallington, and the Interlibrary Loan office at the University of Minnesota.

For permission to reprint images and text, I am grateful to the Archiv der Gedenkstätte Buchenwald, Archiv Industrie- und Filmmuseum Wolfen, Archives of the City of Kingsport, British Library, Brooklyn Museum, Eastman Kodak Company, George Eastman Museum, the Imperial War Museums, McGraw-Hill, the National Museum of Nuclear Science & History and the Atomic Heritage Foundation, the New York Public Library, the Royal Belgian Film Archive, the Science History Institute, and University of Rochester River Campus Libraries Rare Books, Special Collections, and Preservation. Sections of chapter 1 originally appeared in "From Forests to Film: Chemistry, Industry, and the Rise of Nonflammable Film Stock," *JCMS* 62, no. 2 (2023): 151–56. Sections of chapters 2 and 3 appeared in "Celluloid Geopolitics: Film Stock and the War Economy, 1939–1947," *Screen* 60, no. 2 (2019): 224–41. A section of chapter 5 appeared in my coauthored chapter with Katie Trumpener, "Sad and Bitter Landscapes: Ecology and the Built Environment in Czech and East German Documentary Photography and Film," in *Cinema and the Environment in Eastern Europe,* edited by Masha Shpolberg and Lukas Brasikis (New York: Berghahn, 2023), 21–48.

A residency at the Science History Institute's Beckman Center for the History of Chemistry shaped the book in invaluable ways, and for their excellent readings and collegiality, I thank the community of scholars at the Center, including Charlotte Abney Solomon, Armel Cornu, Sarah Hijmans, Gustave Lester, Miriam Lipton, Rohini Patel, Bono Shih, Sean Silver, and Shuko Tamao. Kerri Arsenault offered pivotal tips and guidance, archival and otherwise. I would not have been able to complete the book without the support of the center's Cain Distinguished Fellowship or the George A. and Eliza Gardner Howard Fellowship in Film, or without a Talle Faculty Research Award, Grant-in-Aid, and Imagine Fund Award from the University of Minnesota. Likewise, I would never have begun it if not for discoveries made during a Fulbright fellowship in France, or a Martin Miller and Hannah Norbert-Miller Visiting Fellowship at the University of London. I am deeply appreciative of the opportunities these fellowships and grants offered.

As research assistants, Daniel Aufmann and Dylan Mohr brought their extraordinary knowledge and archival acumen to the book, and Daniel played an essential role in the manuscript's final stages. The Department of Cultural Studies and Comparative Literature and the Program in Moving Image, Media, and Sound at the University of Minnesota are incomparable communities in which to work and to think, and I am grateful to all of my faculty, staff, and student colleagues. The students in my graduate seminar on media technopolitics were wonderful interlocutors at an important stage of writing.

The stories and arguments here were also shaped in conversation with colleagues who generously invited me to share parts of the project at the Media and Extraction series (University College London/University of Southern California); the University of Chicago; the Photographic History Research Centre; Martin-Luther University Halle-Wittenberg; the University of Stockholm; the University of Udine; the Screen Studies Association of Australia and Aotearoa New Zealand; the University of Cambridge; and elsewhere. My thanks especially to Kirsty Sinclair Dootson, Pansy Duncan, Lee Grieveson, Priya Jaikumar, Andrea Mariani, Simona Schneider, Patrick Vonderau, and Kelley Wilder. Regular discussions about film stock with Pansy and Kirsty were a lifeline during years of pandemic isolation and uncertainty. For references, suggestions, and conversation, I also thank Michael Allan, Siobhan Craig, Allyson Nadia Field, Oliver Gaycken, Marsha Gordon, Gary Griffin, Anna Hajková, Martin Johnson, Katerina Korola, Kappy Mintie, Elena Past, Valérie Pozner, Aboubakar Sanogo, Hanna Shell, Emmet von Stackleburg, Jamele Watkins, and Tara Zahra. Douglas O'Reagan and Robert Shanebrook kindly shared documents and materials, and Leslie Thornton graciously took time to talk about Oak Ridge. In many ways, this book really began in Leslie's film classroom and, before that, in Rusty Crump's darkroom.

As the manuscript took shape, I was lucky to receive feedback from brilliant friends and colleagues. Thoughtful comments from Susan Burch, Juliette Cherbuliez, Sheer Ganor, Masha Salazkina, Christophe Wall-Romana, and Margaret Werry helped shape sections and chapters. Sumanth Prabhaker's and Audra Wolfe's insights made this a much better book. The incredible Rick Prelinger, Paula Rabinowitz, Katie Trumpener, Haidee Wasson, Alice Arnold, and Ian McAlpin read the entire thing, in some cases more than once, and offered crucial edits. I owe more than I can say to Haidee, Katie, Paula, and Rick for years of generative conversation about this project and for their own scholarship.

Raina Polivka, my editor at the University of California Press, has been this book's champion for just about as long as I've been working on it, and I am deeply grateful for her keen editorial eye and the push to write it the way I wanted to. The team at the Press, including the fabulous Sam Warren, Francisco Reinking, and Tim DeBold, expertly brought the project to completion, and Alex Trotter produced yet another superb index.

My family—especially Martha, Nathan, Danielle, and David Lovejoy, Mary Lewis, Mary Lovejoy, and John Whistler—patiently talked through all manner of things, and Nathan spent hours reading and discussing the book. They have been a vital source of support, as have Devorah, Ed, and Adie Juda, Eva Enns, Jasmine Foo, Howard Louthan, Colleen Flaherty Manchester, and Leslie Morris. There would be no book at all without the peerless teachers at the University of Minnesota Child Development Laboratory School or without Stella Pearce and Aimee Meller.

My most profound debt is to Igor Tchoukarine, reader, friend, and source of astonishing historical knowledge. It is dedicated with love to our children: Adrien, now a luminous ten-year-old, and joyful Élie, who was born in the middle of it all. The twenty-first century is theirs, after all.

ARCHIVES AND ABBREVIATIONS

BELGIUM

CegeSoma (The Study and Documentation Centre for War and Contemporary Society, Brussels) (CEGES)
Royal Belgian Film Archive, Brussels

BRITAIN

Kodak Archive, British Library, London (KA)
National Archives, Kew (NA)

FRANCE

Archives Jérôme Seydoux-Pathé, Paris (AJSP)
Archives Nationales, Pierrefitte-sur-Seine (AN)

GERMANY

Archiv der Gedenkstätte Buchenwald, Weimar (BwA)
Archiv Industrie- und Filmmuseum Wolfen (AIFM)
Bundesarchiv, Berlin (BArch)

UNITED STATES

Archives of Appalachia, East Tennessee State University, Johnson City, Tennessee (AA)
Rare Book and Manuscript Library, Columbia University Libraries, New York, New York (CU)
George Eastman Museum, Rochester, New York (GEM)
Archives of the City of Kingsport, Kingsport, Tennessee (ACK)
Minnesota Historical Society, St. Paul, Minnesota (MHS)
National Archives, Atlanta, Georgia (NARA Atlanta)
National Archives and Records Administration, College Park, Maryland (NARA)
Oak Ridge Room, Oak Ridge Public Library, Oak Ridge, Tennessee (ORR)
Science History Institute Library and Archives, Philadelphia, Pennsylvania (SHI)
Kodak Historical Collection #D319, University of Rochester River Campus Libraries, Department of Rare Books, Special Collections, and Preservation, Rochester, New York (KHC)

DIGITAL COLLECTIONS

Brooklyn Museum Archives, Brooklyn, New York, United States (BMA)
DOE/NNSA Nuclear Testing Archive, United States (DOE/NNSA)
Field Museum Library Digital Collections, Chicago, Illinois, United States (FML)
Hagley Digital Archives, Hagley Museum & Library, Wilmington, Delaware, United States (HML)
Imperial War Museum, London, United Kingdom
Landeshauptarchiv Sachsen-Anhalt, Merseburg, Germany (LSA)
Media History Digital Library
National Museum of Nuclear Science & History and the Atomic Heritage Foundation, Washington, D.C., United States
New York Public Library Digital Collections, New York, New York, United States

NOTES

INTRODUCTION

1. Williams, *Spies in the Congo*, 6, 77.
2. Minerals and Ores May 43—Sept. 42, 18 September 1942, RG 326, Box 36, MD 410.4, NARA; Minerals and Ores May 43—Sept. 42, Roben to Dean, 11 September 1942, RG 326, Box 36, MD 410.4, NARA; Minerals and Ores May 43—Sept. 42, Nichols to African Metals Corporation, 29 October 1942, RG 326, Box 36, MD 410.4, NARA.
3. Blume, *Fallout*, 2.
4. McQueen, "Flammable Workhorse," 106.
5. Leslie, *Synthetic Worlds*, 16.
6. Horkheimer and Adorno, "The Culture Industry," 96.
7. On media industry studies, see, e.g., Havens and Lotz, eds., *Understanding Media Industries;* Mayer, *Below the Line;* Szczepanik and Vonderau, *Behind the Screen.*
8. See, e.g., Fortmueller and Marzola, *Hollywood Unions;* Grieveson, *Cinema and the Wealth of Nations;* Jacobson, *Studios Before the System;* Marzola, *Engineering Hollywood;* Wasson, *Everyday Movies.*
9. Bozak, *Cinematic Footprint;* Angus, *Camera Geologica.* Scholars in art history and film and media studies are examining film and photography's ecological and material dimensions. On photography, see also Castro et al., eds., "Ecological Histories of Photography"; Dominici, ed., "The Darkroom"; Coleman and James, ed., *Capitalism and the Camera.* On cinema, see also Cubitt, *Finite Media;* Dahlquist and Vonderau, *Petrocinema;* Dootson, *Rainbow's Gravity*; Duncan, *Natural History* and "Towards a Natural History of Film Form"; Fay, *Inhospitable World;* Grieveson and Jaikumar, "Media and Extraction"; Jacobson, *Cinema of Extractions;* LeMenager, *Living Oil;* Maxwell and Miller, *Greening the Media;*

Nieland, "Organic Creativity"; Past, *Italian Ecocinema;* Shukin, *Animal Capital;* Vaughan, *Hollywood's Dirtiest Secret;* and Yue, *Girl Head.*

10. On motion pictures' multiple histories beyond the cinema, see, e.g., Acland and Wasson, *Useful Cinema;* Prelinger, *Field Guide to Sponsored Films;* Orgeron et al., eds., *Learning with the Lights Off;* Hediger and Vonderau, eds., *Films That Work;* and Hediger et al., eds., *Films That Work Harder.*

11. See Arsenault, *Mill Town.*

12. Levi, *Periodic Table,* 78. Key histories of Wolfen and Kingsport, respectively, include Fengler, *Entwickelt und fixiert;* Karlsch and Wagner, *AGFA-ORWO-Story;* Lee, *Tennessee-Virginia Tri-Cities;* and Wolfe, *Kingsport.*

13. "Frank W. Lovejoy, Head of Kodak, Succumbs at 73."

14. "James Charles White," Stedman Families Research Center, accessed September 12, 2024, https://johnlisle.us/genealogy/getperson.php?personID=I91420&tree=stedman_main.

15. Wasson, *Everyday Movies.*

16. "Background info re: Nov. 1, 1951 hot snow," b. 160, f. 13, KHC.

17. Schuppli, "Radical Contact Prints," in O'Brian, *Camera Atomica.* The "black spots" have been discussed elsewhere, e.g., Pringle, "Manufactured Uncertainty," and Graham, "Nature of Risk."

18. "Camphor Industry in Formosa," 288; Hackett, "Coal Tar Began It," 118.

CHAPTER ONE

1. De Grazia, "Mass Culture and Sovereignty"; Smith, "The Man Behind the Film."

2. Wentzel, *Memoirs of a Photochemist,* ix; Amor, "Manufacture of Motion Picture Film," A 71, KA.

3. Smither and Surowiec, *This Film is Dangerous.* See, for instance, the title to Deac Rossell's chapter, "Exploding Teeth, Unbreakable Sheets and Continuous Casting."

4. Brayer, *George Eastman,* 208.

5. Collins, *Story of Kodak,* 68; Usai, *Silent Cinema,* 28.

6. Grieveson, *Cinema and the Wealth of Nations,* 316.

7. *Forty-Fourth Annual Report of the Eastman Kodak Company for the Year Ending December 28, 1946,* 28, A 2866, KA.

8. Eastman to Strong, 11 March 1918, GEM; Shanebrook, *Making KODAK Film,* 123. On silver and Kodak, see also Angus, "The Eastman Kodak Silver Vault."

9. Shanebrook, *Making KODAK Film*, 119; "Dry Gelatine Raw Stocks," b. 97, f. 2, KHC.
10. Brayer, *George Eastman*, 386.
11. Harding, "Kodak," 804.
12. Mees, "Kodak Research Laboratories," 465; Collins, *Story of Kodak*, 116–17, 194–195.
13. Jenkins, *Images and Enterprise*, 188–91.
14. Collins, *Story of Kodak*, 82, 92, 150, 158.
15. Federal Trade Commission v. Eastman Kodak Company, Docket no. 977, 18 April 1924, R8128/16947, BArch. Between 1919 and March 1920, for instance, Kodak made 96 percent of the positive 35 mm film manufactured in the United States. Unless otherwise indicated, all translations from French and German in this book are the author's own.
16. Collins, *Story of Kodak*, 147.
17. Gregory, "Dyes and Dye Intermediates," 42.
18. Haber, *Chemical Industry*, 10; Chandler, *Industrial Century*, 20.
19. Long, "How Mauve Was Her Garment." See also Dootson, *Rainbow's Gravity*.
20. Wentzel, *Memoirs of a Photochemist*, viii; Chandler, *Industrial Century*, 22.
21. Aftalion, *International Chemical Industry*, 69; Cherchi Usai, *Silent Cinema*, 26–27.
22. Karlsch and Wagner, *AGFA-ORWO-Story*, 25–27.
23. Chandler, *Industrial Century*, 21, 162; Haber, *Chemical Industry*, 188.
24. Mees, "Kodak Research Laboratories," 466; Mees, *From Dry Plates to Ektachrome Film*, 142; "Steady Progress of American Dye Industry"; "Eastman Laboratories Assist," b. 189, f. 16, KHC; Collins, *Story of Kodak*, 147–51.
25. Eastman to Philipp, 20 May 1918, GEM.
26. To Herrn. Geheimrat Dr. Oppenheim, 25 September 1922, R8128/16920, BArch.
27. "Brief History of Chemical War." See also Ndiaye, *Nylon and Bombs*, 47.
28. Bustamante, "AGFA, Kullmann, Singer & Co.," 72; Schmelzer and Stein, *Geschichte des VEB Filmfabrik Wolfen*, 17; Löhnert and Mustroph, *Entwicklung der Produktion photographischer Materialien*, 49.
29. Salmon, *Pathé*, 317–19.
30. Kaufmann, "Gas, Gas, Gaas!"
31. See "Calendar of Film Fires," in *This Film Is Dangerous*, esp. p. 436, and Grieveson, *Policing Cinema*.
32. On the history of celluloid, see Friedel, *Pioneer Plastic*.

33. Bustamante, "AGFA, Kullmann, Singer & Co.," 62–63; Wasson, *Everyday Movies,* 43; Mebold and Tepperman, "28mm Film in North America," 140. On other nonflammable films and formats, see Kattelle, "Amateur Motion Picture Equipment," 47, and Salmon, *Pathé,* 212–23. See also Jenkins, *Images and Enterprise,* 289–95; Enticknap, *Moving Image Technology*; and McQueen, "Flammable Workhorse."

34. Eastman to Clarke, 28 April 1909, GEM; see also Le Guern, "European Kodak Research Laboratories," 102. On continuous film casting at Kodak Park, see von Stackleburg, "Wheels of Change," in Lovejoy, Dootson, and Duncan, *Film Stock;* and Rossell, "Exploding Teeth," in Smither and Surowiec, *This Film Is Dangerous.*

35. See, e.g., an advertisement for *The Cattle Thieves,* noting that the film is printed on Eastman nonflammable stock, in *Moving Picture World* 5, no. 19 (November 6, 1911): 632.

36. Eastman to Baker, 27 February 1911, GEM.

37. See, e.g., an advertisement for Agfa nonflammable stock in *Moving Picture World* 11, no. 7 (February 18, 1912): 543. On nonflammable film production at Wolfen, which began in 1911, see Löhnert and Mustroph, *Entwicklung der Produktion photographischer Materialien,* 28–48.

38. Eastman to Gifford, 31 October 1913, GEM; Eastman to Robert Adamson, Fire Commissioner, New York, 15 February 1915, GEM.

39. Eastman to Oppenheim, 18 March 1914, BArch R8128/16947; Eastman to Baker, 27 February 1911, GEM.

40. Karlsch and Wagner, *AGFA-ORWO-Story,* 49–50; Salmon, *Pathé,* 317–19; Collins, *Story of Kodak,* 150. On cellulose acetate airplane dope, see Blanc, *Fake Silk,* 112–16.

41. Eastman to Strong, 14 December 1917, GEM; Eastman to Haught, 9 March 1918, GEM.

42. "Brief History of Chemical War." On the "chemist's war," see Ndiaye, *Nylon and Bombs,* 47.

43. Haber, *Chemical Industry,* 251.

44. Brayer, *George Eastman,* 397. On early vertical integration at Kodak, see Jenkins, *Images and Enterprise.*

45. Smith, "The Man Behind the Film"; Eastman Kodak, "All That Flickers Isn't Gold," 42.

46. "Creative Chemistry," b. 39, f. 7, KHC; "Tennessee Eastman Corporation, Kingsport, Tenn." (1937), 2, Published Collections Department, Trade catalogs and pamphlets, HML.

47. Binnicker, "Carolina, Clinchfield and Ohio Railway"; *Kingsport: City of Industries,* 25; Shuman, "Kingsport: An Unusual City."

48. Egan, "John Bartlett Dennis."
49. Eller, *Miners, Millhands, and Mountaineers*, 43.
50. Garett, "Roads Going South," 60.
51. Long, *Kingsport: A Romance of Industry*, 123.
52. Wolfe, *Kingsport*, 34.
53. Lee, *Tennessee-Virginia Tri-Cities*, 75.
54. Walker, "Gas Warfare," 96.
55. *Kingsport: City of Industries*, 35; Lee, *Tennessee-Virginia Tri-Cities*, 108.
56. Egan, "John Bartlett Dennis."
57. Garrett, "Roads Going South," 61.
58. "Tennessee Eastman Corporation," KC Manuscript Collection 49, box 2, folder 6, ACK.
59. Wolfe, *Kingsport*, 69–71.
60. Shuman, "Kingsport: An Unusual City," 473.
61. Johnson to Eastman, 9 November 1925, KC Manuscript Collection 416, Folder 5, ACK.
62. Jacoby, *Modern Manors*, 70.
63. McKelvey, *Rochester*, 7, 145, 261. On Eastman's support for the eugenics movement, see Brayer, *George Eastman*, 474–476; Feser, *Reproducing Photochemical Life*, chapter 3; and Jacoby, *Modern Manors*, 61.
64. "Tennessee Eastman Corporation," KC Manuscript Collection 49, box 2, folder 6, ACK.
65. Eastman to Dryden, 29 July 1920, GEM. Most of this quotation also appears in "Creative Chemistry," b. 39, f. 7, KHC. On Eastman's arrival in Kingsport, see also Wolfe, *Kingsport*, 70–73.
66. McWhirter, *Red Summer*, 12.
67. Brayer, *George Eastman*, 472, 596–97n2.
68. See McWhirter, *Red Summer*, chapter 16.
69. Lee, *Tennessee-Virginia Tri-Cities*, 118–19.
70. See Arabindan-Kesson, *Black Bodies, White Gold*.
71. Eastman to Olsen, 17 December 1931, GEM.
72. Eastman to Dunn, 28 May 1915, GEM.
73. Eastman to Bartlett, 24 December 1915, GEM. On Eastman and Myrick, see also Brayer, *George Eastman*, 269.
74. Brayer, *George Eastman*, 270.
75. Eastman to Myrick, 19 December 1918, GEM.
76. Field, *Uplift Cinema*, 33–35.
77. Qtd. in Brayer, *George Eastman*, 278.
78. Field, *Uplift Cinema*, 39. Anna Arabindan-Kesson writes that photography itself underscored "the economic equivalency, established through

slavery, between Black people and white cotton." Arabindan-Kesson, *Black Bodies, White Gold,* 18.

79. Johnson to Eastman, 27 August 1921, KC Manuscript Collection 416, folder 2, ACK; Eastman to Johnson, 30 August 1921, KC Manuscript Collection 416, folder 2, ACK.

80. Tennessee Eastman Corporation, *Information for Employees,* 1942, KC Manuscript Collection 81, Folder 6, ACK.

81. Wolfe, *Kingsport,* 71–73. Parts of this section originally appeared in Lovejoy, "From Forests to Film."

82. Wasson, *Everyday Movies,* 58.

83. "Creative Chemistry," b. 39, f. 7, KHC.

84. Collins, *Story of Kodak,* 164; Zimmermann, *Reel Families,* 30; Tepperman, *Amateur Cinema,* 117.

85. Eastman to Baker, 27 February 1911, GEM; Eastman to Oppenheim, 18 March 1914, R8128/16947, BArch.

86. Eastman to Gifford, 8 June 1908, GEM; Eastman to Clarke, 1 June 1910, GEM.

87. "Tennessee Eastman Corp. Will Build New Plant," 1; "Kodak Offering," 2.

88. "Creative Chemistry," b. 39, f. 7, KHC; Eastman Kodak, *Journey,* 25.

89. Blancke, *Celanese Corporation of America,* 8.

90. "Celanese 100 Years Anniversary Timeline," accessed July 2, 2024, https://century.celanese.com/.

91. "Eastman Expansion."

92. "Dr. Crile Sees Clinic He Built Made Shambles." Capitalization of "world" in original.

93. "Safety Film Plant to E-T."

94. "Names Fatal Gases in Cleveland Clinic."

95. "Stress Value of Ventilation," 1848.

96. Collins, *Story of Kodak,* 159; United States National Parks Service, "History of Film Types Timeline"; Schmelzer and Stein, *Geschichte des VEB Filmfabrik Wolfen,* 27.

97. "Work On New Eastman Unit."

98. "Tennessee Eastman Corporation, Kingsport, Tenn." (1937), 2, Published Collections Department, Trade Catalogs and Pamphlets, HML.

99. Salmon, *Pathé,* 161, 220, 224.

100. Bibliothèque municipale de Lyon, "Une fabrique de l'innovation."

101. Keating, "Spatiality of Film Production," 40; "Fassini, Alberto nell'Enciclopedia Treccani," accessed July 2, 2024, https://www.treccani.it/enciclopedia/alberto-fassini.

102. Ndiaye, *Nylon and Bombs*, 102; Marzola, "Better Pictures through Chemistry." On Celanese's history, see "The Beginnings (1912–1920)," accessed July 2, 2024, https://www.celanese.com/en/about-us/who-we-are/the-beginnings.

103. "Japanese Celluloid"; Aftalion, *History*, 205. Dainippon was founded in 1919 through a merger of eight Japanese celluloid companies to "make economical use" of camphor, a plasticizer sourced primarily in Japan's then colony of Formosa (Taiwan). On camphor and film, see Hill, "The Life of a Film."

104. Federal Trade Commission v. Eastman Kodak Company, Docket no. 977, 18 April 1924, R8128/16947, BArch.

105. "Brulatour Files Brief for Film Duty," 35.

106. Letter from Peaslee, Brigham & Gennert, 5 May 1924, R8128/16947, BArch; Federal Trade Commission v. Eastman Kodak Company, Docket no. 977, 18 April 1924, R8128/16947, BArch; Memorandum über die Entwicklung des AGFA ANSCO-Komplexes, 1928–1938, Sekretariat Dr. Gajewski, A 1754, AIFM.

107. Karlsch and Wagner, *AGFA-ORWO-Story*, 41, 58–59; Bode, *Entwicklung des Chemiefaserbereichs der Filmfabrik Wolfen*, 17; Gill, *Jüdische Zwangsarbeiter*, 116; Chandler, *Industrial Century*, 137.

108. Lee, *Tennessee-Virginia Tri-Cities*, 131; Taussig and White, "Rayon and the Tariff."

109. Karlsch and Wagner, *AGFA-ORWO-Story*, 58.

110. "Kodak in West Germany [Kodak Aktiengesellschaft]," b. 59, f. 8, KHC.

111. Karlsch and Wagner, *AGFA-ORWO-Story*, 58.

112. Salmon, *Pathé*, 437, 342, 435. The challenges in building the Ferrania factory are documented in Quartieri La FILM, 1917–1927, b. 1–2, Hist. f. 452, AJSP. On Ferrania, see also Mariani and Schneider, "Elemental Battles," and Past, "Sunlight, Celluloid, Solarity," both in Lovejoy, et al., *Film Stock*.

113. Haber, *Chemical Industry*, 311; Marzola, "Better Pictures through Chemistry," 8–9.

114. See Haber, *Chemical Industry*, 251–279.

115. Salmon, *Pathé*, 437; Kodak in West Germany (Kodak Aktiengesellschaft), b. 59, f. 8, KHC.

116. Taillibert, "Le Pathé-Rural," 127, 139.

117. Fonds Charles Pathé (II), b. 2, f. Kodak-Pathé, Contract Eastman Kodak/Pathé Cinéma/Kodak-Pathé, AJSP; Salmon, *Pathé*, 510.

118. Glanzfilm, 1921–1927, Hist. f. 451, AJSP; "Kodak in West Germany [Kodak Aktiengesellschaft]," b. 59, f. 8, KHC. In 1934, the International Institute of Educational Cinema announced 16 mm as the sole internationally

recognized small-gauge format, not 17.5 mm, as Pathé had hoped. See Taillibert, "Le Pathé-Rural."

119. Memorandum über die Entwicklung des AGFA ANSCO-Komplexes, 1928–1938, Sekretariat Dr. Gajewski, A 1754, IFW.

120. Schröter, "Participation in Market Control," 178; Wentzel, *Memoirs of a Photochemist*, 105; Karlsch and Wagner, *AGFA-ORWO-Story*, 74.

121. Besprechung mit der Kodak Ltd. in Harrow am Donnerstag 29.10.1931, R8128/16949, BArch. Agfa Ansco bought celluloid from companies including the German explosives giant Dynamit Nobel. See Fengler, *Entwickelt und fixiert*, 50.

122. Johnson to Eastman, 1 January 1932, KC Manuscript Collection 416, folder 7, ACK.

123. Johnson to Eastman, 7 January 1932, KC Manuscript Collection 416, folder 7, ACK; Eastman to Johnson, 12 January 1932, KC Manuscript Collection 416, folder 7, ACK.

124. Fengler, *Entwickelt und fixiert*, 50.

125. "Creative Chemistry," b. 39, f. 7, KHC; Chandler, *Industrial Century*, 163.

CHAPTER TWO

1. Othmer interview, 28–29.
2. Spitz, *Petrochemicals*, 237.
3. Press releases, 1931–1936, 10–12; 1936, 131–32, Records of the Department of Public Information, BMA.
4. "Celanese Is Not Rayon," 26–27.
5. Schwarz and Mauersberger, *Rayon and Synthetic Yarn Handbook*, 105.
6. Othmer interview, 51.
7. Zahra, *Against the World*.
8. Lane, "No Fertile Soil for Pathogens," 553.
9. "La lavorazione autarchica."
10. Schnapp, "The Fabric of Modern Times," 197.
11. Levi, *Periodic Table*, 37.
12. On autarky in Fascist Germany and Italy, see Tooze, *Wages of Destruction*; Snyder, *Black Earth*; Saraiva, *Fascist Pigs*; Zahra, *Against the World*.
13. Ungewitter, *Science and Salvage*, 176.
14. Stokes, *Divide and Prosper*, 16; Hayes, *Industry and Ideology*, 20; "Strafanzeige wegen Vergehens gegen 164, 186, 187 StGB," 19 October 1944, R 8128/19680, BArch.

15. DuBois, *Devil's Chemists*, 307; Karlsch, "Fritz Gajewski," 93.
16. Kolbow, "Box Sells," 144; Karlsch and Wagner, *AGFA-ORWO-Story*, 90.
17. Karlsch, "Fritz Gajewski," 127.
18. Karlsch and Wagner, *AGFA-ORWO-Story*, 101–2.
19. Dominik, *Vistra, das weiße Gold Deutschlands*.
20. Leslie, *Synthetic Worlds*.
21. Beckert, *Empire of Cotton*, 355.
22. Tooze, *Wages of Destruction*, 131.
23. To Herrn Geheimrat Dr. Oppenheim, 25 September 1922, BArch R8128/16920.
24. Zischka, *Wissenschaft bricht Monopole*, 7; Lübke, *Das deutsche Rohstoffwünder*, 547–53. See also Baranowski, *Nazi Empire;* and Snyder, *Black Earth*.
25. Zimmerman, *Alabama in Africa*, 1, 177–79. See also Beckert, *Empire of Cotton*, 362–78.
26. Sunseri, "The *Baumwollfrage*," 33.
27. *International Trade in Certain Raw Materials*.
28. "German Photographic Film Base Industry, Final Report, No. 262," A 3024, KA. On the entwining between the histories of colonialism and the Holocaust, see Césaire, *Discours;* and Rothberg, *Multidirectional Memory*.
29. Snyder, *Black Earth,* 12. See also Beckert, "American Danger," and Baranowski, *Nazi Empire*.
30. See, e.g., Furnas, *Storehouse of Civilization;* Hessel et al., *Strategic Materials in Hemisphere Defense*, 224.
31. Black, *Global Interior;* Black, "Interior's Exterior."
32. On Ford and Fordlândia, see Grandin, *Fordlandia;* and Zahra, *Against the World*. On Ford and cinema, see Grieveson, *Cinema and the Wealth of Nations*.
33. Hochschild, *King Leopold's Ghost*.
34. Harp, *World History*, 85.
35. Furnas, *Storehouse of Civilization*, 11; Aftalion, *International Chemical Industry*, 148.
36. "Creative Chemistry," b. 39, f. 7, KHC
37. *Eastman Chemical Company*, 21–22, SHI; *Eastman Chemical Company: Years of Glory, Times of Change, 1920–1990*, Tape 1, SHI.
38. "Confluence of Holston River's North and South Forks," Palmer Room Collection, 1890–1977, ACK.
39. See, e.g., Wolfe, *Competing with the Soviets*, 11.
40. Baxter, *Secret History*, 86.

41. Swanson, *Holston Army Ammunition Plant*, 77.
42. Othmer interview.
43. Waite, "Eastman Kodak Works."
44. Eastman Kodak, *F. W. Lovejoy*, 20.
45. Swanson, *Holston Army Ammunition Plant*, 25, 88; Wolfe, *Kingsport*, 139.
46. Norris, *Racing for the Bomb*, 198.
47. Lee, *Tennessee-Virginia Tri-Cities*, 191–94.
48. Collins, *Story of Kodak*, 255, 247; Lovejoy, "Celluloid Geopolitics."
49. "James Charles White," Stedman Families Research Center, accessed September 12, 2024, https://johnlisle.us/genealogy/getperson.php?personID=I91420&tree=stedman_main.
50. For a detailed discussion of chemical engineering, especially its role in DuPont's roughly simultaneous move from explosives to fibers to the Manhattan Project, see Ndiaye, *Nylon and Bombs*. On DuPont's work in Hanford, Washington, see Brown, *Plutopia*.
51. *Eastman Chemical Company*, 8, SHI; Oak Ridge Operation Office Technical (Declassified) Files of Tennessee Eastman Corporation, 1942–1947, Box 325, Confidential CEW-TEC History, Y-23 Project, January 1943–May 1947, Clinton Engineer Works, Tennessee Eastman Corporation, RG 326, NARA Atlanta.
52. *Manhattan District History, Feed Materials and Special Procurement*, 1.3–1.4, 2.6
53. Memorandum to the President of the United States, 25 August 1944, Roll 2, Target 18, File 35, NARA; Helmreich, *Gathering Rare Ores*, 6.
54. Williams, *Spies in the Congo*, 11; Rhodes, *The Making of the Atomic Bomb*, 427.
55. Helmreich, *Gathering Rare Ores*, 7.
56. US Army Corps of Engineers, "A District Name."
57. Conrad, "Geography and Some Explorers," 272; Frankema and Buelens, "Introduction," in Frankema and Buelens, eds., *Colonial Exploitation and Economic Development*, 6.
58. Dumett, "Africa's Strategic Minerals," 393; Exenberger and Hartman, "Extractive Institutions in the Congo," in Frankema and Buelens, eds., *Colonial Exploitation and Economic Development*, 27; Helmreich, *Gathering Rare Ores*, 396.
59. "Situation des contrats pour les métaux non-ferreux de la colonie," 26 March 1943; "Note pour monsieur Paul Henri Spaak, Ministre des affaires étrangères de Belgique," 1 November 1943; "Non-Ferrous Metal Production in the Belgian Congo," March 1942, b. 1642, f. 105, CEGES.

60. Hecht, *Being Nuclear*, 193.
61. Williams, *Spies in the Congo*, 6.
62. Cauvin, *Congo* (1945); Hochschild, *King Leopold's Ghost*.
63. "Note pour Mr. le Ministre: Le Congo et notre travail de propagande," 16 December 1942, b. 857 f. 2, Courrier 1942, CEGES; Helmreich, *Gathering Rare Ores*, 396.
64. Williams, *Spies in the Congo*, 15.
65. Boulton Expedition Films (Reel 1), FML (https://cdm17032.contentdm.oclc.org/digital/collection/p17032coll5/id/38/rec/1). See also "Marriage, Science, and Secret Intelligence."
66. "De Boma à Tshela (1926)"; Davay, *Cinéma de Belgique*, 83–88.
67. "Rapport sur la Mission Cauvin," b. AA 1940 1–18, f. 4, André Cauvin, CEGES.
68. On the forms and materials of colonial film, see Grieveson and McCabe, *Empire and Film*.
69. Pollack, *Ballad of John Latouche*, 175–77. On *Congo*, see also Gillet, "La 'Mission' Cauvin," and Musser, "Presenting 'a True Idea of the African of To-day.'"
70. "Rapport sur la Mission Cauvin," b. AA 1940 1–18, f. 4, André Cauvin, CEGES.
71. Photograph of André Cauvin and Lucienne Harvey Meurisse, Box 1, Series II, John Latouche Papers, 1930–1960, CU.
72. Latouche and Cauvin, *Congo*, 190–92.
73. Latouche's own commitment to socialist and anticolonial causes flourished after the war. He was active in the Council on African Affairs (Pollack, *Ballad of John Latouche*, 178)—which, in 1943, had been blacklisted by the Manhattan Project as a Communist organization. ("Subject: Russian and Communist Party Activities," February 11, 1943, RG 326, b. 104, f. ORBO-080-Organizations CEW (General), series 8505 (Formerly Classified Correspondence), NARA Atlanta.)
74. Handwritten notes, b. AA 1940 1–18, f. 17, collection André Cauvin, CEGES.
75. *Oak Ridge Journal*, October 26, 1944.
76. Freeman, *Longing for the Bomb*, 17; "US Army Acquires 56,200 Acres."
77. Norris, *Racing for the Bomb*, 327.
78. For a detailed explanation of this process, see Norris, *Racing for the Bomb*, 487–89.
79. *Manhattan District History, Electromagnetic Project, Operation*, 4.3–4.8.

80. Wilcox interview, courtesy of National Museum of Nuclear Science & History and the Atomic Heritage Foundation.

81. Since 1933, a section of the Kodak Research Laboratories in Rochester had been dedicated to Tennessee Eastman. (Mees, "The Kodak Research Laboratories," 476.)

82. Brown, *Plutopia*, 45. On social divisions in Kodak's film manufacturing, see Feser, "Reproducing Photochemical Life."

83. Wilcox interview, courtesy of National Museum of Nuclear Science & History and the Atomic Heritage Foundation.

84. Ellingson interview, courtesy of National Museum of Nuclear Science & History and the Atomic Heritage Foundation.

85. J. Fred McConnell Oral History Collection, undated, p. 22, KC Manuscript Collection 91, ACK. On the continuous reaction process and Hull's role in it, see Baxter, *Secret History,* chapter 8, and *Manhattan District History, Electromagnetic Project, Operation,* 8.4.

86. Oak Ridge Operation Office Technical (Declassified) Files of Tennessee Eastman Corporation, 1942–1947, Box 325, Confidential CEW-TEC History, Y-23 Project, January 1943–May 1947, Clinton Engineer Works, Tennessee Eastman Corporation, RG 326, NARA Atlanta.

87. Atomic Energy Commission, Oak Ridge Operation Office Technical (Declassified) Files of Tennessee Eastman Corporation 1942–47, Box 327, History Report, August 1944, September 27, 1944, RG 326, NARA Atlanta.

88. Slack Report, ORR.

89. FBI Case File, Alfred Dean Slack, 6/2–30/50; Slack to Taylor, 19 September 1950, Colin Baxter Collection, Box 1, AA.

90. "A Heroic and Well-Loved Friend," 44.

91. Freeman, *Longing for the Bomb,* 105.

92. Huddleston interview, courtesy of National Museum of Nuclear Science & History and the Atomic Heritage Foundation; Atomic Energy Commission, Oak Ridge Operation Office Technical (Declassified) Files of Tennessee Eastman Corporation 1942–47, Box 325, CEW-TEC History, Y-12 Project, January 1943-May 1947, RG 326, NARA Atlanta.

93. Kiernan, *Girls of Atomic City,* 118.

94. Whitman interview, courtesy of National Museum of Nuclear Science & History and the Atomic Heritage Foundation.

95. Brown, *Plutopia,* 48.

96. Huddleston interview.

97. Karlsch and Wagner, *AGFA-ORWO-Story,* 56.

98. Mazower, *Hitler's Empire,* 294–95; Walser Smith, "The Workers of Europe," 219.

99. *Nurnberg Military Tribunals*, 44. See also Bode and Gill, *Zwangsarbeiter in der Filmfabrik Wolfen*, 22.

100. Gajewski to Gauobmann Bachmann, D.A.F., Halle, 30 July 1942; to Gajewski, Betr. Urlaub der Polinnen, 28 July 1942, R8128/21163, BArch.

101. To Gajewski and Bürgin, 22 April 1942, R8128/21163, BArch. These programs were organized by General Plenipotentiary for Labor Employment Fritz Sauckel (Mazower, *Hitler's Empire*, 298).

102. "Richtlinien über den Einsatz von Arbeitskräften aus den altsowjetrussischen Gebiet," 26 March 1942, R8128/21163, BArch.

103. These theories drew on the writings of French scholar Gustave Le Bon. See Gonen, *Roots of Nazi Psychology*.

104. Schulze and Ehrig to Kreisobmann der D.A.F., Bitterfeld, 23 December 1942, "Ausländereinsatz—Ostarbeiter," R8128/21163, Barch; Walser Smith, "The Workers of Europe," 216.

105. United States Holocaust Memorial Museum, *Encyclopedia of Camps and Ghettos*, 440; *Femmes oubliées*, 19.

106. "Ukrainian Prisoners at Ravensbrück," Ukrainian Canadian Research & Documentation Centre, accessed July 2, 2024, http://www.ucrdc.org/index_files/RAVENSBRUCK.pdf.

107. *Femmes oubliées*, 89.

108. Betr.: Einsatz weiblicher Häftlinge, 17 May 1943, f. Wolfen (Material Trombke/Schröter), BwA.

109. Lawrik interview, BwA.

110. Ibid.; Benz and Distel, eds., *Sachsenhausen, Buchenwald*, 618–20.

111. Blanc, *Fake Silk*, 143.

112. Vladimir Korolevich, *A Woman in Film* (1928), translated by and quoted in Gadassik, "'A Skillful Isis'," in Malitsky, ed., *A Companion to Documentary Film History*.

113. On the strike, see, e.g., Tedesco, "Claiming Public Space."

114. US National Parks Service, "The Atomic Bombings of Hiroshima and Nagasaki."

115. Leo, "The Mushroom Cloud," 7.

116. "Report on CIOS Trip no 313 to Leipzig Area Leaving United Kingdom on May 29th, 1945," A 3204, KA; "Aktennotiz über die Verhandlungen mit Kodak am 12. und 13. Februar 1941 in Paris," 8128/17430, BArch.

117. Levi, *Periodic Table*, 203.

118. Levi, *Survival in Auschwitz*, 73.

119. Ungewitter, *Use of the Worthless*, 12.

120. See Weinberg, "Impact of Large-Scale Science on the United States"; Wolfe, *Competing with the Soviets*; Galison, *Big Science*.

CHAPTER THREE

1. On the occupation film programs, see Fay, *Theaters of Occupation* and Lovejoy, "A Treacherous Tightrope." Sections of this chapter originally appeared in Lovejoy, "Celluloid Geopolitics."

2. See Jarvie, *Hollywood's Overseas Campaign*.

3. "Kodak-Pathe Societe Anonyme Francaise, History of Losses Written Off," b. 58, f. 6–8, KHC.

4. "Report on CIOS Trip no. 313 to Leipzig Area Leaving United Kingdom on May 29th, 1945," A 3204, KA.

5. "OB Motion Picture Bureau Outpost Report, March 1945," RG 208, b. 2, NARA.

6. Kodak-Pathé to Ministry of Information, Direction Générale du cinéma, 3 November 1944, F/42/123, f. Répartition de la pellicule 1945, AN.

7. "Memorandum to T.L. Barnard from Louis Lober," August 28, 1945, RG 208, b. 2, NARA.

8. Judt, "Exploitation by Integration?," in Ciesla and Judt, *Technology Transfer*, 30.

9. Dos Passos, *Tour of Duty*, 243.

10. Karlsch and Wagner, *AGFA-ORWO-Story*, 119.

11. Hübner, *Die Region Wolfen*, 5.

12. "Protokoll über die Sitzung der Abteilung Kunstseide, Vistra und Zellstoff am 5. April 1943," f. Wolfen (Material Trombke/Schröter), BwA.

13. Benz and Distel, eds., *Sachsenhausen, Buchenwald*, 620; Lawrik interview, BwA.

14. Hübner, *Die Region Wolfen*, 6–7.

15. Gill, "Eine reiche Beute," 46–47.

16. "Agfa Film Factory Wolfen," RG 331, Entry 13D, Box 86, NARA.

17. Levin, *In Search*, 264, 278–79.

18. Hübner, *Die Region Wolfen*, 8; Karlsch and Wagner, *AGFA-ORWO-Story*, 121; "Report on C.I.O.S. Trip no. 313," KA; "Réunion du 4 mai à la DIC," F/42/123, f. Répartition de la pellicule 1945, AN.

19. "Agfa Film Factory Wolfen," RG 331, b. 86, NARA.

20. For a detailed overview of the institutions overseeing investigations in Germany, see O'Reagan, *Taking Nazi Technology*, 29–30.

21. Gimbel, *Science, Technology, and Reparations*, 6–7, 16, 165–166.

22. "R. Leonard Hasche, Tennessee Eastman," Sekretariat Foto, Nr. 2178, AIFM.

23. "Fabrication of Plastics, I.G. Farbenindustrie, Wolfen," RG 331, Entry 13, Box 86, NARA.

24. "Agfa Film Factory Wolfen," RG 331, b. 86, NARA; *The Photographic Industry in Germany during the period 1939–1945*, A 3024, KA.

25. Gill, "Eine reiche Beute," 46.

26. *The Photographic Industry in Germany during the period 1939–1945*, A 3024, KA; "Film Production and Methods Agfa Film Fabrik Plant, Wolfen," RG 331, b. 89, NARA.

27. "Betr.: Agfacolorfilme für Propagandazwecke," 23 June 1945, Wolfen, Sekretariat Foto, Nr. 2178, AIFM; "Betr.: Farbfilm-Geräte für Lt. Col. Cuthbertson," 16 June 1945, Wolfen, Prüfstelle, Nr. 581, AIFM.

28. "Gründe, die dagegen sprechen, unsere Erfahrungen über herstellung der Farbstoffkomponenten für Farbenfilm an USA abzugeben," 8 May 1940, Sekretariat Dr. Gajewski, A 1754, AIFM; Fengler, *Entwickelt und fixiert*, 60–61.

29. Street, *Colour Films in Britain*, 108. On the history of Soviet color film, see Miller, "Soviet cinema, 1929–41." See also Flueckiger, "Timeline of Historical Film Colors."

30. Gimbel, *Science, Technology, and Reparations*, 9.

31. Morin, *L'an zéro*, 23.

32. "Agfa Film Factory Wolfen," RG 331, b. 86, NARA.

33. Morin, *L'an zéro*, 47–48.

34. On the Red Army and rape in occupied Germany, see *Woman in Berlin*, and Grossmann, *Jews, Germans, and Allies*.

35. Hübner, *Die Region Wolfen*, 8.

36. On Allied evacuations of German scientists and technicians, see, e.g., Gimbel, *Science, Technology, and Reparations*, 31, and Maddrell, *Spying on Science*, 17–21.

37. Karlsch, "Capacity Losses, Reconstruction, and Unfinished Modernization," 383.

38. Gill and Löhnert, *Jüdische Chemiker*, 44. On the Nuremberg Race Laws, see, e.g., "Nuremberg Laws."

39. UA Wolfen, Sekretariat Werkleitung, No. 157, qtd. in Gill and Löhnert, *Jüdische Chemiker*, 45; UA Wolfen, BA No. 461, Materialsammlung Eggert, qtd. in Gill and Löhnert, *Jüdische Chemiker*, 46.

40. US Forces European Theater to Medical Supply Officer, 2 February 1946, RG 260, b. 40, NARA; Eggert to Bavarian Control Office (I.G. Farben), 5 February 1946, RG 260, b. 40, NARA.

41. Naimark, *Russians in Germany*, 167; Akinsha, "Stalin's Decrees and Soviet Trophy Brigades," 196.

42. *Woman in Berlin*, 80.

43. Karlsch and Wagner, *AGFA-ORWO-Story*, 123–24; "Intelligence Reports from Berlin, vol. II (November 1946 to January 1947)," FO 1031/60,

NA; DEFA Stiftung, "Rohfilm," accessed July 2, 2024, https://www.defa-stiftung.de/defa/geschichte/daten-und-fakten/filmwesen-der-ddr/11-technik/1170-rohfilm/.

44. Fengler, *Entwickelt und fixiert*, 98–100. On the factory's history, see Valérie Pozner, "Soviet Film's French Origins, 1926–1932," in Lovejoy, Dootson, and Duncan, *Film Stock*.

45. Naimark, *The Russians in Germany*, 169.

46. *Woman in Berlin*, 213, 222.

47. Rose to Orme, 3 December 1945, RG 40, b. 36, NARA.

48. Gimbel, *Science, Technology, and Reparations*, 106.

49. Aster, "On Microfilming," 10; "The Present Status of Equipment," 13; Cady, "Machine Tool."

50. See "René Dagron Operates the Pigeon Post."

51. Cady, "Machine Tool," 51.

52. Wilson, "Historical Perspective," 49.

53. Peiss, *Information Hunters*, 23.

54. Raney, "Through the Eye of the Needle," 242. On the documentation movement, see Farkas-Conn, *From Documentation to Information Science*; Hahn and Buckland, *Historical Studies*; and Peiss, *Information Hunters*.

55. Fayet-Scribe, "Cross-Fertilization," 187.

56. O'Reagan, *Taking Nazi Technology*, 155.

57. Fayet-Scribe, "Cross-Fertilization"; O'Reagan, *Taking Nazi Technology*.

58. Richards, "Aslib at War."

59. "New Microfile Cameras," 51–53. On Allied military photographic projects during the war, see also Wilder, "An American Darkroom."

60. Richards, "Aslib at War," 290.

61. Moholy, "Aslib Microfilm Service," 151–52.

62. Raney, "Through the Eye of the Needle," 235.

63. Bush was also instrumental in the development of the atomic bomb, and his career encapsulates what Jonathan Auerbach and Lisa Gitelman observe in the historical confluence of the bomb and Cold War fascination with microfilm. During this period, they write, "the micro of microfilm and the enormity of the bomb operated on related metaphorical planes, as cynosures of mystery and danger" (Auerbach and Gitelman, "Microfilm," 752).

64. O'Reagan, *Taking Nazi Technology*, 169. On the Rapid Selector, see also Buckland, "Emanuel Goldberg," 286–89.

65. Bush, "As We May Think."

66. United States Bureau of Naval Personnel, *Photographer's Mate*, 423–24; "The Portable Microfile Recordak," 183.

67. Ibid.; Wasson, *Everyday Movies*.
68. "FIAT Operating Procedure, Document Microfilming, Publications Board Program" (8 March 1946), pp. 3, 7, 12, 32, 30, Office of the Chief of Military History, Historical Manuscript File, History of the Field Information Agency, Technical (FIAT), vol. 2, Appendix No. 30, Circular No. 15, FIAT, Ops. Series 1, RG 319, NARA; Gimbel, *Science, Technology, and Reparations*, 62.
69. "FIAT Operating Procedure, Document Microfilming, Publications Board Program" (8 March 1946), p. 7, Office of the Chief of Military History, Historical Manuscript File, History of the Field Information Agency, Technical (FIAT), vol. 2, Appendix No. 30, Circular No. 15, FIAT, Ops. Series 1, RG 319, NARA.
70. Gunther S. Stent, *Nazis, Women, and Molecular Biology: Memoirs of a Lucky Self-Hater* (Kensington, CA: Briones Books, 1998), 43, qtd. in O'Reagan, *Taking Nazi Technology*, 34–35.
71. Hullinger, "World's Greatest Treasure Hunt."
72. O'Reagan, *Taking Nazi Technology*, 164.
73. Gimbel, *Science, Technology, and Reparations*, 135.
74. Peiss, *Information Hunters*, 60.
75. Dr. Bogrow and Wilcox to Mac, 28 December 1945, RG 40, b. 38, NARA.
76. To Ted Haertel, 4 January 1946, RG 40, b. 38, NARA.
77. "Further Investigation of AGFA Filmfabrik," A 3024, KA.
78. There were two waves of dismantling (March–May and October–December 1946). Fengler, *Entwickelt und Fixiert*, 100.
79. Naimark, *The Russians in Germany*, 219, 229.
80. Fengler, *Entwickelt und Fixiert*, 105. The transferred employees were given multi-year contracts in Shostka.
81. "Additional Information on Deportation of German Scientists and Technicians by Soviet Military Administration," 6 December 1946, RG 319, b. 17, NARA.
82. "Memorandum for the Officer in Charge. Subject: Operation 'Mesa'," 2 November 1946, RG 319, b. 31, f. XE 152328, NARA.
83. Special Intelligence Report No. 3 (1–31 January 1947), FO 1031/60, NA.
84. Fengler, *Entwickelt und Fixiert*, 101–4, 66; Karlsch and Wagner, *AGFA-ORWO-Story*, 123, 126.
85. Naimark, *The Russians in Germany*, 168; "Special Report on Agfa Photographic Activities," RG 242, NARA. Firms in the Soviet zone included Agfa, Deutsche Celluloid Fabrik, Schering-Kahlbaum, Zeiss-Ikon, Köbig, and

Haubold. (German Photographic Film Base Industry, Final Report, no. 262, A3024, KA.)

86. Kolbow, "Box Sells," 145.
87. Uhl, *Erinnerungen*, 270; Fengler, *Entwickelt und Fixiert*, 66–68.
88. Lord to Felber, 29 September 1947, RG 260, b. 40, NARA.
89. Uhl, *Erinnerungen*, 274.
90. Hullinger, "World's Greatest Treasure Hunt," 107; Naimark, *The Russians in Germany*, 168.
91. "Conference, present Major Prince, Mr. and Mrs. Uhl, Mr. Felber, February 23, 1946," RG 260, b. 40, NARA.
92. Morin, *L'an zéro*, 244.
93. Lawrik interview, BwA.
94. Karlsch and Schröter, *Strahlende Vergangenheit*, 2–4; Holloway, *Stalin and the Bomb*, 176. On Wismut's history, see Naimark, *The Russians in Germany*, especially 237–38; see also Murdock, "A Gulag" and "Selling Scientific Authority."
95. *Woman in Berlin*, 5.
96. On this idea, see Hecht, *Being Nuclear*, 115.

CHAPTER FOUR

1. Weather data from National Weather Service, www.weather.gov.
2. "Background info re: Nov. 1, 1951 hot snow," b. 160, f. 13, KHC; Eisenbud, "First Years," 566–67; "U of R Survey," 14.
3. Ibid.; Howden, "Snowfall 'Hot' Again," Eisenbud, *Environmental Odyssey*, 64–66; Eisenbud interview, 5.
4. "Nothing to Worry About."
5. Peters, Ralph W., and Harold W. Crouch, Eastman Kodak Company, "Control of Radioactive Contamination in the Pulp, Board, and Paper Industry," b. 160, f. 13, KHC.
6. Mitchell, "The Anthropocene Is Here"; Kaplan, "This Canadian Lake."
7. "A-Dust Forces Changes"; "Background info re Nov. 1, 1951 hot snow," 2 November 1951, b. 160, f. 13, KHC.
8. Eastman Kodak, *Journey*, 92.
9. Webb, "Fogging of Photographic Film," 376, 379.
10. Hennigan, "The Human Toll of Nuclear Testing."
11. Webb, "Fogging of Photographic Film," 375.
12. "Dean Says"; Eisenbud, *Environmental Odyssey*, 66–69.

13. "Summary of Relations Between the AEC and the Photographic Industry Regarding Radioactive Contamination from Atomic Weapons Tests, from January through December 1951," 17 January 1952, NV0072173, DOE/NNSA.

14. Dyer and Sicilia, *Labors of a Modern Hercules*, 205, 157.

15. "Hercules, 'The Legacy'," 19 October 1961, Records & Ephemera of Hercules Incorporated, box 5, SHI.

16. On the photographic equipment and processes at Alamogordo, see O'Brian, "Nuclear Flowers of Hell"; Kuran, *How to Photograph;* Broad, "The Bomb Chroniclers." See also Del Tredici, *At Work in the Fields of the Bomb.*

17. Kuran, *How to Photograph*, 14–16

18. Fay, "Cinema's Hot Chronology."

19. Mack and Brixner, "Mystery of the Black Spots," 26, 29, 58.

20. "Meeting on Atomic Bomb Tests," 23 January 1946, b. 160, f. 13, KHC.

21. Kuran, *How to Photograph*, 27; Kodak Research Laboratories, "Operation Crossroads: Data for Calculating Exposures," February 14, 1946, b. 200, f. 3, KHC.

22. "Meeting on Atomic Bomb Tests," 23 January 1946, b. 160, f. 13, KHC; Creager, *Life Atomic.*

23. "What Science Learned at Bikini," 75–77, 83. See also Pringle, "Manufactured Uncertainty."

24. Warren, "Conclusions," 88.

25. "The Rochester Story," NV0707326, DOE/NNSA; "Stafford L. Warren," accessed September 28, 2024, https://ahf.nuclearmuseum.org/ahf/profile/stafford-l-warren/.

26. Rust, "How the U.S. Betrayed the Marshall Islands."

27. Brown, *Plutopia*, 167.

28. See, e.g., Kuran, *How to Photograph*, 57; and Hamilton and O'Gorman, "Visualities of Strategic Vision." For a broader discussion of film and the US military, see Grieveson and Wasson, eds., *Cinema's Military-Industrial Complex.*

29. "Summary of Relations Between the AEC and the Photographic Industry Regarding Radioactive Contamination from Atomic Weapons Tests, from January through December 1951," 17 January 1952, NV0072173, DOE/NNSA.

30. "Dean Says."

31. "Summary, Medical Research Program, 1943–1946," RG 326, b. 25, f. MD-319.1, series 8505 (Formerly Classified Correspondence), NARA Atlanta. On the idea of a "tolerance dose," see, e.g., Brown, *Plutopia*, 65–66.

32. Tybout to Warren, April 17, 1944, RG 326, b. 38, f. MD-413.53-Photographic Machines and Equipment, series 8505 (Formerly Classified Correspondence), NARA Atlanta. Hart and Hale, *Fast Neutron Monitoring;*

Museum of Radiation and Radioactivity, "Oak Ridge National Laboratory Film Badge (ca. 1953–1958)," accessed September 10, 2023, https://orau.org/health-physics-museum/collection/dosimeters/film/ornl-1950s.html.

33. Pardue and Wollan, "Photographic Film as a Pocket Radiation Dosimeter"; Mitchell et al, "Method for Estimating," 195–207.

34. Eisenbud, *Environmental Odyssey*, 67.

35. Memo, December 23, 1949: Request of FBI re: Uranium, b. 160, f. 13, KHC; Phone conversation—between Mr. Robertson and Mr. Turner of Fulton Lewis, Jr.'s office. Conversation by Mr. Robertson, 14 December 1949, b. 160, f. 13, KHC.

36. Hornblum, *Invisible Harry Gold*, 94, 89; Smith, "Spy Worked at Y-12, Tennessee Eastman Co." On Slack, see also Weinstein and Vassiliev, *The Haunted Wood*.

37. Hornblum, *Invisible Harry Gold*, 95; FBI Case File, Alfred Dean Slack, 6/2–30/50, Colin Baxter Collection, Box 1, AA.

38. "United States of America vs. Alfred Dean Slack, Crim. No. 5593," p. 8, Colin Baxter Collection, AA; Baxter, *Secret History*, 139.

39. Hornblum, *Invisible Harry Gold*, 105–106.

40. FBI Case File, Alfred Dean Slack, 6/2–30/50, Colin Baxter Collection, Box 1, AA.

41. Slack to Taylor, 19 September 1950, Colin Baxter Collection, Box 1, AA.

42. Baxter, *Secret History*, 141.

43. "Tennessee Eastman Corporation," KC Manuscript Collection 49, box 2, folder 6, ACK.

44. Holloway, *Stalin and the Bomb*, 175–176.

45. Fengler, *Entwickelt und fixiert*, 102; Karlsch and Wagner, *AGFA-OWRO-Story*, 125.

46. "Richard Schubert A.G. Sehma, Annaberg," R8128/16022, BArch; Bräunig, *Rummelplatz*.

47. *Chronik der Wismut*, Teil 2, 1244, cited in Zeman and Karlsch, *Uranium Matters*, 164.

48. On labor at Wismut, see Murdock, "A Gulag in the Erzgebirge?"

49. Roeling, "Arbeiter im Uranbergbau," 99.

50. Holloway, *Stalin and the Bomb*, 177.

51. Zeman and Karlsch, *Uranium Matters*, 169.

52. Eisenbud to Bugher, May 28, 1954, NV0405033, DOE/NNSA. On health concerns about fallout elsewhere in the world (in this case, West Germany), see Murdock, "Public Health in a Radioactive Age."

53. Khlopkov and Chekina, "Governing Uranium in Russia."

54. Churchill and LaDuke, "Native America." Hiromitsu Toyosaki offers a global view of the communities harmed by nuclear testing—from Nevada to Kazakhstan and Novaya Zemlya, to the South Pacific and Australia, the Sahara and the Xinjiang Uighur Autonomous Region—in "Hidden and Forgotten Hibakusha," in O'Brian, ed., *Camera Atomica*, 151–163.

55. Yusoff, *A Billion Black Anthropocenes;* Wynter, "Unsettling the Coloniality of Being."

56. "Creative Chemistry," b. 39, f. 7, KHC; Waite, "Eastman Kodak Works at Kingsport, Tenn."

57. *Eastman Chemical Company,* 26, SHI.

58. Stokes, *Opting for Oil,* 3.

59. LeMenager, *Living Oil,* 67.

60. *Eastman Chemical Company,* 18, 24–26, SHI.

61. Fordyce, "Improved Safety Motion Picture Film Support"; "Kodak Wins 'Oscar'" See also Enticknap, "Film Industry's Conversion," 208.

62. *Eastman Chemical Company,* 26, SHI.

63. "The History of Longview," *Now Longview,* accessed October 9, 2023, https://nowlongview.com/history-of-longview/.

64. "Transportation Facilities, Nearby Raw Materials," 6; Rister, *Oil!,* 313.

65. "'Big Inch' and 'Little Inch'," 32.

66. David C. Hull, for instance, who had been instrumental to work at both Holston and Y-12, became Texas Eastman's general manager. ("Creative Chemistry," b. 39, f. 7, KHC).

67. "LONGVIEW—where T.E.C. Will Build New Plant," 5.

68. "Tall Tales from Texas," *TEC News,* January 18, 1951; "Texas Eastman News," *TEC News,* April 19, 1951.

69. "The Texas Eastman Company," b. 39, f. 7, KHC.

70. *A Glimpse of Texas Eastman,* SHI.

71. "Manufacture of Perlon and Experiments with Yellow Cross at Agfa-Wolfen," accessed September 12, 2024, https://www.cia.gov/readingroom/document/cia-rdp82-00457r011700110006-8.

72. *Eastman Chemical Company,* 28, SHI.

73. Spitz, *Petrochemicals,* 271–281. On nylon and its introduction during the war years, see Ndiaye, *Nylon and Bombs.*

74. In 1950, Kodak began researching synthetic film base technologies. DuPont licensed Kodak to use its polyester process for film base, and Kodak began manufacturing PET film base at the end of the 1950s, beginning with X-ray film. (Shanebrook, *Making KODAK Film,* 95; *Eastman Chemical Company,* 30, SHI; Spitz, *Petrochemicals,* 286.)

75. Letter from J. Massis to P. Braunberger, 16 January 1957 (Archives des Films du Jeudi), qtd. in Buiré, "Genese," 4.
76. See, e.g., Ungar, "Scenes in a Library," Dimendberg, "These Are Not Exercises in Style," and Wilson, *Alain Resnais*.
77. Dimendberg, "'These Are Not Exercises in Style,'" 85.
78. "The Texas Eastman Company," b. 39, f. 7, KHC.
79. Lippit, *Atomic Light*, 4.
80. On X-rays, see Cartwright, *Screening the Body*.
81. Levi, *Periodic Table*, 200–10.
82. Shanebrook, *Making KODAK Film*, 95; *Eastman Chemical Company*, 30, SHI.
83. "Extract from the report of the Kontinentale Treuhandgesellschaft m.b.H. Düsseldorf, dated August 20, 1947 on the audit of the balance-sheet of the film factory Berlin-Köpenick as of December 31, 1945," b. 58, f. 2, KHC; "Sworn statement by Erich Haiber," June 1964, b. 58, f. 2, KHC; "Bericht uber die Besprechungen bei der Filmfabrik Kodak am 1. und 2. August 1950 wegen Errechnung des ausländischen Kapitalanteils," DG2/19562, BArch.
84. "Jahresbericht 1953 der Kodak A.G. Filmfabrik Köpenick," DF4/56348, BArch.
85. See Wright, *Iron Curtain*, 66–73, and Vatulescu, *Reading the Archival Revolution*, 157–58.
86. "Background info re: Nov. 1, 1951 hot snow," b. 160, f. 13.
87. "Nothing to Worry About."
88. In October 1997, the AEC's agreement with the photographic industry, coupled with its denial of fallout's danger to humans, was the subject of a heated hearing at the US Senate, where Iowa senator Tom Harkin put it bluntly: "The Government protected rolls of film, but not the lives of our kids." (US Congress, Senate, Committee, *Radioactive Fallout*.) See also Wald, "U.S. Alerted Photo Film Makers."

CHAPTER FIVE

1. Reynolds, "Nuclear Plant May End Ashford's Pastoral Era."
2. On meteorology and the related field of nuclear weapons research, see Edwards, "Entangled Histories."
3. Fordyce to McCool, 18 February 1963, b. 160, f. 13, KHC.
4. Statement by Dr. Charles R. Fordyce, b. 160, f. 13, KHC.
5. "Wesley Lewis Named NFS Plant Manager."

6. "Charles Fordyce Retires," 370.

7. On the evolution of public perceptions of radiation and fallout, see Creager, *Life Atomic*.

8. Press release, US Department of Health, Education, and Welfare, 6 September 1961, b. 160, f. 13, KHC.

9. Reynolds, "Nuclear Plant May End Ashford's Pastoral Era."

10. Carson, *Silent Spring*, 6. On Rachel Carson and fallout, see Solnit, *Savage Dreams*; Lutts, "Chemical Fallout"; and Lear, "Rachel Carson's 'Silent Spring.'"

11. Warren interview, 3.

12. Hayes, "Eastman Chemical Co."; Kiss, "Day Kingsport Wept." See also the Archives of the City of Kingsport's posts on the explosion, accessed December 18, 2024: https://kingsportarchives.wordpress.com/2010/10/04/the-day-kingsport-wept-eastman-explosion-october-4-1960/; https://kingsportarchives.wordpress.com/2010/10/02/tennessee-eastman-explosion-october-4-1960/.

13. Feser, "Reproducing Photochemical Life." On the environmental and human toll of chemicals in Rochester and at Kodak Park, see also Miller, "Environmental Ruin of Eastman Kodak," and the website "Kodak's Toxic Colors," accessed September 12, 2024, https://kodakstoxiccolors.wordpress.com/.

14. Foderaro, "Pollution by Kodak Brings Sense of Betrayal."

15. Impressions of the factory's late-socialist history are in artist Tobias Zielony's "Wolfen."

16. "Aktennotiz: Arbeitseinsatz," 1 April 1942, R8128/21163, Barch.

17. ARD Fernsehen, Sendung "Kontraste" am 27.9.1988, Abteilung Merseburg, M Rat des Bezirkes Halle, 4. Abl. Nr. 6572, Bl. 197, LSA; Argumentationsmaterial zur Sendung "Kontraste" am 27.09.1988, Abteilung Merseburg, M Rat des Bezirkes Halle, 4. Abl. Nr. 6572, Bl. 197, LSA. This discussion of *Bitterness* is adapted from Lovejoy and Trumpener, "Sad and Bitter Landscapes."

18. "Holston Army Ammunition Plant," b. 160, f. 8, KHC; "Holston Supplies Many Vital Defense Items."

19. Richard Lawson, "Holston Defense gets a Shorter Fuse," *The Business Journal*, May 1, 1996, 16–18, Colin Baxter Collection, Box 1, AA; Center for Land Use Interpretation, "Holston Army Ammunition Plant," accessed July 2, 2024, https://clui.org/ludb/site/holston-army-ammunition-plant.

20. James H. Sterner, M.D., Medical Director, b. 160, f. 13, KHC.

21. Vaughn to Brereton, 4 May 1964, b. 160, f. 13, KHC.

22. US EPA, OECA, "Case Summary: Bankruptcy Settlements."

23. "Eastman Kodak Now Has 70 Subsidiaries."

24. "This is Eastman Gel . . .," b. 39, f. 7, KHC.

25. Manion, "Local 21's Quest for a Moral Economy," 2, 34.

26. Jacoby, *Modern Manors*, 63; "A Handbook for the Men and Women of Eastman Gelatine Corporation, Peabody, Massachusetts, 1945," b. 97, f. 2, KHC.

27. "This is Eastman Gel...," b. 97, f. 2, KHC.

28. In 1921, Kodak had co-founded the Odin Gelatine Works in Eberbach, Germany, creating a self-contained company town that echoed Eastman's efforts in Rochester and Kingsport. The Odin works closed in 1940. ("Commentary on Dry Gelatine Raw Stocks," b. 97, f. 2, KHC.)

29. Mees, "Kodak Research Laboratories," 468; Shanebrook, *Making KODAK Film*, 163; Shukin, *Animal Capital*.

30. "Commentary on Dry Gelatine Raw Stocks," b. 97, f. 2, KHC.

31. "This is Eastman Gel," b. 97, f. 2, KHC.

32. Klein, "Who Knew Kodak Would Keep So Many Skeletons in its Closet?"

33. Manion, "Local 21's Quest for a Moral Economy," p. 34.

34. Forman, "Stories of Noxious Odors Fill Lawsuit against Rousselot."

35. Bigelow, "The Great Peabody Flood of 1954"; Massachusetts Department of Public Health, "An Investigation into Pancreatic Cancer Mortality"; Breathe Clean North Shore, "Rousselot's Plant Emits 21,000 Metric Tons MORE CO_2 than the Waters River Substation," December 29, 2023, https://breathecleannorthshore.org/2023/12/29/rousselots-plant-emits-38000-metric-tons-of-co2-more-than-the-waters-river-substation/.

36. U.S. Department of Energy Legacy Management, "Fact Sheet: Beverly, Massachusetts Site," accessed September 12, 2024, https://www.energy.gov/lm/beverly-massachusetts-site; Ventron Corporation SEC Petition Evaluation Report," 52.

37. Leighton, "Compensation Increasing for Former Manhattan Project Workers in Beverly"; *SEC Petition Evaluation Report*, 27–30.

EPILOGUE

1. "Filmotec—Kompetenz in schwarz und weiss," accessed September 12, 2024, https://filmotec.de/; "A Brief History of Ferrania," accessed September 12, 2024, https://www.filmferrania.it/pages/about; News release, June 3, 1964, f. 10, 3M Historical Corporate Records, MHS.

2. Quentin Tarantino, Tom Cruise, J. J. Abrams, P. T. Anderson, Ken Loach, Christopher Nolan, Martin Scorsese, Zach Snyder, and James Gray are

all rumored to only shoot or act on film. (Rizov, "24 Films [More or Less] Shot on 35mm Released in 2018.")

3. See Starosielski, *Media Hot and Cold,* and Crawford, *Atlas of AI.* See also Parikka, *A Geology of Media;* Cubitt, *Finite Media;* Gabrys, *Digital Rubbish;* Peters, *The Marvelous Clouds;* Taffel, "Towards an Ethical Electronics?"

4. Zahiga, "Uranium, Cobalt, Copper"; Searcey et al., "A Power Struggle Over Cobalt."

5. O'Carroll, "The East German Town."

6. "Deponie Grube Johannes—ein Projekt der MDSE," accessed September 12, 2024, https://grubejohannes.mdse.de/.

7. "Wismut GmbH—Sanierung, Wasserreinigung, Grube, Umweltüberwachung," accessed September 12, 2024, https://www.wismut.de/de/sanierung_aufgaben.php.

8. *Femmes oubliées,* 90. On Soviet reprisals against returnees from the West, see Judt, *Postwar,* 30.

9. Eastman Chemical, "Circularity | Sustainability," accessed September 15, 2024, https://www.eastman.com/en/sustainability/environmental/circularity.

10. Keeling, "Eastman Execs See Lucrative Future"; Keeling, "National Resources Defense Council"; Winters and Sanders, "'Plastics Are Awesome.'"

11. Levi, *Periodic Table,* 142.

12. Ibid., 232.

ACKNOWLEDGEMENTS

1. Reich, "Trump Has No Problem."

BIBLIOGRAPHY

INTERVIEWS

Eisenbud, Merril. Interview by J. Newell Stannard, July 9, 1979. NV0716552, transcript. DOE/NNSA Nuclear Testing Archive.

Ellingson, Robert. Interview, September 22, 2005. *Voices of the Manhattan Project,* digital audio and transcript. Washington, DC: Atomic Heritage Foundation. https://ahf.nuclearmuseum.org/voices/oral-histories/robert-ellingsons-interview/.

Huddleston, Ruth. Interview by Nathanial Weisenberg, April 25, 2018. *Voices of the Manhattan Project,* digital video and transcript. Washington, DC: Atomic Heritage Foundation. https://ahf.nuclearmuseum.org/voices/oral-histories/ruth-huddlestons-interview/.

Lawrik, Oleksandra. Interview by Dr. Irmgard Seidel, April 12, 1988. Weimar, Germany: Archive of the Buchenwald Memorial.

Othmer, Donald F. Interview by James J. Bohning. Oral History #0034, digital audio and transcript. Philadelphia: Chemical Heritage Foundation. https://digital.sciencehistory.org/works/6969z1940.

Warren, Stafford. Interview by J. Newell Stannard, February 7, 1979. NV07050146, transcript. DOE/NNSA Nuclear Testing Archive.

Whitman, Lucille. Interview, September 22, 2005. *Voices of the Manhattan Project,* digital video and transcript. Washington, DC: Atomic Heritage Foundation. https://ahf.nuclearmuseum.org/voices/oral-histories/lucille-whitmans-interview/.

Wilcox, William J., Jr. Interview, June 17, 2006. *Voices of the Manhattan Project,* digital video and transcript. Washington, DC: Atomic Heritage Foundation. https://ahf.nuclearmuseum.org/voices/oral-histories/william-j-wilcox-jrs-interview-2006/.

PUBLISHED PRIMARY SOURCES

Diaries, Memoirs, Fiction, and Nonfiction

Bräunig, Werner. *Rummelplatz*. Translated by Samuel P. Willcocks. London: Seagull Books, 2016.
Carson, Rachel. *Silent Spring*. Boston: Houghton Mifflin, 1962.
Dos Passos, John. *Tour of Duty*. Boston: Houghton Mifflin, 1946.
Eisenbud, Merril. *An Environmental Odyssey: People, Pollution, and Politics in the Life of a Practical Scientist*. Seattle: University of Washington Press, 1990.
Latouche, John, and André Cauvin. *Congo*. New York: Willow, White, and Co., 1945.
Levi, Primo. *The Periodic Table*. Translated by Raymond Rosenthal. Reissue edition. New York: Schocken, 1995.
———. *Survival in Auschwitz: The Nazi Assault on Humanity*. Translated by Stuart Woolf. New York: Simon and Schuster, 1996.
Levin, Meyer. *In Search: An Autobiography*. New York: Horizon Press, 1950.
Morin, Edgar. *L'An zéro de l'Allemagne*. Paris: Éditions de la Cité Universelle, 1946.
Uhl, Bruno. *Erinnerungen*. Privatdruck, 1970.
Wentzel, Fritz. *Memoirs of a Photochemist*. Edited by Louis Walton Sipley. Philadelphia: American Museum of Photography, 1960.
A Woman in Berlin: Eight Weeks in the Conquered City. Translated by Philip Boehm. New York: Picador/Henry Holt, 2006.

Government, Corporate, Institutional, and Scientific Documents and Publications

Army Corps of Engineers. *Manhattan District History*, book V, vol. 6, *Electromagnetic Project: Operation*. 1948. https://www.osti.gov/opennet/manhattan_district.
Army Corps of Engineers. *Manhattan District History*, book VII, vol. 1, *Feed Materials, Special Procurement, and Geographical Exploration: Feed Materials and Special Procurement*. 1948. https://www.osti.gov/opennet/manhattan_district.
Blancke, Harold. *Celanese Corporation of America, the Founders and the Early Years*. New York: Newcomen Society in North America, 1952.
Brooklyn Museum Department of Industrial Art. *A Brooklyn Museum Handbook Compiled for the Industrial Art Exhibition of Rayon and Synthetic Yarns*. New York: J. B. Watkins, 1936.

"Celanese Is Not Rayon: A Reply to Bulletin No. 21 of the Better Business Bureau of New York City, Inc." September 26, 1928, in Foster, *The Cleaning and Dyeing of Celanese and Rayon.*

Dominik, Hans. *Vistra, das weiße Gold Deutschlands: die Geschichte einer weltbewegenden Erfindung.* Leipzig: Koehler und Amelang, 1936.

Eastman Chemical Company. *Eastman Chemical Company: Years of Glory, Times of Change, 1920–1990.* Kingsport, TN: Eastman Chemical Company, 1991.

Eastman Kodak Company. *Journey: 75 Years of Kodak Research.* Rochester, NY: Eastman Kodak Company, 1989.

———. *F. W. Lovejoy: The Story of a Practical Idealist.* Rochester, NY: Eastman Kodak, 1947.

Foster, L. E., ed. *The Cleaning and Dyeing of Celanese and Rayon.* York, NE: L. E. Foster, 1929.

Furnas, C. C. *The Storehouse of Civilization.* New York: Teachers' College, 1939.

Hart, R. S., and J. P. Hale, Jr. *Fast Neutron Monitoring with NTA Film Packets.* Canoga Park, CA: Atomics International, 1956.

Hessel, Mary Stanley, W. J. Murphy, Frederick Adam Hessel, and Harold J. Wasson. *Strategic Materials in Hemisphere Defense.* New York: Hastings House, 1942.

International Trade in Certain Raw Materials and Foodstuffs by Countries of Origin and Consumption: Summary of Proceedings. Geneva: League of Nations, 1936.

Kingsport: City of Industries, Schools, Churches, and Homes. Rotary Club of Kingsport, Tennessee, 1937.

Long, Howard. *Kingsport: A Romance of Industry.* Johnson City, TN: Overmountain Press, 1928.

Lübke, Anton. *Das deutsche Rohstoffwünder: Wandlungen der deutschen Rohstoffwirtschaft.* Stuttgart: Forkel, 1938.

Massachusetts Department of Public Health. "An Investigation into Pancreatic Cancer Mortality." Boston: Massachusetts Department of Public Health, 1984.

Nurnberg Military Tribunals: Indictments. Nuremberg: Office of Military Government for Germany (US), 1946.

Schwarz, E. W. K., and Herbert R. Mauersberger, eds. *Rayon and Synthetic Yarn Handbook: A Practical Reference Book for the Rayon Yarn Producer, Technician, Processor, Salesman, Engineer, Economist, and Student.* New York: Rayon Publishing Company, 1934.

SEC Petition Evaluation Report, Petition SEC-00198. Washington, DC: National Institute for Occupational Safety and Health, 2012.

U.S. Congress. Senate. Subcommittee of the Committee on Appropriations. *Radioactive Fallout from Nuclear Testing at Nevada Test Site,* 1950–1960. 105th Cong., 1st sess., October 1, 1997.

Ungewitter, Claus. *Science and Salvage, from the German "Verwertung des Wertlosen."* Translated by L. A. Ferney and G. Haim. London: Crosby, Lockwood, and Son, 1944.

United States Bureau of Naval Personnel. *Photographer's Mate 3 & 2*. Washington, DC: US Government Printing Office, 1966.

United States Environmental Protection Agency, OECA. "Case Summary: Bankruptcy Settlements Reached with the Eastman Kodak Company Worth $49 Million." May 13, 2014. https://www.epa.gov/enforcement/case-summary-bankruptcy-settlements-reached-eastman-kodak-company-worth-49-million.

Zischka, Anton. *Wissenschaft bricht Monopole*. Leipzig: Wilhelm Goldmann Verlag, 1936.

PERIOD NEWSPAPER, MAGAZINE, AND JOURNAL ARTICLES

"A-Dust Forces Changes in Kodak Paper Mills." *Democrat and Chronicle* (Rochester, NY), Nov. 6, 1951.

Advertisement for Agfa Film. *Moving Picture World* 11, no. 7 (February 17, 1912): 543.

Amor, A. E. "The Manufacture of Motion Picture Film." Reprinted from *The Photographic Journal,* vol. LXXVIII (July 1938): 459–73.

Aster, A. K. "On Microfilming." *Photo Technique,* September 1939.

"Brulatour Files Brief for Film Duty; Belgian and German Films are Feared." *Moving Picture World* 49, no. 1 (March 5, 1921): 35.

Bush, Vannevar. "As We May Think." *The Atlantic,* July 1945.

"The Camphor Industry in Formosa: An Important Japanese Monopoly." *Scientific American Supplements,* November 1, 1913.

"Charles Fordyce Retires." *Journal of the SMPTE* 78, no. 78 (May 1969): 370.

Conrad, Joseph. "Geography and Some Explorers." *National Geographic Magazine* 45 no. 3 (1924): 239–74.

"Dean Says Atom Blasts Hurt Rochester Film, Nothing Else." *Evening Star* (Washington, DC), May 13, 1952.

"Dr. Crile Sees Clinic He Built Made Shambles." *The Columbus Dispatch* (Columbus, OH), May 16, 1929.

"Eastman Expansion Was Great During Last Year." *The Kingsport Times* (Kingsport, TN), March 30, 1930.

Eastman Kodak Company, "All That Flickers Isn't Gold: How Motion Picture Film is Manufactured." *Photoplay* XIV, no. 2 (July 1918).

"Eastman Kodak Now Has 70 Subsidiaries." *Wall Street Journal,* August 22, 1928.

Foderaro, Lisa W. "Pollution By Kodak Brings Sense of Betrayal: Company Town Feels Betrayed by Kodak Pollution." *The New York Times,* March 8, 1989.

Fordyce, Charles R. "Improved Safety Motion Picture Film Support." *Journal of the Society of Motion Picture Engineers* 51 (October 1948): 331–50.

"Frank W. Lovejoy, Head of Kodak, Succumbs at 73." *Democrat and Chronicle* (Rochester, NY), September 17, 1945.

Garett, Garet. "Roads Going South." *Saturday Evening Post,* September 3, 1938.

Hackett, Charles M. "Coal Tar Began It: Vast Increase in U.S. Organic Chemicals Industry." *Scientific American,* September 1940.

"Holston Supplies Many Vital Defense Items for A.E.C., N.A.S.A., Military." *TEC News,* January 18, 1962.

Howden, Norman M. "Snowfall 'Hot' Again, UR Atom Men Report." *Democrat and Chronicle* (Rochester, NY), November 2, 1951.

Hullinger, Edwin Ware. "World's Greatest Treasure Hunt." *Nation's Business,* October 1945.

"Industry Needs Tariff to Maintain Living Standard Set, Mr. Eastman Argues." *Democrat and Chronicle* (Rochester, NY), October 31, 1926.

"Japanese Celluloid." *The Times of India,* January 30, 1920.

Kirkpatrick, Sidney D. "Building an Integrated Industry in Times of Depression." *Chemical & Metallurgical Engineering* 40 no. 5 (1933): 236–40.

"Kodak Offering to Net $30,800,000." *Wall Street Journal,* August 4, 1929.

"Kodak Wins 'Oscar' for Safety Film." *TEC News,* April 6, 1950.

"Longview—Where T.E.C. Will Build New Plant." *TEC News,* January 26, 1950.

Mack, Julian Ellis, and Berlyn Brixner. "The Mystery of the Black Spots." *US Camera* (November 1945): 26, 29, 58.

Mees, C. E. Kenneth. "The Kodak Research Laboratories." *Proceedings of the Royal Society of London, Series A: Mathematical and Physical Sciences* 192, no. 1031 (March 18, 1948): 465–79.

Moholy, Lucia. "The Aslib Microfilm Service: The Story of its Wartime Activities." *Journal of Documentation* 2, no. 3 (April 1946): 147–73.

———. "A Few Remarks on Documentary Reproduction in General and Microfilm in Particular." *Journal of Documentation* 1, no. 1 (June 1945): 31–40.

"Names Fatal Gases in Cleveland Clinic." *The New York Times,* June 16, 1929.

"New Microfile Cameras Installed." *Journal of Documentary Reproduction* 3, no. 1 (March 1940): 53.

"Nothing to Worry About: A-Blasts to Send Radioactive Rain." *Democrat and Chronicle* (Rochester, NY), March 12, 1953.

Pardue, L. A., N. Goldstein, and E. O. Wollan. "Photographic Film as a Pocket Radiation Dosimeter." In *Metallurgical Laboratory Report CH*-1553. Oak Ridge, TN: Technical Operations Division, Oak Ridge Directed Operations, 1944.

"The Portable Microfile Recordak, Model E." *Journal of Documentary Reproduction* 4, no. 3 (March 1941): 183–87.

"The Present Status of Equipment and Supplies for Microphotography." *Journal of Documentary Reproduction* 1, no. 3 (Summer 1938): 4–56.

Raney, M. L. "Through the Eye of the Needle." *Journal of Documentary Reproduction* 1, no. 3 (Summer 1938): 233–42.

Reynolds, Marian. "Nuclear Plant May End Ashford's Pastoral Era." *Olean Times Herald* (Olean, NY), June 5, 1963.

"Safety Film Plant to E-T: Product Would Avert X-Ray Yellow Death Disaster such as at Cleveland." *Knoxville News-Sentinel,* June 21, 1929.

Shuman, Isaac. "Kingsport: An Unusual City, Built to Make Business for a Railroad: How Vision Backed by Science is Creating a Model City in the Tennessee Mountains." *American City* 22, no. 5 (May 1920): 471–73.

Smith, Frederick James. "The Man Behind the Film—George Eastman." *Motion Picture Magazine,* September 1918.

"Steady Progress of American Dye Industry." *Manufacturers Record,* December 17, 1925.

"Stress Value of Ventilation as Means of Reducing Fire Hazards." *Motion Picture News* 39, no. 22 (June 1, 1929): 1848.

"Tall Tales from Texas." *TEC News,* January 18, 1951.

Taussig, F. W., and H. D. White. "Rayon and the Tariff: The Nurture of an Industrial Prodigy." *The Quarterly Journal of Economics* 45, no. 4 (August 1931): 588–621.

"Tennessee Eastman Corp. Will Build New Plant." *The Kingsport Times* (Kingsport, TN), June 19, 1929.

"Texas Eastman News." *TEC News,* April 19, 1951.

"Transportation Facilities, Nearby Raw Materials Led to Longview's Selection." *TEC News,* January 26, 1950.

"U of R Survey Parties Test Snow for Radioactivity in 100-Mile Area." *Democrat and Chronicle* (Rochester, NY), February 3, 1951.

"US Army Acquires 56,200 Acres in E-T for Training Center." *Knoxville Journal,* October 7, 1942.

Waite, Andrew. "Eastman Kodak Works at Kingsport, Tenn." *The Kingsport Times* (Kingsport, TN), April 9, 1951.
Walker, W. H. "Gas Warfare and the Development of Edgewood Arsenal." *Manufacturers Record,* April 10, 1919, 96.
Warren, Stafford L. "Conclusions: Tests Proved Irresistible Spread of Radioactivity." *Life* 23, no. 6 (August 11, 1947): 86–88.
Webb, J. H. "The Fogging of Photographic Film by Radioactive Contaminants in Cardboard Packaging Materials." *Physical Review (U.S.) Superseded in Part by Phys. Rev. A, Phys. Rev. B: Solid State, Phys. Rev. C, and Phys. Rev. D* 76, no. 3 (1949): 375–80.
Weinberg, Alvin M. "Impact of Large-Scale Science on the United States." *Science* 134, no. 3473 (July 21, 1961): 161–64.
"Wesley Lewis Named NFS Plant Manager." *Ellicottville Post,* March 6, 1963.
"What Science Learned at Bikini: Latest Report on the Results." *Life* 23, no. 6 (August 11, 1947): 74–85.
"Work on New Eastman Unit to Begin Next Week." *The Kingsport Times* (Kingsport, TN), February 22, 1931.

SECONDARY SOURCES

"A Heroic and Well-Loved Friend and Colleague Passes On." *For Your Information* (Y-12 National Security Complex) 6, no. 1 (April 1994): 1–53.
Acland, Charles R., and Haidee Wasson, eds. *Useful Cinema.* Durham, NC: Duke University Press, 2011.
Aftalion, Fred. *A History of the International Chemical Industry.* Philadelphia: University of Pennsylvania Press, 1991.
Akinsha, Konstantin. "Stalin's Decrees and Soviet Trophy Brigades: Compensation, Restitution in Kind, or 'Trophies' of War?" *International Journal of Cultural Property* 17, no. 2 (May 2010): 195–216.
Andrew, Dudley. "The Post-War Struggle for Colour." In *The Cinematic Apparatus,* edited by Teresa de Laurentis and Stephen Heath. New York: St. Martin's, 1980.
Angus, Siobhan. *Camera Geologica: An Elemental History of Photography.* Durham, NC: Duke University Press, 2024.
———. "The Eastman Kodak Silver Vault." In *Mining Photography: The Ecological Impact of Image Production,* edited by Boaz Levin, Esther Ruelfs, and Tulga Beyerle. Leipzig: Spector Books, 2022.

Arabindan-Kesson, Anna. *Black Bodies, White Gold: Art, Cotton, and Commerce in the Atlantic World*. Durham, NC: Duke University Press, 2021.

Arsenault, Kerri. *Mill Town: Reckoning with What Remains*. New York: St. Martin's Griffin, 2021.

Auerbach, Jonathan, and Lisa Gitelman. "Microfilm, Containment, and the Cold War." *American Literary History* 19, no. 3 (Autumn 2007): 745–68.

Baranowski, Shelley. *Nazi Empire: German Colonialism and Imperialism from Bismarck to Hitler*. Cambridge, UK: Cambridge University Press, 2010.

Baxter, Colin F. *The Secret History of RDX: The Super-Explosive that Helped Win World War II*. Lexington: University Press of Kentucky, 2018.

Beckert, Sven. "American Danger: United States Empire, Eurafrica, and the Territorialization of Industrial Capitalism, 1870–1950." *American Historical Review* 122, no. 4 (October 2017): 1137–70.

———. *Empire of Cotton: A Global History*. New York: Alfred A. Knopf, 2014.

Benz, Wolfgang, and Barbara Distel, eds. *Sachsenhausen, Buchenwald*. Vol. 3 of *Der Ort des Terrors: Geschichte der nationalsozialistischen Konzentrationslager*, edited by Benz and Distel. Munich: C. H. Beck, 2005.

Bibliothèque municipale de Lyon. "Une fabrique de l'innovation: Trois siècles de révolutions industrielles en Rhône-Alpes." Accessed July 2, 2024. https://www.bm-lyon.fr/expositions-en-ligne/une-fabrique-de-l-innovation/.

"'Big Inch' and 'Little Inch' Pipelines: 1942–1944." *Energy Markets Supplement: 100 Most Influential People*, 32. Houston, TX: Energy Markets, 2000.

Bigelow, Nora. "The Great Peabody Flood of 1954." Peabody Historical Society, https://peabodyhistorical.org/2023/05/the-great-peabody-flood-of-1954/.

Binnicker, Margaret D. "Carolina, Clinchfield and Ohio Railway." *Tennessee Encyclopedia*. Accessed July 2, 2024. http://tennesseeencyclopedia.net/entries/carolina-clinchfield-and-ohio-railway/.

Black, Megan. *The Global Interior: Mineral Frontiers and American Power*. Cambridge, MA: Harvard University Press, 2018.

———. "Interior's Exterior: The State, Mining Companies, and Resource Ideologies in the Point Four Program." *Diplomatic History* 40, no. 1 (January 2016): 81–110.

Blanc, Paul David. *Fake Silk: The Lethal History of Viscose Rayon*. New Haven, CT: Yale University Press, 2016.

Blume, Lesley. *Fallout: The Hiroshima Cover-Up and the Reporter Who Revealed It to the World*. New York: Simon & Schuster, 2021.

Bode, Herbert. *Entwicklung des Chemiefaserbereichs der Filmfabrik Wolfen von den Anfängen bis 1935*. Wolfen: Komm. für Betriebsgeschichte d. Zentralen Parteiltg. d. VEB Filmfabrik Wolfen, 1986.

Bode, Herbert, and Manfred Gill. *Zwangsarbeiter in der Filmfabrik Wolfen 1939–1945: Ihre ökonomisch-soziale Lage und Unterbringung dargestellt mit postalischen Belegen*. Wolfen: Kommission für Betriebsgeschichte der Zentralen Parteileitung und Betriebsarchiv des VEB Filmfabrik Wolfen, Stammbetrieb des VEB Fotochemisches Kombinat Wolfen, 1982.

Bozak, Nadia. *The Cinematic Footprint: Lights, Camera, Natural Resources*. New Brunswick, NJ: Rutgers University Press, 2012.

Bravo, Monica. "Mercury Rising: US-Mexican Conflict in Alexander Edouart's Blessing of the Enrequita Mine." *Art History* 46, no. 3 (June 2023): 540–67.

Brayer, Elizabeth. *George Eastman: A Biography*. Baltimore, MD: Johns Hopkins University Press, 1996.

"A Brief History of Chemical War." *Science History Institute*, May 11, 2015. https://www.sciencehistory.org/distillations/a-brief-history-of-chemical-war.

Broad, William. "The Bomb Chroniclers." *The New York Times*, September 13, 2010.

Brown, Kate. *Plutopia: Nuclear Families, Atomic Cities, and the Great Soviet and American Plutonium Disasters*. Oxford: Oxford University Press, 2013.

Buckland, Michael K. "Emanuel Goldberg, Electronic Document Retrieval, and Vannevar Bush's Memex." *Journal of the American Society for Information Science* 43, no. 4 (1992): 284–94.

Buiré, Jean-François. "Genese: En partant de l'objet retrouvons ses aïeux." In *Lycéens au cinéma*. Paris: CNC, 2003.

Bustamante, Carlos. "AGFA, Kullmann, Singer & Co. and Early Cine-Film Stock." *Film History* 20, no. 1 (2008): 59–76.

Cady, Susan A. "Machine Tool of Management: A History of Microfilm Technology." PhD diss., Lehigh University, 1994.

"Calendar of Film Fires." In Smither and Surowiec, *This Film Is Dangerous*.

Cartwright, Lisa. *Screening the Body: Tracing Medicine's Visual Culture*. Minneapolis: University of Minnesota Press, 1995.

Castro, Teresa, Brenda Lynn Edgar, and Estelle Sohier, eds. "Ecological Histories of Photography." Special issue, *Transbordeur* 8 (2024).

Césaire, Aimé. *Discours sur le colonialisme*. Paris: Présence africaine, 1955.

Chandler, Alfred D., Jr. *Shaping the Industrial Century: The Remarkable Story of the Evolution of the Modern Chemical and Pharmaceutical Industries*. Cambridge, MA: Harvard University Press, 2005.

Cherchi Usai, Paolo. *Silent Cinema: A Guide to Study, Research, and Curatorship*, 3rd ed. London: BFI, 2019.

Coleman, Kevin P., and Daniel James, eds. *Capitalism and the Camera: Essays on Photography and Extraction*. London: Verso, 2021.

Collins, Douglas. *The Story of Kodak*. New York: H. N. Abrams, 1990.

Crawford, Kate. *The Atlas of AI: Power, Politics, and the Planetary Costs of Artificial Intelligence*. New Haven, CT: Yale University Press, 2021.

Creager, Angela N. *Life Atomic: A History of Radioisotopes in Science and Medicine*. Chicago: The University of Chicago Press, 2013.

Cubitt, Sean. *Finite Media: Environmental Implications of Digital Technologies*. Durham, NC: Duke University Press, 2017.

Dahlquist, Marina, and Patrick Vonderau. *Petrocinema: Sponsored Film and the Oil Industry*. New York: Bloomsbury Academic and Professional, 2021.

Davay, Paul. *Cinéma de Belgique*. Gembloux, BE: Duculot, 1973.

"De Boma à Tshela (1926)." *Filmgeschiedenis*. Accessed July 2, 2024. http://filmgeschiedenis.be/portfolio/de-boma-a-tshela-1926.

de Grazia, Victoria. "Mass Culture and Sovereignty: The American Challenge to European Cinemas, 1920–1960." *The Journal of Modern History* 61, no. 1 (March 1989): 53–87.

Del Tredici, Robert. *At Work in the Fields of the Bomb*. New York: Perennial Library, 1987.

Dimendberg, Edward. "'These Are Not Exercises in Style': Le Chant du Styrène." *October* 112 (Spring 2005): 63–88.

Dominici, Sara, ed. "The Darkroom: Chemical, Cultural, Industrial." Special issue, *Photo Researcher* 41 (2024).

Dootson, Kirsty Sinclair. *The Rainbow's Gravity: Colour, Materiality and British Modernity*. London: Paul Mellon Centre for Studies in British Art, 2023.

DuBois, Josiah E. *The Devil's Chemists: 24 Conspirators of the International Farben Cartel Who Manufacture Wars*. Boston: The Beacon Press, 1952.

Dumett, Raymond. "Africa's Strategic Minerals During the Second World War." *Journal of African History* 26, no. 4 (1985): 381–408.

Duncan, Pansy. *A Natural History of Film Form*. Edinburgh: Edinburgh University Press, forthcoming.

———. "Towards a Natural History of Film Form: Silver Salts and the Aesthetics of Early Studio-Era Hollywood Cinema." *Screen* 63, no. 4 (2022): 411–26.

Dyer, Davis, and David B. Sicilia. *Labors of a Modern Hercules: The Evolution of a Chemical Company*. Boston: Harvard Business School Press, 1990.

Edwards, Paul N. "Entangled Histories: Climate Science and Nuclear Weapons Research." *Bulletin of the Atomic Scientists* 68, no. 4 (July 2012): 28–40.

Egan, Martha Avaleen. "John Bartlett Dennis." *Tennessee Encyclopedia*. Accessed July 2, 2024. http://tennesseeencyclopedia.net/entries/john-bartlett-dennis/.

Eisenbud, Merril. "The First Years of the Atomic Energy Commission New York Operations Office Health and Safety Laboratory." *Environment International*, 20, no. 5 (1994): 561–71.

Eller, Ronald D. *Miners, Millhands, and Mountaineers: Industrialization of the Appalachian South, 1880–1930.* Knoxville: University of Tennessee Press, 1982.

Enticknap, Leo. "The Film Industry's Conversion from Nitrate to Safety Film in the Late 1940s: A Discussion of the Reasons and Consequences," in Smither and Surowiec, *This Film is Dangerous*.

———. *Moving Image Technology: From Zoetrope to Digital.* New York: Wallflower Press, 2005.

Exenberger, Andreas, and Simon Hartmann. "Extractive Institutions in the Congo: Checks and Balances in the *longue durée*." In *Colonial Exploitation and Economic Development*, edited by Ewout Frankema and Frans Buelens. London: Routledge, 2013.

Farkas-Conn, Irene Sekely. *From Documentation to Information Science: The Beginnings and Early Development of the American Documentation Institute-American Society for Information Science.* New York: Greenwood Press, 1990.

Fay, Jennifer. "Cinema's Hot Chronology (5:29:21 Mountain War Time, July 16, 1945)." *JCMS* 58, no. 2 (Winter 2019): 146–52.

———. *Inhospitable World: Film in the Time of the Anthropocene.* Oxford: Oxford University Press, 2018.

———. *Theaters of Occupation: Hollywood and the Reeducation of Postwar Germany.* Minneapolis: University of Minnesota Press, 2008.

Fayet-Scribe, Sylvie. "The Cross-Fertilization of the U.S. Public Library Model and the French Documentation Model (IIB, French Correspondent of FID) through the French Professional Associations between World War I and World War II." In Hahn and Buckland, *Historical Studies*.

Femmes oubliées de Buchenwald. Paris: Association Paris-Musées, 2005.

Fengler, Silke. *Entwickelt und fixiert: zur Unternehmens- und Technikgeschichte der deutschen Fotoindustrie, dargestellt am Beispiel der Agfa AG Leverkusen und des VEB Filmfabrik Wolfen (1945–1995).* Essen: Klartext, 2009.

Feser, Alison. "Reproducing Photochemical Life in the Imaging Capital of the World." PhD diss., The University of Chicago, 2020.

Field, Allyson Nadia. *Uplift Cinema: The Emergence of African-American Film and the Possibility of Black Modernity.* Durham, NC: Duke University Press, 2015.

Flueckiger, Barbara. "Timeline of Historical Film Colors." Accessed July 2, 2024. https://filmcolors.org/.

Forbes, Meghan. "'What I Could Lose: The Fate of Lucia Moholy." *Michigan Quarterly Review* 55, no. 1 (Winter 2016): 24.

Forman, Ethan. "Stories of Noxious Odors Fill Lawsuit Against Rousselot." *The Salem News* (Salem, MA), January 7, 2020.

Forster, Ralf, and Jeanpaul Goergen. "Ozaphan: Home Cinema on Cellophane." *Film History* 19, no. 4 (2007): 372–83.

Fortmueller, Kate, and Luci Marzola. *Hollywood Unions.* New Brunswick, NJ: Rutgers University Press, 2024.

Frankema, Ewout, and Frans Buelens. "Introduction." In *Colonial Exploitation and Economic Development,* edited by Frankema and Buelens. London: Routledge, 2013.

Freeman, Lindsey A. *Longing for the Bomb: Oak Ridge and Atomic Nostalgia.* Chapel Hill: University of North Carolina Press, 2016.

Friedel, Robert. *Pioneer Plastic: The Making and Selling of Celluloid.* Madison: University of Wisconsin Press, 1983.

Gabrys, Jennifer. *Digital Rubbish: A Natural History of Electronics.* Ann Arbor: University of Michigan Press, 2011.

Gadassik, Alla. "'A Skillful Isis': Esfir Shub and the Documentarian as Caretaker." In *A Companion to Documentary Film History,* edited by Joshua Malitsky. Hoboken, NJ: Wiley Blackwell, 2020.

Galison, Peter, and Bruce Hevly. *Big Science: The Growth of Large-Scale Research.* Stanford, CA: Stanford University Press, 1992.

Gill, Manfred. "Eine reiche Beute—die Filmfabrik Agfa Wolfen." *Photo Antiquaria* 144 (2020): 46–53.

———. "Jüdische Zwangsarbeiter im Aceta-Werk Berlin-Lichtenberg." *Mitteilungen* 16 (2002): 116–33.

Gill, Manfred, and Peter Löhnert. *Jüdische Chemiker aus Dessau in der Filmfabrik Wolfen: ein Beitrag zum Schicksal der jüdischen Wissenschaftler und der jüdisch verheirateten Wissenschaftler der Filmfabrik Wolfen in der Zeit des Nationalsozialismus.* Dessau: Moses-Mendelsson-Gesellschaft, 1997.

Gillet, Florence. "La 'Mission' Cauvin: La propagande coloniale du gouvernement belge aux États-Unis pendant la Seconde Guerre mondiale." *Les Cahiers d'histoire du temps présent* 15 (2005): 357–83.

Gimbel, John. *Science, Technology, and Reparations: Exploitation and Plunder in Postwar Germany.* Stanford, CA: Stanford University Press, 1992.

Gonen, Jay Y. *The Roots of Nazi Psychology: Hitler's Utopian Barbarism.* Lexington, KY: University Press of Kentucky, 2000.

Graham, Lindsey. "The Nature of Risk." Podcast. *American History Tellers,* season 1, episode 4, January 10, 2018. MP3 audio, 41:15. https://wondery.com/shows/american-history-tellers/episode/5279-the-cold-war-the-nature-of-risk/.

Grandin, Greg. *Fordlandia: The Rise and Fall of Henry Ford's Forgotten Jungle City*. New York: Metropolitan Books, 2009.

Gregory, Peter. "Dyes and Dye Intermediates." In *Kirk-Othmer Encyclopedia of Chemical Technology*. September 18, 2009. https://onlinelibrary.wiley.com/doi/10.1002/0471238961.0425051907180507.a01.pub2.

Grieveson, Lee. *Cinema and the Wealth of Nations: Media, Capital, and the Liberal World System*. Berkeley: University of California Press, 2017.

———. *Policing Cinema: Movies and Censorship in Early Twentieth-Century America*. Berkeley: University of California Press, 2004.

Grieveson, Lee, and Priya Jaikumar. "Media and Extraction: A Brief Research Manifesto." *Journal of Environmental Media* 3, no. 2 (December 2022): 197–206.

Grieveson, Lee, and Colin MacCabe, eds. *Empire and Film*. London: Palgrave MacMillan, 2011.

Grieveson, Lee, and Haidee Wasson, eds. *Cinema's Military-Industrial Complex*. Oakland: University of California Press, 2018.

Grossmann, Atina. *Jews, Germans, and Allies: Close Encounters in Occupied Germany*. Princeton, NJ: Princeton University Press, 2009.

Haber, L. F. *The Chemical Industry, 1900–1930: International Growth and Technological Change*. Oxford: Clarendon Press, 1971.

Hahn, Trudi Bellardo, and Michael Keeble Buckland, eds. *Historical Studies in Information Science*. Medford, NJ: Information Today, 1998.

Hamilton, Kevin, and Ned O'Gorman. "Visualities of Strategic Vision: Lookout Mountain Laboratory and the Deterrent State from Nuclear Tests to Vietnam." *Visual Studies* 30, no. 2 (2015): 195–208.

Harding, Colin. "Kodak." In *Encyclopedia of Nineteenth-Century Photography*, edited by John Hannavy. New York: Routledge, 2013.

Harley, John H. "A Brief History of Long-Range Fallout (Report HASL-306)." *US Atomic Energy Commission, Environmental Quarterly* (July 1976): 1–8.

Harp, Stephen L. *A World History of Rubber: Empire, Industry, and the Everyday*. Malden, MA: Wiley Blackwell, 2015.

Havens, Timothy, and Amanda D. Lotz, eds. *Understanding Media Industries*, 2nd ed. New York: Oxford University Press.

Hayes, Peter. *Industry and Ideology: IG Farben in the Nazi Era*. Cambridge, UK: Cambridge University Press, 1987.

Hayes, Sharon. "Eastman Chemical Co. Marked Its Darkest Day 50 Years Ago." *Kingsport Times-News* (Kingsport, TN), October 3, 2010.

Haynes, Williams. *American Chemical Industry*, vol. 3. New York: Van Nostrand, 1945.

Hecht, Gabrielle. *Being Nuclear: Africans and the Global Uranium Trade.* Cambridge, MA: MIT Press, 2012.

Hediger, Vinzenz, Florian Hoof, Yvonne Zimmermann, and Scott Anthony, eds. *Films That Work Harder: The Circulation of Industrial Film.* Amsterdam: Amsterdam University Press, 2023.

Hediger, Vinzenz, and Patrick Vonderau. *Films That Work: Industrial Film and the Productivity of Media.* Amsterdam: Amsterdam University Press, 2009.

Helmreich, Jonathan E. *Gathering Rare Ores: The Diplomacy of Uranium Acquisition, 1943–1954.* Princeton, NJ: Princeton University Press, 1986.

Hennigan, W. J. "Opinion: The Human Toll of Nuclear Testing." *The New York Times,* June 20, 2024.

Hill, W. Z. "The Life of a Film: Medianatures, Camphor, and the Ideology of Technological Modernity." *JCMS* 61, no. 4 (Summer 2022), 85–105.

Hochschild, Adam. *King Leopold's Ghost: A Story of Greed, Terror, and Heroism in Colonial Africa.* London: Picador, 2019.

Holloway, David. *Stalin and the Bomb: The Soviet Union and Atomic Energy, 1939–1956.* New Haven, CT: Yale University Press, 1994.

Hornblum, Allen M. *The Invisible Harry Gold: The Man Who Gave the Soviets the Atom Bomb.* Yale University Press, 2010.

Horkheimer, Max, and Theodor W. Adorno. "The Culture Industry: Enlightenment as Mass Deception." In *Dialectic of Enlightenment: Philosophical Fragments.* Edited by Gunzelin Schmid Noerr. Translated by Edmund Jephcott. Stanford, CA: Stanford University Press, 2002.

Hübner, Bernhard. *Die Region Wolfen, die Filmfabrik und das Jahr 1945.* Bitterfeld: Industrie- und Filmmuseum Wolfen, 2009.

Jacobs, Nancy J. "Marriage, Science, and Secret Intelligence in the Life of Rudyerd Boulton (1901–1983): An American in Africa." *Kronos* 11, no 41 (2015): 287–313.

Jacobson, Brian. *The Cinema of Extractions: Film Materials and Their Forms.* New York: Columbia University Press, 2025.

———. "Crude Designs for an Oil-Built World." *Post45* 6 (March 2021).

———. *Studios Before the System: Architecture, Technology, and the Emergence of Cinematic Space.* New York: Columbia University Press, 2015.

Jacoby, Sanford M. *Modern Manors: Welfare Capitalism Since the New Deal.* Princeton, NJ: Princeton University Press, 1997.

Jarvie, I. C. *Hollywood's Overseas Campaign: North Atlantic Movie Trade, 1920–50.* Cambridge, UK: Cambridge University Press, 1993.

Jenkins, Reese. *Images and Enterprise: Technology and the American Photographic Industry, 1839 to 1925.* Baltimore, MD: Johns Hopkins University Press, 1987.

Johnson, Jeffrey Allan. "Military-Industrial Interactions in the Development of Chemical Warfare, 1914–1918: Comparing National Cases Within the Technological System of the Great War." In *One Hundred Years of Chemical Warfare: Research, Deployment, Consequences,* edited by Bretislav Friedrich, Dieter Hoffmann, Jürgen Renn, Florian Schmaltz, and Martin Wolf. Cham, CH: Springer International Publishing, 2017.

Judt, Matthias. "Exploitation by Integration? The Re-Orientation of the Two German Economies After 1945. The Impact of Scientific and Production Controls." In *Technology Transfer Out of Germany After 1945,* edited by Burghard Ciesla and Matthias Judt. London: Routledge, 1996.

Judt, Tony. *Postwar: A History of Europe Since 1945.* New York: Penguin, 2005.

Kaplan, Sarah. "This Canadian Lake Should Mark the Start of the Anthropocene, Scientists Say." *Washington Post,* July 11, 2023.

Karlsch, Rainer. "Capacity Losses, Reconstruction, and Unfinished Modernization: The Chemical Industry in the Zone of Occupation (SBZ)/GDR, 1945–1965." In *The German Chemical Industry in the Twentieth Century,* edited by John E. Lesch. Boston: Kluwer Academic, 2000.

———. "Fritz Gajewski (1885–1965)—charismatiker Manager in einem multidivisionalen Konzern?" In Karlsch and Maier, *Studien zur Geschichte der Filmfabrik Wolfen.*

Karlsch, Rainer, and Helmut Maier, eds. *Studien zur Geschichte der Filmfabrik Wolfen und der IG Farbenindustrie AG in Mitteldeutschland.* Essen: Klartext, 2014.

Karlsch, Rainer, and Harm G. Schröter, eds. *Strahlende Vergangenheit: Studien der Geschichte des Uranbergbaus der Wismut.* St. Katherinen: Scripta Mercaturae Verlag, 1996.

Karlsch, Rainer, and Paul Werner Wagner. *Die AGFA-ORWO-Story: Geschichte der Filmfabrik Wolfen und ihrer Nachfolger.* Berlin: Verlag für Berlin-Brandenburg, 2010.

Kattelle, Alan D. "Evolution of Amateur Motion Picture Equipment 1895–1965." *Journal of Film and Video* 38, nos. 3 and 4 (Summer–Fall 1986), 47–57.

Kaufmann, Doris. "'Gas, Gas, Gaas!' The Poison Gas War in the Literature and Visual Arts of Interwar Europe." In *One Hundred Years of Chemical Warfare: Research, Deployment, Consequences,* edited by Bretislav Friedrich, Dieter Hoffmann, Jürgen Renn, Florian Schmaltz, and Martin Wolf. Cham, CH: Springer Nature, 2017.

Keating, Carla Mereu. "The Spatiality of Film Production and the Politics of Urban Planning: Rome's Pioneering Film Studio Cines (1905–37)." *Film History* 33, no. 3 (2021), 37–65.

Keeling, Jeff. "Eastman Execs See Lucrative Future for Molecular Recycling." *WJHL Tri-Cities News & Weather* (Johnson City, TN), May 23, 2024. https://www.wjhl.com/news/local/environmental-group-has-major-concerns-about-eastman-chemicals-plastic-recycling-process/.

———. "National Resources Defense Council (NDRC) Director of Plastics and Environmental Group Has Major Concerns about Eastman Chemical's Plastic Recycling Process." *WJHL Tri-Cities News and Weather* (Johnson City, TN), May 24, 2024. https://www.wjhl.com/news/local/eastman-execs-see-lucrative-future-for-molecular-recycling/.

Khlopkov, Anton, and Valeriya Chekina. *Governing Uranium in Russia*. Copenhagen: Danish Institute for International Studies, 2014.

Kiernan, Denise. *The Girls of Atomic City: The Untold Story of the Women Who Helped Win World War II*. New York: Simon and Schuster, 2013.

Kiss, Mary. "The Day Kingsport Wept." *Kingsport Times-News* (Kingsport, TN), October 5, 1975.

Klein, Alec. "Who Knew Kodak Would Keep So Many Skeletons in Its Closet?" *Wall Street Journal*, January 18, 1999.

Kolbow, Berti. "Box Sells: Die 'Amerikanisierung' des Kamera-Marketings der Agfa, 1925–1945." In Karlsch and Maier, *Studien zur Geschichte der Filmfabrik Wolfen*.

Kuran, Peter. *How To Photograph an Atomic Bomb*. 1st edition. Santa Clarita, Calif: vce.com, 2007.

LaDuke, Winona, and Ward Churchill. "Native America: The Political Economy of Radioactive Colonialism." *Journal of Ethnic Studies* 13, no. 3 (Fall 1985): 107–32.

Lane, Yvette Florio. "'No Fertile Soil for Pathogens': Rayon, Advertising, and Biopolitics in Late Weimar Germany." *Journal of Social History* 44, no. 2 (Winter 2010): 545–62.

Le Guern, Nicolas. "Contribution of the European Kodak Research Laboratories to Innovation Strategy at Eastman Kodak." PhD diss., De Montfort University, 2017.

Lear, Linda J. "Rachel Carson's 'Silent Spring.'" *Environmental History Review* 17, no. 2 (Summer 1993): 23–48.

Lee, Tom. *The Tennessee-Virginia Tri-Cities: Urbanization in Appalachia, 1900–1950*. Knoxville: University of Tennessee Press, 2005.

Leighton, Paul. "Compensation Increasing for Former Manhattan Project Workers in Beverly." *The Salem News* (Salem, MA), December 21, 2016.

LeMenager, Stephanie. *Living Oil: Petroleum Culture in the American Century*. Oxford: Oxford University Press, 2014.

Leo, Vincent. "The Mushroom Cloud Photograph." *Afterimage* 13 (June 1985): 6–12.

Leslie, Esther. *Synthetic Worlds: Nature, Art, and the Chemical Industry*. London: Reaktion, 2005.

Lippit, Akira Mizuta. *Atomic Light (Shadow Optics)*. Minneapolis: University of Minnesota Press, 2005.

Löhnert, Peter, and Heinz Mustroph. *Die Entwicklung der Produktion photographischer Materialien. Der Aufbau und die ersten Jahre der Filmfabrik Wolfen von der Gründung 1909 bis 1918*. Wolfen: Kommission für Betriebsgeschichte der Zentralen Parteileitung und Betriebsarchiv des VEB Filmfabrik Wolfen, Stammbetrieb des VEB Fotochemisches Kombinat Wolfen, 1987.

Long, Priscilla. "How Mauve Was Her Garment." *The American Scholar*, June 19, 2013. https://theamericanscholar.org/how-mauve-was-her-garment/.

Lovejoy, Alice. "'A Treacherous Tightrope': The US Office of War Information, Psychological Warfare, and Film Distribution in Liberated Europe." In Grieveson and Wasson, *Cinema's Military-Industrial Complex*.

———. "Celluloid Geopolitics: Film Stock and the War Economy, 1939–1947." *Screen* 60, no. 2 (2019): 224–41

———. "From Forests to Film: Chemistry, Industry, and the Rise of Nonflammable Film Stock." *JCMS* 62, no. 2 (2023): 151–56.

Lovejoy, Alice, Kirsty Sinclair Dootson, and Pansy Duncan, eds. *Film Stock: A Global History*. Minneapolis: University of Minnesota Press, forthcoming.

Lovejoy, Alice, and Katie Trumpener. "Sad and Bitter Landscapes: Ecology and the Built Environment in Czech and East German Photography and Film." In *Cinema and the Environment in Eastern Europe: From Communism to Capitalism*, edited by Lukas Brasikis and Masha Shpolberg. New York: Berghahn Books, 2023.

Lutts, Ralph H. "Chemical Fallout: Rachel Carson's Silent Spring, Radioactive Fallout, and the Environmental Movement." *Environmental Review* 9, no. 3 (Autumn 1985): 210–25.

Maddrell, Paul. *Spying on Science: Western Intelligence in Divided Germany, 1945–1961*. Oxford, UK: Oxford University Press, 2006.

Manion, Lynne Nelson. "Local 21's Quest for a Moral Economy: Peabody, Massachusetts, and its Leather Workers, 1933–1973." PhD diss., University of Maine, 2003.

Mariani, Andrea, and Simona Schneider. "Elemental Battles: Film Stock Production in the Italian Market of the Late 1920s and '30s." In Lovejoy, Dootson, and Duncan, *Film Stock*.

Marzola, Luci. "Better Pictures through Chemistry: DuPont and the Fight for the Hollywood Film Stock Market." *The Velvet Light Trap* 76 (Fall 2015): 3–18.

———. *Engineering Hollywood: Technology, Technicians, and the Science of Building the Studio System.* New York: Oxford University Press, 2021.

Maxwell, Richard, and Toby Miller. *Greening the Media.* New York: Oxford University Press, 2012.

Mayer, Vicki. *Below the Line: Producers and Production Studies in the New Television Economy.* Durham, NC: Duke University Press, 2011.

Mazower, Mark. *Hitler's Empire: How the Nazis Ruled Europe.* New York: Penguin, 2008.

McKelvey, Blake. *Rochester: The Quest for Quality, 1890–1925.* Cambridge, MA: Harvard University Press, 1956.

McQueen, Amanda. "Flammable Workhorse: A History of Nitrate Film from the Screen to the Vault." In *The Routledge Companion to Media Technology and Obsolescence,* edited by Mark J. P. Wolf. New York: Routledge, 2019.

McWhirter, Cameron. *Red Summer: The Summer of 1919 and the Awakening of Black America.* New York: Henry Holt, 2011.

Mebold, Anke, and Charles Tepperman. "Resurrecting the Lost History of 28mm Film in North America." *Film History* 15, no. 2 (2003): 137–51.

Mees, C. E. Kenneth. *From Dry Plates to Ektachrome Film: A Study of Photographic Research.* New York: Ziff-Davis, 1961.

Megargee, Geoffrey P. *The United States Holocaust Memorial Museum Encyclopedia of Camps and Ghettos, 1933–1945.* Bloomington: Indiana University Press, 2009.

Miller, Jamie. "Soviet Cinema 1929–41: The Development of Industry and Infrastructure." *Europe-Asia Studies* 58, no. 1 (January 2006): 103–24.

Miller, Toby. "The Environmental Ruin of Eastman Kodak." *Psychology Today,* April 12, 2018. https://www.psychologytoday.com/us/blog/greening-the-media/201804/the-environmental-ruin-eastman-kodak.

Mitchell, Alanna. "The Anthropocene Is Here—and Tiny Crawford Lake Has Been Chosen as the Global Ground Zero." *Canadian Geographic,* July 11, 2023. https://canadiangeographic.ca/articles/the-anthropocene-is-here-and-tiny-crawford-lake-has-been-chosen-as-the-global-ground-zero/.

Mitchell, Toby J., George Ostrouchov, Edward L. Frome, and George D. Kerr. "A Method for Estimating Occupational Radiation Dose to Individuals, Using Weekly Dosimetry Data." *Radiation Research* 147, no. 2 (February 1997): 195–207.

Murdock, Caitlin E. "A Gulag in the Erzgebirge? Forced Labor, Political Legitimacy, and Eastern German Uranium Mining in the Early Cold War,

1946–1949." *Central European History* 47, no. 4 (December 2014): 791–821.

———. "Public Health in a Radioactive Age: Environmental Pollution, Popular Therapies, and Narratives of Danger in the Federal Republic of Germany, 1949–1970." *Central European History* 52, no. 1 (2019): 45–64.

———. "Selling Scientific Authority: Radium Spas, Advertising, and Popular Understandings of Radioactivity in Germany, 1900–1937." *German History* 35, no. 1 (March 2017): 21–42.

Musser, Charles. "Presenting 'a True Idea of the African of To-day': Two Documentary Forays by Paul and Eslanda Robeson." *Film History* 18, no. 4 (2006): 412–39.

Naimark, Norman M. *The Russians in Germany: A History of the Soviet Zone of Occupation, 1945–1949*. Cambridge, MA: Belknap Press of Harvard University Press, 1995.

Ndiaye, Pap. *Nylon and Bombs: DuPont and the March of Modern America*. Translated by Elborg Forster. Baltimore, MD: Johns Hopkins University Press, 2007.

Nieland, Justus. "Organic Creativity: Alden B. Dow's Small-Gauge Architecture." *JCMS* 62, no. 2 (2023): 157–61.

Norris, Robert S. *Racing for the Bomb: The True Story of General Leslie R. Groves, the Man Behind the Birth of the Atomic Age*. New York: Skyhorse, 2014.

"Nuremberg Laws." *Holocaust Encyclopedia*. Accessed July 2, 2024. https://encyclopedia.ushmm.org/content/en/article/nuremberg-laws.

O'Brian, John, ed. *Camera Atomica*. Toronto: Art Gallery of Ontario, 2015.

———. "Nuclear Flowers of Hell." In O'Brien, *Camera Atomica*, 75–106.

O'Carroll, Lisa. "The East German Town at the Centre of the New 'Gold Rush' ... for Lithium." *The Observer*, September 20, 2023.

O'Reagan, Douglas. *Taking Nazi Technology: Allied Exploitation of German Science After the Second World War*. Baltimore, MD: Johns Hopkins University Press, 2019.

Oakes, Leimomi. "Terminology: Rayon, Viscose, Acetate, Cuprammonium and All Those Other Manufactured Naturals." *The Dreamstress*, January 18, 2014. https://thedreamstress.com/2014/01/terminology-rayon-viscose-acetate/.

Orgeron, Devin, Marsha Orgeron, and Dan Streible, eds. *Learning with the Lights Off: Educational Film in the United States*. New York: Oxford University Press, 2012.

Parikka, Jussi. *A Geology of Media*. Minneapolis: University of Minnesota Press, 2015.

Past, Elena. *Italian Ecocinema Beyond the Human*. Bloomington: Indiana University Press, 2019.

———. "Sunlight, Celluloid, Solarity: Photosensitive Ferrania Film Stock in the Anthropocene." In Lovejoy, Dootson, and Duncan, *Film Stock*.

Peiss, Kathy. *Information Hunters: When Librarians, Soldiers, and Spies Banded Together in World War II Europe*. New York: Oxford University Press, 2020.

Peters, John Durham. *The Marvelous Clouds: Toward a Philosophy of Elemental Media*. Chicago: University of Chicago Press, 2015.

Pollack, Howard. *The Ballad of John Latouche: An American Lyricist's Life and Work*. New York: Columbia University Press, 2017.

Pozner, Valérie. "Soviet Film's French Origins, 1926–1932." In Lovejoy, Dootson, and Duncan, *Film Stock*.

Prelinger, Rick. *The Field Guide to Sponsored Films*. San Francisco: National Film Preservation Foundation, 2006.

Pringle, Thomas. "Manufactured Uncertainty and the Media History of Risk." *Institute on the Formation of Knowledge,* May 13, 2021. https://ifk.uchicago.edu/news/manufactured-uncertainty-and-the-media-history-of-risk/.

Reich, Robert. "Trump Has No Problem Letting Billionaires Profit Off the Pandemic." *The Guardian,* August 9, 2020.

"René Dagron Operates the Pigeon Post into Paris: The First Important Application of Microfilm." *History of Information*. Accessed August 19, 2024. https://www.historyofinformation.com/detail.php?id=2072.

Rhodes, Richard. *The Making of the Atomic Bomb*. New York: Simon and Schuster, 1986.

Richards, Pamela Spence. "Aslib at War: The Brief but Intrepid Career of a Library Organization as a Hub of Allied Scientific Intelligence, 1942–1945." *Journal of Education for Library and Information Science* 29, no. 4 (Spring 1989): 279–96.

Rister, Carl Coke. *Oil! Titan of the Southwest*. 1st ed. Norman: University of Oklahoma Press, 1949.

Rizov, Vadim. "The 24 Films (More or Less) Shot on 35mm Released in 2018." *Filmmaker,* April 24, 2019. https://filmmakermagazine.com/107353-23-films-35mm-released-in-2018/.

Roeling, Rob. "Arbeiter im Uranbergbau: Zwang, Verlocken, und soziale Umstände (1945–1952)." In Karlsch and Schröter, *Strahlende Vergangenheit*.

Rossell, Deac. "Exploding Teeth, Unbreakable Sheets, and Continuous Casting." In Smither and Surowiec, *This Film is Dangerous*.

Rothberg, Michael. *Multidirectional Memory: Remembering the Holocaust in the Age of Decolonization*. Palo Alto, CA: Stanford University Press, 2009.

Rust, Susanne. "How the U.S. Betrayed the Marshall Islands, Kindling the next Nuclear Disaster." *Los Angeles Times,* November 10, 2019.
Salmon, Stéphanie. *Pathé: A la conquête du cinéma, 1896–1929.* Paris: Tallandier, 2014.
Saraiva, Tiago. *Fascist Pigs: Technoscientific Organisms and the History of Fascism.* Cambridge, MA: MIT Press, 2016.
Schmelzer, Janis, and Eberhard Stein. *Geschichte des VEB Filmfabrik Wolfen, 1850–1945.* Berlin: Verlag Tribüne, 1969.
Schnapp, Jeffrey T. "The Fabric of Modern Times." *Critical Inquiry* 24, no. 1 (Autumn 1997): 191–245.
Schröter, Verena. "Participation in Market Control through Foreign Investment: IG Farbenindustrie AG in the United States: 1920–38." In *Multinational Enterprise in Historical Perspective,* edited by Alice Teichova, Maurice Lévy-Leboyer, and Helga Nussbaum. Cambridge, UK: Cambridge University Press, 1986.
Schuppli, Susan. "Radical Contact Prints." In O'Brien, *Camera Atomica.*
Searcey, Dionne, Michael Forsythe, Eric Lipton, and Ashley Gilbertson. "A Power Struggle Over Cobalt Rattles the Clean Energy Revolution." *The New York Times,* November 20, 2021.
Shanebrook, Robert. *Making KODAK Film.* 2nd ed. Self-published, 2016.
Shukin, Nicole. *Animal Capital: Rendering Life in Biopolitical Times.* Minneapolis: University of Minnesota Press, 2009.
Smith, D. Ray. "Spy Worked at Y-12, Tennessee Eastman Co." *Oak Ridger,* December 29, 2014. https://www.oakridger.com/story/news/2014/12/29/spy-worked-at-y-12/35641282007/.
Smither, Roger, and Catherine A. Surowiec, eds. *This Film is Dangerous: A Celebration of Nitrate Film.* Brussels: Fédération Internationale des Archives du Film, 2002.
Snyder, Timothy. *Black Earth: The Holocaust as History and Warning.* New York: Tim Duggan Books, 2015.
Solnit, Rebecca. *Savage Dreams: A Journey into the Hidden Wars of the American West.* Berkeley: University of California Press, 2014.
Spitz, Peter H. *Petrochemicals: The Rise of An Industry.* New York: Wiley, 1988.
Starosielski, Nicole. *Media Hot and Cold.* Durham, NC: Duke University Press, 2021.
Stokes, Raymond. *Divide and Prosper: The Heirs of I.G. Farben under Allied Authority, 1945–1951.* Berkeley: University of California Press, 1988.
———. *Opting for Oil: The Political Economy of Technological Change in the West German Industry, 1945–1961.* Cambridge, UK: Cambridge University Press, 2006.

Street, Sarah. *Colour Films in Britain: The Negotiation of Innovation, 1900–1955*. London: Palgrave MacMillan, 2012.
Sunseri, Thaddeus. "The *Baumwollfrage*: Cotton Colonialism in German East Africa." *Central European History* 34, no. 1 (2001): 31–51.
Swanson, Mark. *Holston Army Ammunition Plant*. Vol. 9B of *U.S. Army Materiel Command Historic Context Series: Report of Investigations*. Plano, TX: Geo-Marine, 1996.
Szczepanik, Petr and Patrick Vonderau. *Behind the Screen: Inside European Production Cultures*. New York: Palgrave Macmillan, 2013.
Taffel, Sy. "Towards an Ethical Electronics? Ecologies of Congolese Conflict Minerals." *Westminster Papers in Communication and Culture* 10, no. 1 (2015): 18–33.
Taillibert, Christel. "Le Pathé-Rural ou les aléas du 17,5 mm." *1895, revue d'histoire du cinéma* 21, no. 1 (1996), 125–45.
Tedesco, Marie. "Claiming Public Space, Asserting Class Identity, and Displaying Patriotism: The 1929 Rayon Workers' Strike Parades in Elizabethton, Tennessee." *Journal of Appalachian Studies* 12, no. 2 (Fall 2006): 55–87.
Tepperman, Charles. *Amateur Cinema: The Rise of North American Moviemaking, 1923–1960*. Berkeley: University of California Press, 2015.
Tooze, Adam. *The Wages of Destruction: The Making and Breaking of the Nazi Economy*. New York: Viking, 2007.
Toyosaki, Hiromitsu. "Hidden and Forgotten Hibakusha." In O'Brien, *Camera Atomica*.
Vaughan, Hunter. *Hollywood's Dirtiest Secret: The Hidden Environmental Costs of the Movies*. New York: Columbia University Press, 2019.
Ungar, Steven. "Scenes in a Library: Alain Resnais and 'Toute la mémoire du monde.'" *SubStance* 41, no. 2 (2012): 58–78.
United States Army Corps of Engineers. "A District Name Intended to Hide the Development of the Atomic Bomb." Accessed July 22, 2024. https://www.usace.army.mil/About/History/Historical-Vignettes/Military-Construction-Combat/113-Atomic-Bomb/.
United States National Parks Service. "The Atomic Bombings of Hiroshima and Nagasaki." Accessed July 2, 2024. https://www.nps.gov/articles/000/the-atomic-bombings-of-hiroshima-and-nagasaki.htm.
———. "History of Film Types Timeline." Accessed July 2, 2024. https://www.nps.gov/subjects/hfc/history-of-film-types-timeline.htm.
Vatulescu, Cristina. *Reading the Archival Revolution: Declassified Stories and their Challenges*. Palo Alto, CA: Stanford University Press, 2024.

von Stackleburg, Emmet. "Wheels of Change: Eastman Kodak, Continuous Flow, and the Origins of Mass-Produced Film Stock." In Lovejoy, Dootson, and Duncan, *Film Stock*.

Wald, Matthew L. "U.S. Alerted Photo Film Makers, Not Public, About Bomb Fallout." *The New York Times*, September 30, 1997.

Walser Smith, Helmut. "The Workers of Europe and a Dye Factory in Germany, 1940–1945." In *Die mittledeutsche Chemieindustrie und ihre Arbeiter im 20. Jahrhundert*, edited by Rupieper, Hermann-Josef, Friederike Sattler, and Georg Wagner-Kyora, eds. Halle (Saale): Mitteldeutscher Verlag, 2005.

Wasson, Haidee. *Everyday Movies: Portability and the Transformation of American Culture*. Berkeley: University of California Press, 2020.

Weinstein, Allen, and Alexander Vassiliev. *The Haunted Wood: Soviet Espionage in the United States—The Stalin Era*. New York: Random House, 1999.

Wilder, Kelley. "An American Darkroom in Paris. In "The Darkroom: Chemical, Cultural, Industrial."

Williams, Susan. *Spies in the Congo: America's Atomic Mission in World War II*. New York: PublicAffairs, 2016.

Wilson, Emma. *Alain Resnais*. Manchester, UK: Manchester University Press, 2006.

Wilson, Paul. "Historical Perspective on the Use of Microfilm in Libraries and Archives." In *Preservation Microfilming: Does it Have a Future? Proceedings of the First National Conference of the National Preservation Office, at the State Library of South Australia, 4–6 May 1994*. Canberra: National Library of Australia, 1995.

Winters, Joseph, and Emily Sanders. "'Plastics Are Awesome': Inside the Energy Department's Partnership with the Plastics Industry." *Grist*, February 3, 2025. https://grist.org/accountability/energy-department-american-chemistry-council-chemical-recycling/

Wolfe, Audra J. *Competing with the Soviets: Science, Technology, and the State in Cold War America*. Baltimore, MD: Johns Hopkins University Press, 2013.

Wolfe, Margaret Ripley. *Kingsport, Tennessee: A Planned American City*. Lexington: University Press of Kentucky, 1987.

Wright, Patrick. *Iron Curtain: From Stage to Cold War*. Oxford: Oxford University Press, 2007.

Wynter, Sylvia. "Unsettling the Coloniality of Being/Power/Truth/Freedom: Towards the Human, After Man, Its Overrepresentation—An Argument." *CR: The New Centennial Review* 3, no. 3 (Fall 2003): 257–337.

Yue, Genevieve. *Girl Head: Feminism and Film Materiality.* New York: Fordham University Press, 2020.
Yusoff, Kathryn. *A Billion Black Anthropocenes or None.* Minneapolis: University of Minnesota Press, 2018.
Zahiga, Remy. "Uranium, Cobalt, Copper: The Painful Legacy of the Shinkolobwe Mines in the DRC." Heinrich Böll Stiftung. Accessed August 19, 2024. https://www.boell.de/en/2023/10/09/uranium-cobalt-copper-painful-legacy-shinkolobwe-mines-drc.
Zahra, Tara. *Against the World: Anti-Globalism and Mass Politics Between the World Wars.* New York: W. W. Norton, 2023.
Zeman, Zbyněk, and Rainer Karlsch, *Uranium Matters: Central European Uranium in International Politics,* 1900–1960 New York: Central European University Press, 2008.
Zielony, Tobias. *Wolfen.* Leipzig: Spector Books, 2023.
Zimmerman, Angela. *Alabama in Africa: Booker T. Washington, the German Empire, and the Globalization of the New South.* Princeton, NJ: Princeton University Press, 2010.
Zimmermann, Patricia. *Reel Families: A Social History of Amateur Film.* Bloomington: Indiana University Press, 1995.

FILMOGRAPHY

Eastman Chemical Company. *Eastman Chemical Company: Years of Glory, Times of Change,* 1920–1990. United States, 1991. VHS.
Cauvin, André, dir. *L'agneau mystique.* Belgium, 1939. Film.
Cauvin, André, dir. *Congo.* Belgium, 1942. Film.
Cauvin, André, dir. *Congo, terre d'eaux vives.* Belgium, 1939. Film.
Cauvin, André, dir. *Hans Memling, peintre de la Vierge.* Belgium, 1940. Film.
Cauvin, André, dir. *Nos soldats d'Afrique.* Belgium, 1939. Film.
CBS Reports. *The Silent Spring of Rachel Carson.* United States. Aired April 3, 1963. Television.
Fenton, Paul, dir. *A Movie Trip through Filmland.* United States, 1921. Film.
Hällfritzsch, Rainer, Margit Miosga, Ulrich Neumann, dirs. *Bitteres aus Bitterfeld: Eine Bestandsaufnahme.* GDR, 1988. VHS.
Harlan, Veit, dir. *Die goldene Stadt.* Germany, 1942. Film.
Jacoby, Georg, dir. *Die Frau meiner Träume.* Germany, 1944. Film.
———. *Bunter Reigen.* Germany, 1942. Film.
"La lavorazione autarchica per estrarre la lana del latte." *Giornale Luce,* Italy. November 24, 1937. Film.
Resnais, Alain, dir. *Le Chant du styrène.* France, 1958. Film.
Resnais, Alain, dir. *Hiroshima mon amour.* France, 1959. Film.
Resnais, Alain, dir. *Nuit et brouillard.* France, 1957. Film.
Resnais, Alain, dir. *Toute la mémoire du monde.* France, 1957. Film.
Wolf, Konrad, dir. *Sonnensucher.* GDR 1958. Film.

INDEX

Aceta company, 42, 43
acetic acid, 3, 33, 62, 76, 141, 169; acetic anhydride made from, 35; role in production of cellulose acetate, 49
acetic anhydride, 3, 33, 76; imported from Germany, 35; RDX explosive and, 62
acetone, 33, 49, 97, 156
acid rain, 156
Adorno, Theodor, 6–7
AEC (Atomic Energy Commission), 122–23, 126–28, 132, 158; danger of radioactive fallout denied by, 151, 153, 200n88; film manufacturers and, 128, 139; Fordyce's appeal to, 152, 153; as successor to Manhattan Project, 133; US Department of Energy as successor to, 164
Africa, colonial cotton farming in, 58
Agfa (Aktien-Gesellschaft für Anilin-Fabrikation), 2, 5–6, 15; contraction of, 166; as dye maker, 19; as Kodak competitor, 40, 41–42; Nazi autarky and, 57; as part of IG Farben cartel, 6, 43–44; rayon produced by, 36, 43, 150; standard-gauge (35 mm) film of, 23; Vistra rayon of, 56–57, 56*fig.*, 163; West German film factory in Leverkusen, 116, 157; World War I and, 20, 23

Agfa Ansco Corporation, 45, 55, 113, 186n121
Agfacolor, 99*fig.*, 104, 105; formulas seized by T-Forces, 99; history of, 98; postwar reparations and, 112, 120
Agfa Wolfen factory, 6, 7, 8, 41*fig.*, 45, 73, 142; aviation film made in, 20; beginnings of, 19; Cold War and, 115–18; color film research/specialists at, 99, 114–15; cotton sourced from abroad by, 57; employees and parts transferred to Soviet Ukraine, 112, 114, 143, 195n80; expansion during World War I, 40; forced laborers at, 9, 81–83; IG Farben Division III headquartered in, 54–55; looting of, 94, 95–97; nylon (Perlon) made by, 144; ORWO ("Original Wolfen"), 157, 167; poison gas produced in, 21; seized by Allies at end of World War II, 93, 94–103; in Soviet zone of occupation, 100, 101, 103–4, 105*fig.*, 115, 195n85; T-Forces and, 98; ventilation at, 22; women workers at, 81–85
Agneau mystique, L' [*The Sacred Lamb*] (film, dir. Cauvin), 69
All the Memory in the World [*Toute la mémoire du monde*] (film, dir. Resnais, 1957), 145

American Bemberg factory, 42–43
American Cyanamid Company, 158
American Glanzstoff factory (Elizabethton, Tenn.), 43, 86
American Glue Company, 161
American Library Association, 106
AMG (Dutch company), 168
AMS (Aslib Microfilm Service), 107–8
Amtorg [Amerikanskaya Torgovlya] (Soviet trade agency), 111, 135
Anchors Aweigh (film musical, dir. Sidney, 1945), 2
Angus, Siobhan, 7
aniline, 5, 19, 155, 160
Ansco, 15, 45, 98, 152; Agfa color film technology and, 113; Ansco Color, 99
Anthropocene, 123–24, 129, 139, 140
Aslib [Association of Special Libraries and Information Bureaus] (Britain), 107
Astrograph machines, 64
"As We May Think" (Bush, 1945), 109
atomic bomb, 1, 10, 65, 79, 167; Bikini Atoll tests, 130–31, 153–54; Little Boy, 87; microfilm and, 194n63; photographing first atomic explosion, 129; Soviet Union and, 119, 121, 138–39; Trinity test, 10, 126, 128, 129, 138; tsunamis and underwater nuclear explosions, 130–31. *See also* Bikini Atoll; Hiroshima; Manhattan Project; radiation
"Atomic Energy for Society and the Balance Between Hazard and Gain" (Sterner, 1964), 159
Atomic Weight 500 [*Atomgewicht* 500] (Dominik, 1935), 56
"Atoms for Peace" program, 152, 158
Auerbach, Jonathan, 194n63
Auschwitz death camp, 8, 88, 145
autarky, in Fascist Italy, 53, 88
autarky, in Nazi Germany, 53–54, 55, 56, 82, 85, 93; military conquest funded by, 58; United States as model, 58–59; Vistra as cotton substitute, 56–57, 56*fig.*, 85
automobile industry, 141

Babbit, William C., 126
Bachmann, Werner, 62
"Ballad for Americans" (Robinson, 1939), 69
Bartlett, Murray, 32
BASF (Badische Anilin- und Soda Fabrik), 19, 22, 55
Bauhaus, 51, 108
Bausch & Lomb, 130
Bavarian Film Company, 105
Bayer company, 19, 22
Belgian Congo, 1, 2, 60, 67, 138, 170; filmmakers in, 68–72; uranium mined for Manhattan Project, 66, 67, 74; violent history of, 67–68. *See also* Katanga province
Bell and Howell, 124
Beloschenko, Pelageja, 83
Bent, W. G., 92
beta rays, 125, 128–29
Bibliography of Scientific and Industrial Reports, 111
Big Inch oil pipeline, 142
Bikini Atoll, atomic testing at, 130–31, 132, 153–54, 159
Bitterness from Bitterfeld: A Stocktaking [*Bitteres aus Bitterfeld: Eine Bestandsaufnahme*] (documentary film, dir. Hällfritzsch, Miosga, and Neumann), 156–57
Black Americans, 38, 58; cotton and Black labor, 31; in Kingsport, Tennessee, 30; soldiers in World War I, 30; "uplift" ideology and, 31–32, 73
black spots (fogging), from radioactive fallout, 122, 128–34, 134*fig.*, 139, 149, 152, 158, 167; AEC reassurance over hot snow, 151; cause of, 125–26; from

Ore Mountains uranium, 139; Trinity test and, 130
Bobseine, Mark, 154–55
Bondarenko, Tatjana, 83
Bouchard, Thomas, 51
Boulton, Rudyerd, 68
Boundy, Ray H., 98
Bowles, Paul, 71
Bozak, Nadia, 7
Brayer, Elizabeth, 31
Brazil, Fordlândia project in, 59–60, 72
Briggs, Richard, 135
Brixner, Berlyn, 130
Brock, Sgt. Leader, 95, 97, 100, 101
Brown, Kate, 77
Brownie camera, 35
Brulatour, Jules, 41, 42
Buchenwald concentration camp, 9, 82, 85, 94
Bugajewa, Walentina, 83
Bush, Vannevar, 108–9, 110, 120, 194n63

cadmium, 68, 72
camphor, 10, 15, 48, 185n103
Canadian Radium and Uranium Corporation, 1
cancer, from chemical and nuclear waste, 154, 155–56, 159, 163, 164
Carolina, Clinchfield, and Ohio (CC&O) Railway, 25–26, 29, 35, 136
Caron, George, 87–88
Carson, Rachel, 155, 156, 158, 159, 165
Cauvin, André, 69, 70, 73–74
Celanese Corporation, 36, 40, 52, 97
cellulose acetate (nonflammable) "safety" film, 3–4, 4*fig.*, 5, 9, 151; change in raw materials of, 140; chemical foundations of, 33; cost of, 35; deadly consequences associated with, 10; early development of, 22–23; Kodak Academy Award and, 142; mass production of, 62; microfilm and growth of, 106; petrochemicals and, 124; production process of, 49–50; synthetic materials and, 144, 150, 199n74; X-ray film made from, 38
cellulose nitrate (flammable) film, 3, 4, 10, 150; Cleveland Clinic fire (1929) and, 37; danger of, 13–14, 22; poison gas and, 21–22; production process, 25
cellulose triacetate, 142, 150
Chaplin, Charlie, 13
Chapman, Albert K., 131
Checkograph, 106
chemical engineering, 66
chemical industry, 7, 10, 141, 165; brief slump after World War I, 24; conglomerates, 43–44; in Germany, 19, 20, 40, 54; widespread pollution from, 159–60, 163
Chemical Warfare Service, US, 24, 37–38
chlorine, 20, 38, 55
Chornobyl Nuclear Power Plant (Ukraine), 168
Churchill, Ward, 139
Churchill, Winston, 93, 150–51
cigarettes, 2, 7, 22, 144, 170
Ciné-Kodak 16 mm camera, 34*fig.*, 35, 44, 140
cinema (motion pictures), 3, 6, 13, 35, 129; chemical history of, 2; first motion pictures, 19; importance of safety film to, 22–23; in Weimar Germany, 7
Cines Seta Artificiale, 40
Civil War, American, 25, 30, 32
Civil War, Russian, 30
Cleveland Clinic fire (1929), 36–38, 106, 149, 153
climate crisis, 167, 169
Clinton Engineer Works, 74, 77, 79
coal, 3, 20, 120, 136, 141, 146, 156; CC&O Railway and, 25, 136; cellulose acetate film production process and, 36, 38, 92–93; Charket product, 33; coal mines, 14; coal tar, 5, 18, 19;

coal *(continued)*
: dyes made from, 18, 20; German autarky and, 57; Kingsport and, 28, 29; nylon and, 144; Ore Mountains and, 137; replaced by oil as core raw material, 140, 144; shortage in postwar Europe, 92

cobalt, 68, 72, 73, 168

Cold War, 115–20, 124, 135, 139; "Iron Curtain," 150, 151; military-civilian partnerships during, 158

color film: Ansco and, 99, 113; Ferrania film factory and, 99, 112; Gevaert company and, 99, 112; Kodak and, 112; Sovcolor, 99; Trinity test photographed with, 129. *See also* Agfacolor

Colorful Dance [*Bunter Reigen*] (film, dir. Jacoby, 1942), 99

Communism, 53, 134, 137, 189n73

Composition B (explosive), 62, 63, 158

Comprehensive Environmental Response, Compensation, and Liability Act, 160

concentration camps, 6, 9, 82, 94

Congo (film and book, Cauvin, 1942), 70–73, 71*fig.*, 74

Congo, terre d'eaux vives [*Congo, Land of Living Waters*] (film, dir. Cauvin, 1939), 69

Conrad, Joseph, 67

copper, 1, 54, 67, 70, 71–73

cotton, 15, 25, 136; cotton linters, 3–4, 13, 25, 49, 57, 58, 127, 132; German autarky and, 57; inseparability from Black labor in American South, 31, 48; slavery and, 139

Crawford Lake (Canada), 123–24

Crile, George W., 37, 38

Cuba, manganese from, 60

Cuban Missile Crisis, 154

culture industry, 6–7

Curie, Marie, 119

Cuthbertson, Lt. Col., 97, 99, 113

Dagron, René, 106

Dainippon Celluloid Company, 40, 185n103

de Boe, Gérard, 69

Denis, Armand, 68

Dennis, John B., 25, 27–28

Densten Felt Hair Company, 160

Department of Energy, US, 164

Deutsche Celluloid Fabrik, 114, 195n85

digital technologies, 167

Dimendberg, Edward, 146

DiNic Chemical Company, 152

Dominik, Hans, 56–57

Dos Passos, John, 93, 95

Dow Chemical, 98

Dreyfus brothers, 36

Dreyfus cellulose acetate, 40

Dryden, George B., 29, 31

Du Bois, W.E.B., 32

Dumett, Raymond, 67

DuPont company, 40, 43, 75, 124; nylon sold by, 144; polyester film factory of, 150; T-Forces and, 98, 104

DuPont-Pathé Film Manufacturing Corporation, 43

dyes, 3, 5–6, 20, 27, 120, 158; gas and, 21; German dyes imported by Kodak, 18; in IG Farben Division II, 54; synthetic, 19

Dynacolor, 125

Dynamit Nobel, 55, 186n121

Eastman, George, 15–19, 64, 169; Agfa as competitor and, 40, 41–42, 44–45; anxiety about control, 24, 47, 59; Bolshevism opposed by, 30; cellulose acetate market and, 36; with Ciné-Kodak 16 mm camera, 34*fig.*; death of, 47; in failing health, 45; Kingsport venture and, 28, 29, 33, 142; nonflammable film and future of cinema, 23; North Carolina farm of, 31–32; Pathé's agreement with, 44;

234 · INDEX

Progressive worldview of, 28, 31; public life of Rochester and, 28–29; as supporter of Black "uplift" project, 31–32, 58, 73; vertical integration and, 24; World War I and, 20, 23–24 Eastman Chemical Company, 158, 169 Eastman Gelatine factory, 7, 160–63, 162*fig.*, 164, 166, 170; Kodak Park as model for, 161; odors emanating from, 3, 162–63; range of products made at, 5 Eastman Kodak Company: antitrust troubles of, 5, 19, 28; bankruptcy declaration (2012), 166; color film technology and, 112; court-ordered consent decree and, 17, 38, 40; diversification of, 5, 6; dyes imported from Germany, 18; factory site cleanup settlement (2014), 160; Glanzfilm purchased by, 113; Manhattan Project and, 66, 158; mass production and, 63, 65; microfilm and, 113; reputation of, 16–17; as supplier to US military, 23; T-Forces and, 98; uranium from Katanga and, 1; vertical integration of, 5, 28; "welfare capitalism" of, 28–29. *See also* Kodak Park; Rochester, New York (Kodak headquarters)
Eastman Photographic Materials, 16
Edgewood Arsenal, 27
Edison company, 22, 23
Eggert, John, 101–3
Eggert, Margarete, 101–2
Eisenbud, Merril, 123, 126–27, 133–34, 139, 148
Eisenhower, Dwight, 152
Elizabethton (Tennessee) Glanzstoff factory, 86
Eller, Ronald D., 25
Ellingson, Robert, 77
Enola Gay warplane, 87–88
Environmental Protection Agency, 160
ethanol, 141, 142
ethylene, 141

explosives, 7, 21–22, 55, 186n121. *See also* Composition B; RDX (Research Development Explosive)

"Fabrication of Plastics at I.G. Farbenindustrie, Wolfen" (Hasche and Boundy), 98
Fairchild Camera, 130
Fascism. *See* Italy, Fascist; Nazism
Fay, Jennifer, 129
FBI (Federal Bureau of Investigation), 134–35, 137, 139
Federal Dyestuff and Chemical Corporation, 27
Federal Trade Commission, 42
Felber, Fritz, 116, 117, 118
Ferrania (Italy) film factory, 43, 167; autarky in Fascist Italy and, 88; color film technology and, 99, 112
fertilizers, 19
Feser, Alison, 155
FIAT (Field Information Agency), 97, 110, 111, 115; Enemy Personnel Exploitation Section, 114
Field, Allyson Nadia, 32
film: artificial silk and, 39–42; chemical history of, 8; damaged by radiation, 125; digital turn, 167; film developing, 3; Kodachrome, 77, 167; Kodak 70 mm, 167; materials in composition of, 3; as product of chemical industry, 10
FILM (Fabbrica Italiana Lamine Milano), 43
film, 8 mm, 68, 69, 142; magnetic tape as replacement for, 157; Super 8, 167
film, 16 mm, 35, 44, 45, 142; as internationally recognized small-gauge format, 185–86n118; magnetic tape as replacement for, 157; for military mail in World War II, 64; Trinity test photographed with, 129; World War I military technology and, 47

film, 17.5 mm, 35, 44
film, 35 mm, 23, 35; cellulose triacetate formula and, 142; Kodak share of US market, 42, 181n15; Trinity test photographed with, 129
FilmoTec company, 167, 168
Fisher, Arthur, 69, 70
Ford, Henry, 59
Fordney-McCumber Tariff Act, 42
Fordyce, Charles, 152–53, 155, 158, 159
French Kodak SAF, 16
Fuchs, Erwin, 114
Fuchs, Klaus, 135
Fuji Photo Film Co., Ltd., 40

Gajewski, Fritz, 8–9, 55, 101, 116
gamma rays, 125, 128–29
Garrett, Garet, 27–28
Gaumont company, 23
gelatin, photographic, 5, 8, 115, 117–18, 119; contamination in, 132–33; sources of, 15, 160–61
General Advisory Committee on Atomic Energy (New York State), 159
General Electric, 16
Genval, Ernest, 69
Gérard, Jean, 107
Germany, East [GDR] (German Democratic Republic), 120, 138; chemical pollution in, 156–58; Kodak AG Filmfabrik Köpenick, 150; Soviet uranium supplies from, 139
Germany, West, 148, 150, 157
Gevaert company, 15, 88, 97; color film technology and, 112; Gevacolor, 99
Gill, Manfred, 98
Gitelman, Lisa, 194n63
Glanzfilm factory (Berlin), 44, 45, 151, 160; housing on former site of, 166; Kodak AG, 150; "Kodak World" and, 47; as response to Agfa's rayon production, 43

gold, 67, 68
Gold, Harry, 135, 136
Golden City, The [*Die goldene Stadt*] (film, dir. Veit, 1942), 98
Graham, Martha, 51
Great Depression, 45, 54, 57
Greenglass, David, 135, 136
Grierson, Lee, 15
Groves, General Leslie R., 1, 65–66, 67, 77–78, 131
Grube Johannes mine pit (Silbersee, Germany), 157, 168

Haber, Fritz, 107
Haloid company, 125
Hanford Engineer Works, 75, 80, 132
Hankins, Sue, 46–47, 49, 52
Hans Memling, peintre de la Vierge [*Hans Memling, Painter of the Virgin*] (film, dir. Cauvin), 69
Hargrave, Thomas J., 132, 133, 134
Harlan, Veit, 98
Hasche, R. Leonard, 98
Hauff company, 19
Hecht, Gabrielle, 68
Hercules, Inc., 127
Higgins, C. A., 127
Hillers, Marta, 104, 120
Hiroshima, atomic bombing of, 2, 87, 125, 126. *See also* Manhattan Project
Hiroshima mon amour (film, dir. Resnais, 1959), 148
Hitler, Adolf, 52, 53, 55
Hoechst company, 19
Hogue, Dock, 68, 69
Hollywood Colorfilm Corporation, 98
Hollywood film industry, 7, 17, 41, 68; retaking of European subsidiaries in World War II, 91; Tennessee Eastman and, 142
Holston Defense Corporation, 158
Holston Ordnance Works, 9, 62, 65, 73, 86, 135, 143; aerial view of,

64*fig.*; nitric acid division, 78; workers at, 63
Holston River, 61, 61*fig.*
Holston Trading Company, 60, 61–65
Home Kinetoscope, 22
Hoover, J. Edgar, 134
Horkheimer, Max, 6–7
HUAC (House Un-American Activities Committee), 134, 139
Hull, David C., 77, 199n66
Humbert, Agnès, 85
hydroquinone, 60, 140

IG Farben chemical cartel, 6, 43–44, 45; Allied Control Council's dismantling of, 115, 117; Division I, 54; Division II, 54; Division III, 8, 54–55, 85, 98, 116, 138; slave labor used during World War II, 81; synthetics and, 54
Ilford company, 15, 97
iodine 131, 154, 170
Iordanskij, Lt. Col., 104
"Iron Curtain," idea of, 150–51, 156
Italy, Fascist, 8, 53, 54, 88

Jáchymov mines (Czechoslovakia), 67, 119, 139
Jacoby, Georg, 98, 99
Jacoby, Sanford, 28
Japan, 40, 60, 185n103
Johnson, J. Fred, 25–26, 26*fig.*, 31, 33, 46, 52; persuasive influence of, 27–28; relationship with George Eastman, 45, 64; young Kingsport neighbors of, 47, 73
Jones, Dorothy, 79–80
Journal of Documentary Reproduction, 106

Kalischkin, Col., 104
Kaminska, Henryka, 82
Karlsch, Rainer, 138

Kastner, Lacy, 91, 93, 97
Katanga province (Congo), 1, 9, 71, 82, 86; cobalt mined in, 168; uranium deposits, 67. *See also* Belgian Congo
Kid, The (film, dir. Chaplin, 1921), 13
Kiernan, Denise, 79
Kingsport, Tennessee, 1, 8, 47, 142; Black population of, 30; explosion and fire in (1960), 155, 160; Kodak methanol plant in, 5, 25, 27, 28, 33; as planned model city, 26, 27–28; Slack at, 9
Kingsport Extract Corporation, 26
Kingsport Improvement Corporation, 27, 31
Kingsport Tannery, 26–27
Klein, Alec, 163
Kodak, Ltd., 16, 47, 92, 97, 122–23
Kodakery (Kodak employee magazine), 161, 162
Kodak GmbH, 16
Kodak Park (Rochester), 13, 22, 36, 64, 73, 132; air filters at, 128*fig.*; atomic fallout at, 133; chemical leaks and accidents at, 155–56; Eastman Gelatine modeled after, 161. *See also Movie Trip Through Filmland, A* (film, 1921)
Kodak-Pathé company, 44, 88, 91–92, 97, 120, 123
Kodak-Pathé Vincennes factory, 40, 44, 47, 88; poison gas produced in, 21; repossessed by Kodak at end of World War II, 92–93, 92*fig.*
Kodak Research Laboratories, 16, 23, 52, 60, 76; experiments with nonflammable film, 35; problem of black spots and, 130; Synthetic Organic Chemicals Department, 20
"Kodak World," at New York World's Fair (1939), 46*fig.*, 47
Koda yarn, 38, 52, 140

INDEX · 237

Korolevich, Vladimir, 86
Kreutzberg, Harald, 51

LaDuke, Winona, 139
Lane, Yvette, 53
Lanital, 53, 57
Latouche, John, 69, 71, 189n73
Lawrence, Ernest, 75
Lawrik, Oleksandra, 9, 84–85, 84*fig.*, 119, 137; escape from Agfa Wolfen, 94; journey home, 119, 121; sent to Soviet work camp, 168
Lee, Tom, 30
LeMenager, Stephanie, 141
Leopold II, king of Belgium, 67, 70, 72
Leslie, Esther, 6, 57
Leverkusen paper plant, 115
Levi, Primo, 8, 53, 88, 148–49, 169–70
Levin, Meyer, 95–96
Lewis, Wesley H., 153
Limited or Partial Test Ban Treaty (1963), 154
Lippit, Akira Mizuta, 148
lithium hydroxide, 168
Los Alamos, 76, 86–87, 132, 135
Los Alamos Laboratories Weapons Physics Division, 129
Lovejoy, Frank, 8, 29, 63
Lower, William Edgar, 36–38
Lumière brothers, 19
Lumière company, 15, 40

Mack, Julian, 130
Maison de la Chimie [House of Chemistry] (Paris), 107
Maji Maji rebellion (German East Africa [Tanzania], 1904), 58
manganese, 61, 68
Manhattan Project, 2, 65–67, 108, 130, 155, 189n73; AEC as successor to, 133; *Oppenheimer* film (2023) and, 167; radioactive fallout and, 126, 131–32; uranium for, 66, 67, 74

Marshall Islands, 130, 170
Matadi (port city in Congo), 1, 66, 71*fig.*
Mays, Maurice, 30
McCarthy, George, 105, 106
McMaster, Donald, 92, 97
McWhirter, Cameron, 30
Mees, C. E. Kenneth, 16, 20
Metal Hydrides Corporation, 163–64, 166
methanol, 5, 9, 25, 49, 141, 169
methylene chloride, 156
Meurisse, Lucienne Harvey, 69
Micro-File (Model D), 108
Micro-File (Model E), 110
microfilm, 7, 9, 64, 105–11, 142, 194n63; Bush's imaginary Memex, 109–10, 111; Dagron's Stanhope, 106; documentation and, 106–7; Recordak, 105–6, 108, 109
Moholy, Lucia, 108, 110, 120
Morin, Edgar, 100, 101, 114, 118
Motion Picture Magazine, 24
Movie Trip Through Filmland, A (film, 1921), 13–14, 16, 17, 21, 24; exterior view of Kodak Park, 14*fig.*; global reach of Kodak film, 18*fig.*; *The Song of Styrene* compared with, 146
MPPC (Motion Picture Patents Company), 17, 18, 23
Mumzhiev, Lt. Col., 104
Munich Camera Works, 115, 116
Mussolini, Benito, 53
mustard gas, 38
Myrick, Henry, 31–32, 47

Naimark, Norman, 117
National Association of Photographic Manufacturers, 126
National Defense Research Committee, 62, 110
Navaux, Pierre, 69
Nazism, 6, 9, 53, 55, 81, 100. *See also* autarky; Third Reich

238 · INDEX

Ndiaye, Pap, 66
New Deal, 69
Newell and Knowlton Extracting Works, 160
"New South," 25, 30, 48, 74
New York World's Fair (1939), 46*fig.*, 47, 69
Night and Fog [*Nuit et brouillard*] (film, dir. Resnais, 1957), 145
nitric acid, 3, 4, 22, 25, 78; in cellulose nitrate, 14; in RDX explosive, 62; role in filmmaking process, 13
nitrocellulose, 21–22, 40, 43, 55
nitrous oxide, 37
Nolan, Christopher, 167
Nolen, John, 28, 30
Nordhausen concentration camp, 94
Nos soldats d'Afrique [*Our African Soldiers*] (film, dir. Cauvin, 1939), 69
nuclear waste, 152, 155, 158, 163
nylon, 144

Oak Lodge (Eastman's North Carolina farm), 31, 45
Oak Ridge, Tennessee, 1, 2, 8, 9, 76, 132, 170; cinemas and film society at, 74; Manhattan Project and, 65, 78; secrecy at, 80*fig.*; toxicity of chemicals used at, 155
Oak Ridge National Laboratory, 88
Odin Gelatine Works (Eberbach, Germany), 202n28
Office of Scientific Research and Development, 110
Office of Strategic Services, US, 68, 107
Office of Technical Services, 110
olefins, 141
Operation Crossroads, 130
Oppenheimer (film, dir. Nolan, 2023), 167
O'Reagan, Douglas, 111
Ore Mountains (Germany and Czechoslovakia), 137–38, 156, 168; silver mined in, 119; Soviet uranium supplies from, 139
Osoaviakhim (Soviet operation to relocate Agfa employees), 114
Othmer, Donald F., 52
Ovakimian, Gaik, 135

Pathé, Charles, 44
Pathé company, 15, 36, 91–92; artificial silk produced by, 39–40; Kok 28 mm film, 22, 23, 44; poison gas produced by, 21; VGF Glanzfilm and, 43; World War I and, 23. *See also* Kodak-Pathé company
Pathé Rural projector, 44
Pathéscope, 22, 33, 44
Pechiney (French company), 145, 146
Periodic Table, The (Levi, 1975), 8, 169–70
Perkin, William, 19
pesticides, chemical, 6, 155, 158, 159
petrochemicals, 10, 124, 145
petroleum, 6, 7, 54, 142, 169
pharmaceuticals, 19, 54
phosgene, 20, 22, 36, 38, 55
photochemistry, 19
Photographic Industry in Germany during the period 1939-1945, *The* (British report), 112*fig.*
photography, 15, 17, 35, 109, 110, 142; aviation/aerial, 20, 136; chemical and culture industry of, 6–7; chemical history of, 2; Eastman Gel and, 161; Kodak products for amateurs, 35; Memex and, 109; military and civilian, 152; range of Kodak products and, 47; slavery and, 183–84n78; synthetic dye industry and, 19; T-Forces and, 110
photolithography, 64
Photoplay magazine, 25, 31
photo shops, 3, 6
Planchon, Victor, 40

plasticizers, 115, 140, 144
plastics, 2, 7, 8, 64, 141; in Nazi Germany, 57; in *The Song of Styrene*, 145–46
plutonium, 75, 126, 152
poison gas, 6, 10, 20–21, 21*fig.*, 149; death toll of World War I and, 107; kinship with celluloid, 36–38
Poland, forced laborers in Germany from, 81–82, 83
political economy, liberal, 15
polyester, 144, 199n74
polyethylene terephthalate (PET), 4, 199n74
polypropylene, 141
potassium bromide, 3
Potsdam Conference (1945), 103
Power, Eugene, 107
Prince, Elmer W., 116–18
Progressivism, 25, 27, 28, 31, 48, 118
Publication Board, US Department of Commerce, 110
pyroligneous acid, 49

Queneau, Raymond, 146

radiation, 122–27, 133–34, 164; in Chornobyl accident, 168; "radioactive colonialism," 139
radium, 66, 72, 119, 125; alpha rays and, 126; in Ore Mountains, 137
Raney, M. Llewellyn, 107, 108
rare earth minerals, 168
Ravensbrück concentration camp, 9, 83, 85
raw materials, 7, 10, 16, 23, 42, 48, 170–71; of the Belgian Congo, 70; of cellulose acetate, 36; control over, 24; diversification and, 5; Eastman Gelatine factory and, 162; Eastman's social philosophy and, 32–33; of flammable and nonflammable film, 4; Kodak's suppliers of, 17; looting of, 100; waste of, 14; World War II and, 74
rayon, 2, 7, 8, 9, 76; Aceta company production of, 42; Agfa production of, 36, 85; Eastman acetate yarn, 39*fig.*; film editing and, 86; Kodak international expansion and, 38; Nazi autarky and, 55; patent wars over, 150; spooling of, 87*fig.*
Rayon and Synthetic Yarns in Textiles (Brooklyn Museum exhibit, 1936-37), 51, 51*fig.*, 53
RDX (Research Development Explosive), 9, 64, 76, 77, 86, 120, 151; cellulose acetate technology and, 5; Holston as sole producer of, 158; Slack's espionage activity and, 136; World War II use of, 62–63; World War I use of, 137
Reconstruction period, 25, 30
Recordak, 105–6, 107, 108, 109
Red Summer (1919), 30, 32, 142
Resnais, Alain, 144–45, 148
Reynolds, Marian, 154
Robeson, Paul, 69
Robinson, Earl, 69
Rochester, New York (Kodak headquarters), 3, 13, 47, 143, 146; Chemical Group, 76, 78; demographics of, 29; experimental chemistry centered in, 77; George Eastman and, 28–29, 45; Manhattan Project and, 66; radioactive fallout from atomic tests in, 122–23, 124, 151, 154; raw materials sent to, 15; school of aviation photography in, 20. *See also* Kodak Park; Kodak Research Laboratories
Rockefeller Foundation, 107
Roosevelt, Franklin D., 72, 93
Rose, C. E., 104
Rosenberg, Ethel, 135
Rosenberg, Julius, 135

Rousselot (French gelatin company), 163, 167
Rozenau, Dorote, 82
rubber, 59–60, 67, 70, 72
rubber, synthetic, 60, 88, 141, 144, 150; autarky policy of Third Reich and, 54, 98; produced at Auschwitz, 169–70
Rubber [*Kautschuk*] (Dominik, 1930), 56

"safety" film. *See* cellulose acetate (non-flammable) "safety" film
SAG (Sowjetisch Aktiengesellschaft) Photoplenka, 138, 144
Schering company, 19
Schnapp, Jeffrey, 53
Schuppli, Susan, 10
Schützenberger, Paul, 22
Schweinfurt Gelatin Works, 115
Sehma rayon works, 138
Semyonov, Semyon Markovich, 135
Sengier, Edgar, 67, 72
SHAEF (Supreme Headquarters Allied Expeditionary Force), 97, 103
Sheik, The (film, dir. Melford, 1921), 13
Sherman Antitrust Act, 17
Shinkolobwe mine (Katanga, Congo), 1, 66, 72, 139
Shostka (Ukraine), Agfa Wolfen transferred to, 104, 112, 114, 143
Shukin, Nicole, 161
Silent Spring (Carson), 6, 159
Silent Spring of Rachel Carson, The (CBS Reports documentary, 1963), 155, 158
silver, 8, 25, 48, 59, 137, 169; from Belgian Congo, 68; in calutron magnets, 76; in postwar Germany at outset of Cold War, 117–20; purity of ore used by Kodak, 15; slavery and, 139
"Silver" (Levi), 148–49
silver nitrate, 3, 97, 117

Slack, Alfred Dean, 9, 78–79, 135, 136–37
Smoot-Hawley Act, 42
Snyder, Timothy, 58
Société des Celluloses Planchon, 40
Société Générale, 1
Soie de Chardonnet, 40
Song of Styrene, The [*Le Chant du Styrène*] (film, dir. Resnais, 1958), 144–46, 148
Sovcolor, 99
Soviet Union, 9, 53, 60; atomic weapons testing by, 10, 122, 123, 138–39, 154; forced laborers in Germany from, 81, 82; Nazi occupation of, 82, 83, 104; nuclear espionage of, 135–36; relations with Western powers in occupied Germany, 113–14, 115–18; reparations taken from Germany, 103–4, 111, 119, 139; "trophy brigades" in Germany, 103; uranium mined in, 137; wartime alliance with United States, 136
Spaak, Paul-Henri, 69
Stalin, Joseph, 93
Standard Oil, 17, 141
Stanhope, 106
steel industry, 6, 7
Steel Secret, The [*Das stählerne Geheimnis*] (Dominik, 1934), 56
Stent, Gunther, 111
Sterner, James H., 159
strontium 90, 154, 170
Sun Seekers [*Sonnensucher*] (film, dir. Wolf, 1958), 138
Superfund sites, 160, 163, 164
Svema film factory (Ukraine), 99, 104
synthetic materials, 52, 53–54, 60

Taiwan, 10, 185n103
Taylor, Robert L., 137
tear gas, 27
Teca fiber, 38, 52, 140

Tenite, 38, 63, 140
Tennessee Eastman, 1–2, 5, 6, 8, 73, 137, 160; chemical weapons industry and, 47; expansion into rayon, 129; growth of, 140; "Kodak World" and, 47; Manhattan Project and, 65–67, 167; move into cellulose acetate, 44; origin as lumber company, 33; petrochemicals and, 141–42; postwar view of, 140*fig.*; "production men" at, 77, 78; Protestant ideology and, 52; raw materials extraction and, 7; raw materials for safety film and, 35–36; research laboratory of, 38; safety film mass-produced at, 9; separation from Kodak, 158; synthetic rubber and, 60; Texas Eastman as subsidiary, 4. *See also* Holston Ordnance Works; Texas Eastman; Y-12 uranium separation plant (Oak Ridge)
Tennessee Valley Authority, 61
Texas Eastman, 4, 142; aerial view of, 147*fig.*; Longview (Texas) facility, 142–44, 146, 150, 160; petrochemicals from Gulf Coast and, 10; *TEC News*, 124, 143
textiles, film and, 86–88
T-Forces, American and British, 97–98, 99, 100, 104, 109
Third Reich, 6, 53, 104, 118; chemistry and German empire, 57–58; "synthetic world" of, 57, 86; uranium acquired by, 67. *See also* autarky; Nazism
3M (Minnesota Mining and Manufacturing Company), 167
tin, 8, 67, 68, 71
Tinian Island, 2, 87
Tsar Bomba test (1961), 154
Tuskegee Institute, 32, 58

Uhl, Bruno, 115–18
Uhl, Greti, 116, 117

Ukraine, forced laborers in Germany from, 83–85, 84*fig.*
Union Carbide Corporation, 74–75
Union Minière du Haut-Katanga, 1, 66, 67, 72, 73
United States: atomic weapons testing by, 122–23, 126–27; domestic chemical dye industry, 19–20; German admiration for, 101; migration of textile industry to South, 42; synthetic rubber industry, 60; wartime alliance with Soviet Union, 136
University Microfilm, Inc., 107, 108
University of California, Berkeley, 75
uranium, 1–2, 8, 9, 88, 121, 152, 170; alpha rays and, 126; in calutrons, 76; Manhattan Project and, 66–67, 77, 163–64; silver mining and, 119–20; Soviet acquisition of, 134, 135
US Steel, 17

Valentino, Rudolph, 13
Vatulescu, Cristina, 150–51
vertical integration, 5, 24, 59, 132
VGF (Vereinigte Glanzstoff-Fabriken), 42, 44, 150; Nazi ideology and, 53; rayon factories in Tennessee, 42–43. *See also* Glanzfilm factory (Berlin)
Victoria, Queen, 19
Viscose Society, 40
Vistra (autarkic rayon, cotton substitute), 56–57, 56*fig.*, 85, 163
Vistra: The White Gold of Germany [*Vistra, das weiße Gold Deutschlands*] (Dominik, 1936), 56–57, 56*fig.*
Vogel, H. W., 19

Warner Brothers, 98
War Production Board, US, 60, 79
Warren, Stafford L., 131, 132, 133, 155
Washington, Booker T., 31, 32, 58
Wasson, Haidee, 9, 110
Webb, Julian H., 125–26, 127, 130, 148

Weinberg, Alvin M., 88
Wells, H. G., 107
West Valley (New York), nuclear waste processing in, 152–53, 154, 155, 159, 164, 170
White, James C., 8, 65–66, 77
White-Stevens, Robert, 158
Whitman, Lucille, 79–80
Wigman, Mary, 51
Wilcox, Bill, 76, 77, 80
Wilcox, Perley S., 28, 29, 137
Williams, Susan, 68
Wilson, Woodrow, 30
Wismut (Soviet military zone in Germany), 119, 138, 139, 168
Wolf, Konrad, 138
Wolfe, Margaret, 29
Woman in Film, A (Korolevich, 1928), 86
Woman of My Dreams, The [*Die Frau meiner Träume*] (film, dir. Jacoby, 1944), 98, 99
wood, film manufacturing and, 24, 132, 136
World Congress of Universal Documentation, 107
World War I, 27, 30, 36, 137, 141; airplane dope as use for cellulose acetate, 36, 40, 47, 132, 149; cellulose acetate (nonflammable) film and, 23–24; documentation movement and, 107; German colonies lost after, 58; imports of German chemical products stopped by, 19–20; poison gas used during, 6, 20–21, 21*fig.*, 37, 55, 149; synthetic materials and, 52
World War II, 1, 6, 22, 48, 60; "big science" of, 88; European film factories taken by Allies, 92–103, 92*fig.*, 95*fig.*, 99*fig.*; Holston Ordnance Works and, 62–65; impact on sources of gelatin, 161; interwar internationalist projects upended by, 107; radiation damage of film and, 125; strategic minerals and, 66–73; synthetic rubber in, 150
World War II, film as reparations following, 120, 139; in American and British zones, 105, 106, 115; color film and, 105, 112; diplomacy and, 113; looting and, 97; Potsdam Agreement and, 103; in Soviet zone of occupation, 103–4, 111, 119
Wratten and Wainwright, 16
Wright, Patrick, 150–51
Wynter, Sylvia, 139

X-ray film, 7, 9, 37, 38, 65, 142, 148–49; atomic fallout recorded on, 131, 148; dental, 133; PET film base and, 149, 169, 199n74; radioactive fogging of, 125
X-10 graphite reactor, 75

Y-12 uranium separation plant (Oak Ridge), 1–2, 5, 78, 86, 161; "calutrons" at, 75–76, 75*fig.*, 80–81, 80*fig.*; Chemical Group, 77; electromagnetic separation method at, 74; number of employees, 79; Slack at, 9, 135; women employees, 79–81, 80*fig*. *See also* Oak Ridge, Tennessee; Tennessee Eastman
Yusoff, Kathryn, 139

Zahra, Tara, 52
Zimmerman, Angela, 58
zinc, 8, 68, 72

Founded in 1893,
UNIVERSITY OF CALIFORNIA PRESS
publishes bold, progressive books and journals
on topics in the arts, humanities, social sciences,
and natural sciences—with a focus on social
justice issues—that inspire thought and action
among readers worldwide.

The UC PRESS FOUNDATION
raises funds to uphold the press's vital role
as an independent, nonprofit publisher, and
receives philanthropic support from a wide
range of individuals and institutions—and from
committed readers like you. To learn more, visit
ucpress.edu/supportus.